CHURCH BUILDERS

CHURCH BUILDERS

EDWIN HEATHCOTE AND IONA SPENS

A.D. ACADEMY EDITIONS

Acknowledgements

We would like to express our appreciation to the architects who provided material for this publication and our gratitude to Andrew Mead and the Architectural Press archive (now EMAP Construct) for kindly lending us a number of photographs. We would also like to thank G E Kidder Smith for allowing us to reproduce illustrative material; Robert Elwall at the British Architectural Library, RIBA, for his assistance; Maggie Toy at Academy Editions for her support, and Mario and Andrea Bettella of Artmedia for designing the book.

Photographic credits

All photographs are courtesy of the architects or from the Architectural Press archive, unless stated otherwise; every effort has been made to locate sources and credit material but in the very few cases where this has not been possible our apologies are extended: Marco D'Anna pp142-3; BAL, RIBA pp6, 12 (centre), 18 (left), 20, 27 (left, centre), 29 (above, centre), 30, 37, 38 (left, centre), 47 (above), 53 (below); H Baranger p49 (centre); Benda p164 (below); Mario Bettella pp2, 22; Hedrich Blessing p55; Frederico Brunetti pp94-7; Enrico Cano pp144, 146-7; Arno de la Chapelle pp148, 150-3, 155, 158-9 (above); Martin Charles pp14, 70 (above); Arrigo Coppitz p50 (below); Wim Cox p26 (right); Richard Einzig p62 (above right); Jamie Eynon p59; A Fethulla p102; Geleta & Geleta pp162, 166, 168; Edwin Heathcote pp12 (above), 14 (right), 18 (right), 19, 39 (centre), 65 (right), 164 (above); Tom Heinz p53 (above); Lucien Hervé p62 (below left); Timothy Hursley pp176-8; Karhu p101 (below); G E Kidder Smith pp42, 44 (above), 45 (above), 47 (centre, below), 50 (above, centre); Toshiharu Kitajima pp194, 196, 198, 200-1; Lourdes Legorreta pp170, 172, 174-5; Mitsuo Matsuoka pp130-1, 134-6; Pino Musi pp138, 140-1; V Niemela p107; Tomio Ohashi p211; Richard Payne pp118-9, 121-2, 124-7; Pietinen p62 (below right), 74, 82, 85; Jock Pottle/Esto pp218, 219 (right); Simon Rista pp154, 157; Michael Rogol p116; Inge and Arved van der Ropp p44 (centre); Friedrich St Florian pp42, 44, 62 (illustrations); Jussi Tiainen p159 (below); Kelf Treuner p167 (illustration right); T P Tukianen p98; Bernard Tulkens pp202-7; Michael Wolgensinger pp86-8; Yan p49 (below).

Cover: Myyrmäki Church and Parish Centre, Vantaa, Finland, 1980-4, Juha Leiviskä; photograph: Simon Rista
Frontispiece: Church of the Sagrada Familia, Barcelona, Antoni Gaudí, 1884-; photograph: Mario Bettella

First published in Great Britain in 1997 by
ACADEMY EDITIONS

A division of
JOHN WILEY & SONS
Baffins Lane
Chichester
West Sussex PO19 1UD

ISBN: 0 471 97755 1

Other Wiley Editorial Offices
New York • Weinheim • Brisbane • Singapore • Toronto

Printed and bound in Singapore

CONTENTS

PREFACE

Edwin Heathcote and Iona Spens

If the world is to be lived in, it must be founded – and no world can come to birth in the chaos of the homogeneity and relativity of profane space. The discovery or projection of a fixed point – the center – is equivalent to the creation of the world.

We will use an example that is accessible to everyone – a church in a modern city. For a believer, the church shares in a different space from the street on which it stands. The door that opens on the interior of the church actually signifies a solution of continuity. The threshold that separates the two spaces also indicates the distance between two modes of being, the profane and the religious. The threshold is the limit, the boundary, the frontier that distinguishes and opposes two worlds – and at the same time the paradoxical place where those two worlds communicate, where passage from the profane to the sacred world becomes possible.
Mircea Eliade, *The Sacred and the Profane.*[1]

Eliade eloquently points out the critical position of sacred space in our existential situation and the role it has played in societal development. In a century of massive intellectual upheaval the role of the Church and of the church's place in the physical fabric have been questioned and examined. This book attempts to take a broad look at some of the symptoms of this questioning of fundamental precepts and at the effects on architecture and the changing nature of sacred space in the Christian world.

The church is merely a house. It is the house of God, but the congregation is the real *House of God*; God dwells within them, not within the building. At its most basic it is a recreation of the room in which the Last Supper was held, a dining room in which the sacred time is infinitely recycled to allow the repetition of Christ's last supper, his sacrifice. The congregation are as the apostles, partaking of that meal around the table or the altar.

The twentieth century saw a massive reappraisal of sacred space; an analysis of the meaning of the liturgy such as had not happened since the Reformation. It coincided with a reassessment of man's place within the world and his relationship to God; with the emergence of psychoanalysis, a new vision of the soul, with existentialism and the rise of Marxism. It also coincided with the momentous changes in architecture which this existential upheaval had helped to bring about: the emergence of modernism.

This book attempts to touch on the ground which lies at this threshold, the junction of architecture and sacred space and the physical forms which developed as an expression of these intellectual, theological and architectural upheavals: the modern church and its builders.

Anglican Cathedral, Liverpool, 1903-78, Giles Gilbert Scott

THE TWENTIETH-CENTURY CHURCH

THE ENIGMA OF SACRED OBJECTIVITY

Edwin Heathcote

I. A MATTER OF MORALITY

About 1835, in England, Augustus Welby Pugin (1812-52) transferred the equation of Christianity and Gothic into architectural theory and practice. With him, to build in the forms of the Middle Ages was a moral duty. And he went further. He contended that, as the medieval architect was an honest workman and a faithful Christian, and as medieval architecture is good architecture, you must be an honest workman and a good Christian to be a good architect.[1]

With this Aristotelian syllogism, Pevsner dealt with the issue of the basis of the gothic revival in simplistic Puginian terms. Note the appearance of the words 'moral' and 'honest'. These two words have underpinned the great majority of the literature which deals with the fundamental change in architecture which emerged from the nineteenth century to inform the architecture of the early twentieth century. As Robert Furneaux-Jordan states in his summation of *Victorian Architecture*: 'Architecture, thereafter [after Pugin] ceased to be a matter of taste, it became a matter of morality'.[2]

As Furneaux-Jordan points out, this removal of architecture from the realms of the aesthetic to the ethical persists to this day in a lingering trace of the moralising nature of criticism from which the modern artistic and architectural spheres have never recovered. Pugin and later Ruskin were credited with this change in spirit, whereby it was claimed that the gothic was the only moral style for churches, the classical style having been derived from the pagan civilisations. This was combined with a nascent functionalism (a rejection of the classical language as a system devised for timber which had been transposed to stone) regarding structure which had been inspired by the French eighteenth-century position and an aspiration for an *architecture parlante*:

The great test of architectural beauty is the fitness of the design to the purpose for which it is intended, and that the style of the building should so correspond with its use that the spectator may at once perceive the purpose for which it was intended. *A W N Pugin.*[3]

Gothic alone was perceived to be a style which had derived from the desire to build for God. For Pugin, the verticality of the gothic was an 'emblem of the resurrection'. What other style could a church possibly be? God was on the side of the gothic.

This was not merely a stylistic debate however. The plan of the English church, derived from the Protestant preaching house and the currency of all British church architecture from Christopher Wren onwards was abandoned in favour of a plan which could accommodate the fundamentally Catholic ritual espoused by the Ecclesiologists. The emancipation of Catholics and a spate of high-profile conversions including cardinal Newman, Pugin himself and Schlegel in Germany prompted a reassessment of Catholic liturgy and the perceived shortcomings of the Anglican mass. The Ecclesiologists and the Oxford Movement essentially rediscovered the sacraments (particularly communion) and sought spirituality through the continuity of the historic ritual of the church.

The arrangement of chancel, aisles and side-chapels became as important as the gothic ornamentation. This was gothic as generator of the plan, not merely as a stylistic device. The principal proponent of this approach was William Butterfield, a functionalist gothicist (not necessarily a paradox); his buildings revelled in their ugliness. Yet they have lasted well; All Saints, Margaret Street in London, 1849-59 (see p12) was a key structure, a bold piece of urban infill design and an important example to others.

Although it is easy to see a rational route, as many have done, between Pugin's writings, Ruskin's plea for honesty and the happy craftsman, Butterfield's modern gothic idiom and Morris' idealistic medievalising socialism through to the Bauhaus and functionalism, the path is in fact much less clear cut. Le Corbusier's *Vers une Architecture* (1923) is bristling with studies of the Parthenon while the neo-classicists of revolutionary France and later Schinkel in Germany exerted a great influence on the emerging modernism, just as did the British Arts and Crafts. The most admired British classicists, Wren and Hawksmoor, lingered in spirit, if not in language, close to the gothic. No Athenian or Florentine building ever had steeples like those that defined London's skyline.

Britain was not alone in the debates which were raging about style and morality at the end of the nineteenth century. Goethe encouraged the lyrical in architecture ('It is the poetical part, the fiction, that makes a building into a work of art')[4] in a manner which was also close to the French revolutionary architects. However, his heart lay with Winckelmann; he greatly admired the world of antiquity and expounded his views with great authority and learning to an eager audience. Goethe was fundamentally of a different age to Pugin and Ruskin. He was perplexed by the completion of Cologne Cathedral in a gothic style after the original plans had been found; he tried but failed to appreciate it and could not bring himself to understand the passion for the medieval.

Schinkel appreciated the gothic as the language of spirituality and inspiration but remained firmly neo-classical in his convictions, while Hegel saw in gothic or 'romantic' architecture: that which 'is peculiarly appropriate to the Christian rite, together with a harmony between the architectural form and the inner spirit of Christianity' (*Vorleisungen über die Ästhetik*). Schopenhauer, however, advocated neo-classicism as an unsurpassable architectural language and saw the many gothic projects as 'trying to embalm the dead body of Christianity'.[5]

Gottfried Semper, one of the key names in nineteenth-century architectural theory, concerned himself with a symbolism of construction, material and colour and, although often cited as a proto-functionalist, remained unable to find a new style. He condemned neo-gothic largely because of its associations in Germany in the second half of the nineteenth century with Catholicism and the conservatism which he saw as a suffocating influence on German culture.

Although there was a proliferation and high level of architectural debate in the German-speaking countries, many of the actual innovations in ecclesiastical architecture during the nineteenth century (and those which would have the greatest influence in the next century) came out of France. Despite the pervasive influence of the École des Beaux-Arts and the preponderance of a neo-renaissance language on the French architectural scene, some remarkable and visionary leaps were made. The romantic Byzantine language of the Sacré Coeur at Montmartre in Paris (1875-7) by Paul Abadie predates Bentley's Westminster Cathedral by a couple of decades and the age saw the predominance of one of Europe's great nineteenth-century architectural theorists, Eugène Viollet-le-Duc.

Victor Hugo's novel *Notre Dame de Paris, 1482* (1831) featured the eponymous cathedral as its central character; the other figures appeared like humorous gargoyles existing within the great structure's shadow (it is interesting to note that Hugo believed that printing and reading by the masses would lead to the end of the church building as a text in stone as people's ability to read its language would be lost). In his novel Hugo analysed the architecture of the city and its relationship to the cathedral, discussed attitudes towards conservation and also interpreted the gothic as an expression of the liberty and fulfilment of the French nation:

> Upon the face of this ancient queen of French cathedrals, beside each wrinkle we constantly find a scar. *Tempus edax, homo edacior* (time is destructive, man more destructive) – which we would willingly render thus – Time is blind but man is stupid.

But as Hugo bemoaned the insensitive 'restorations' of the great gothic buildings a tide of such work was about to engulf the northern European countries. In France the inspiration behind many of these schemes (if not the actual work itself) came from Viollet-le-Duc. He was responsible for setting apart the gothic as *le style* among *les styles*. His 'restorations' which now seem dubious were based not on an actual past stage in the building's life but on an idealised model.

For Viollet the gothic was a celebration of technology and was 'flexing, free and questing like the modern spirit', in contrast to the classical which was static and immobile. His *Dictionnaire raisonné de l'architecture française* (1854-68), an encyclopaedia of French gothic architecture, and *Entretiens sur l'architecture* (1863-72) were seminal works. Despite his medievalising œuvre, his rational theories and faith in technology (he appreciated machines in a way that was unheard of in

England where they were the preserve of the engineer and the philistine, not 'high art') are a direct predecessor of the worship of technology and its use as a paradigm in Le Corbusier's *Vers une Architecture*, and once the stylistic trappings had been disposed of by his pupils, a fundamental impulse for the growth of modernism. For a modern espousal of Viollet's views it is worth reading Jean Gimpel[6] who also advocated the theory that Western civilisation reached its greatest moment in the Middle Ages and that the Renaissance merely saw the artist lifted to demi-god status and art replacing religion as the fundamental impulse.

The use of technology and new materials was the impetus which led to drastic changes in architecture. In England while Deane and Woodward were building the Oxford University Museum using structural ironwork and gothic decoration of the structure with the help of Ruskin, Louis-Auguste Boileau was building an iron church in Paris. At the Church of St Eugène (1854-5) Boileau used iron columns and iron vaulting ribs to create a gothic structure of a lightness and slenderness which the medieval church builders would have greatly envied. The church was in a poor area of Paris and iron was used for reasons of economy rather than theory and, although it was not the first time that iron had been used for ecclesiastical architecture, it was the first time it had been used so visibly.

At the same time Victor Baltard was building Les Halles Centralles with its magnificent iron structure (comparable to the Crystal Palace in London), often cited as an early example of rationalism; yet his Church of St Augustin in Paris (1860-71), which also utilises structural iron, is a tragic blend of styles which dress the building in an eclectic sauce, disguising the flavour of its structure (which even features an iron dome). The rationalism which could be brought to bear on a station or a market hall rarely made it intact through to churches.

This timidity when applying modern principles to church architecture prevailed until around the turn of the century when the crucial jumps were made. In France the spectacular progress is illustrated best by two buildings. The first of these is the Church of Notre-Dame-du-Travail, Paris (1899-1901), by Zacharie Astruc which finally utilised the unsentimental iron structures which had been defining the stations and sheds of the last half century. The result is a powerful and light interior, bold and expressive, and a highly influential building which is completely articulated by its unadorned structure. But as this building was rising another Paris church was in progress which would have even greater repercussions.

The mantle of structural innovation was moving from iron to concrete and Paris was very firmly in the vanguard. Work had begun on St Jean de Montmartre in 1894. Although it was not finished until 1904 it proved a sensational building to open the century with. Not only was it the first church to use reinforced concrete, it was perhaps the first building of any type to display its concrete structure so boldly and so proudly. It was designed by Anatole de Baudot, a pupil of Viollet-le-Duc, and its execution is closer to a twentieth-century Art Nouveau œuvre than it is to neo-gothic. The pointed arches are still apparent but so are rounded arches. The architectural vocabulary expresses the structure more than the style. The use and celebration of structure remains faithful to Viollet-le-Duc's gothic principles and the use of new structural technology is also sympathetic to his ideals but Baudot managed to shed the clutter and stylistic baggage which had bound architecture to the nineteenth century and ecclesiastical architecture to the Middle Ages. While François Hennebique pioneered concrete structures in the ensuing years in Paris it was left to Perret to take these developments in ecclesiastical architecture to a truly modern conclusion.

The scene in Europe at the turn of the century was cluttered with styles. Gothic, classical and neo-renaissance vied with each other and innovation in ecclesiastical architecture was rare. The emerging Arts and Crafts movement (see chapter II) in Britain had a powerful effect on European architecture and encouraged architects to explore the vernacular, resulting in a spate of national romantic buildings while new styles emerged to take their place next to the established ones. Many fine churches had sprung from the Arts and Crafts Movement in an almost direct line from Butterfield's All Saints, Margaret Street, while a vein of largely stultifyingly dull gothic continued to dominate British ecclesiastical design, along with a few other historical styles which cropped up less frequently but nevertheless regularly.

Ninian Comper's uncluttered gothic carried on the style and approach of his master, G F Bodley resulting in some fine, simple spaces, such as St Cyprian's at Clarence Gate (1901-3), London. He continued building in gothic until the middle of the twentieth century: St Mary's, Wellingborough for instance was not finished until 1950. Gothic was blended with Arts and

ABOVE: All Saints, Margaret St, London, 1859, W Butterfield
CENTRE: St Mary's, Wellingborough, 1950, N Comper
BELOW: Westminster Cathedral, London, 1903, J F Bentley

Crafts to good effect at Holy Trinity, Sloane Street, London, by J D Sedding (1888-90) and other churches across the country with varying effects; some innovations were made but usually only the familiar motifs and vernacular details were added to an already overcrowded stylistic catalogue of features.

Two huge cathedrals defined the turn of the century in Britain. The first of these was the Catholic Westminster Cathedral (1895-1903) designed by J F Bentley, a convert as had been Pugin before him. Despite Pugin's zeal, the Catholic establishment and many of the new converts had been wary of the gothic which had become so associated with the Church of England over the past half century. At Westminster a compromise was found between the Italian Baroque of Herbert Gribble's Brompton Oratory and the nearby Westminster Abbey in the shadow of Pugin's gothic parliament, the symbol of the established Anglican state. That compromise was a monumental Byzantine, perhaps influenced by Abadie's Sacré Coeur but wholly different, taking its cue as much from Norman Shaw's nearby Scotland Yard and its stripey bricks, the Hagia Sophia and Ruskin's beloved Venetian gothic. It was a substantial building, boldly massed and with dark, cavernous interiors and a huge campanile.

The other structure which was taking shape was Giles Gilbert Scott's precocious design for Liverpool Cathedral (see p8). Scott, the grandson of Gilbert Scott (maltreater of many medieval churches and prolific architect) had entered a competition of which the rules decreed that all entries must be gothic in execution. A wave of protest had ensued from architects to whom the idea of imposing a historical style seemed anathema. The 22-year-old Scott won and his design, a powerful composition in a stripped, stark, free gothic, matured as he developed until his death in 1960. It was only completed in 1978, probably the last cathedral to be made fully of stone and a fine epitaph to the great age of gothic revival.

Although impressive these last great sighs of historicism proved a dead end. The historical revivals were no longer a part of any living theological impulse and lacked the vitality inherent in a movement which comes from within. Churches continued to be built all over the continent and the USA in every conceivable revived style but the energy and the future lay with the French structural innovators and the architects of the late Arts and Crafts in England. These were the link to the next phase, the century of modernism.

II. ARTS AND CRAFTS

> The modern way of building must be flexible and vigorous, even smart and hard. We must give up designing the broken-down picturesque which is part of the ideal of make believe. The enemy is not science but vulgarity, a pretence to beauty at second-hand . . . Much has to be done; it is a time of beginning as well as of making an end. *W R Lethaby* [1]

William Morris could not be envisaged without John Ruskin, just as Lethaby owed a huge debt to Morris but there was a century and a world between them. Morris' socialism and his violent reaction to the vulgarity and uselessness of the objects at the Great Exhibition led to his Arts and Crafts vision, a vision which inspired many pupils and followers. But whereas some of those followers became stuck in the pleasant pastoral and paternalistic idyll of Morris' *News from Nowhere*, Lethaby and a few others were able to free themselves from the vestiges of historicism and project their architecture into the twentieth century.

Apart from Lethaby the other critical figure in the move to a modern church idiom was Edward Prior. Prior designed two churches that embody a simplicity and clarity of intent which is in stark contrast to the highly decorated, fussy structures of even the Arts and Crafts architects, let alone the gothic revivalists. The first of these was Holy Trinity, Bothenhampton (1884-9). The forms of the gothic were retained in the pointed arch of the building's structural ribs and in the windows but this was a powerfully elemental church. The structure alone defines the form of the building, which was the inspiration behind Prior's next church, St Andrew's, Roker.

This church (built 1906-7) was a response both to Prior's own rational architectural convictions and the new spirit of the Anglican Church which had in places once more begun to comprehensively examine its liturgy and rites in the wake of the excessive medievalism which had swept the country through the pervasive influence of the Ecclesiologists. It had led to a heightened awareness of the word and the corporate nature of the mass. The excessive segregation of the clergy and the congregation which had resulted in chancel arches, half-invisible altars shrouded in mists of incense, screens and choirs acting as barriers between the laity and the ordained was increasingly seen as unacceptable.

Prior's response was an austere church, devoid of distracting decoration and clearly focused on the altar.

The space created is a stark barn defined by the huge structural ribs which form arches across the nave. All questions of style and decoration have been banished. The pointed form of the arches may be reminiscent of gothic and the architect was almost certainly influenced by Saxon forms but these are abstracted to the extent that they melt into an organic image. Prior wrote that 'Church architecture, least of all, has been able to go beyond the trivial efforts of traditional picturesqueness; least of all our buildings has it been monumental'.[2] The sentiments precisely correspond with those of his friend Lethaby whose quote begins the chapter.

At St Andrew's, Prior made no effort to prettify the building. It is a tough church for an industrial, dockside community and monumentality and presence is achieved through its scale and the solidity of its construction. Prior also used reinforced concrete in the arches and the roof structure in an early application of the material in English ecclesiastical work (Bentley was in fact using concrete for the domes at Westminster Cathedral at the same time). The only relief to the rough textured austerity of the interior is the painted chancel ceiling, executed twenty years after the building's completion. An electric sun at its centre and a cosmological scheme of stars, creation and representations of the tree of life and Eden echo Lethaby's preoccupation with symbolism and the archetypal temple, a 'Ceiling like the Sky'.

This phrase is taken from Lethaby's book *Architecture, Mysticism and Myth* (1891), in which he attempts to survey the ancient civilisations and cultures and derive a typology of symbolic elements which he subsequently splits into common themes which run universally across cultures. It is a lyrical exploration of architecture as the embodiment of *Weltanschauung* and can help us understand the impetus behind his remarkable œuvre

Lethaby, like his contemporary Adolf Loos in Austria, was concerned with the stripping down of ornament and a rational approach to building and construction. His writing presages modernist manifestoes:

> A gothic cathedral may be compared to a great cargo ship which has to attain a balance between speed and safety. The church and the ship were both designed in the same way by a slow perfecting of parts; all was effort acting on custom, beauty was mastery, fitness, size with economy of material.[3]

The comparison with the ship is reminiscent of Le Corbusier while the following leaves Loos ringing in our ears:

All Saints, Brockhampton, 1902, W R Lethaby

Queen's Cross Church, Glasgow, 1899, C R Mackintosh

We must remember that beauty may be unadorned and it is possible that ornamentation, which arises in such arts as tattooing, belongs to the infancy of the world, and it may still be that it will disappear from our architecture as it has from our machinery.[4]
Loos' *Ornament and Crime* (1908) echoes these sentiments in precisely the same terms. But Lethaby is also something of a paradox. His writing is lyrical and exposes a depth of knowledge into primitive symbolism and archetypes which is more than a peripheral interest, yet his attitude to architecture is firmly practical to the extent that he preferred the term 'building' as it didn't carry the same connotations as 'art'. It has often been pointed out that despite regarding himself as a humanist he advocated a severe and joyless architecture. But *Architecture, Mysticism and Myth* can be interpreted as a search for meaning in architecture which is independent of ornament but relies on a Jungian collective unconscious as the basis of a language of archetypal elements, the use of which will lead to a freeing of architecture from historicism and sham detailing due to the universal nature of the typology of the structures' fundamental elements. 'Old architecture lived because it had a purpose. Modern architecture, to be real, must not be a mere envelope without contents.'[5]

Of all his buildings, that which illustrates this point of view most clearly is his Church of All Saints, Brockhampton of 1902. The building lies at the start of the new century and ushers in a new mode of thinking and a new architectural epoch. Lethaby's architectural swan-song was his masterpiece. After the completion of this church he devoted himself entirely to teaching. The church is left to speak of his architectural vision and it does so eloquently. The space inside is one of primaeval simplicity and is imbued with a curious sacrality which could belong to the temple of an ancient cult. It is a

powerful expression of Lethaby's conviction that a truly modern architecture could only emerge from a developing tradition in an evolutionary rather than a revolutionary way. Although his writings may lead the reader to assume that he would have become an ardent modernist, this was not the case and he condemned functionalism as 'a *style*, instead of seeking the truly modern, which expands and forms itself'. This church is his interpretation of the fruitful union of an evolving vernacular tradition, new building technology and his own symbolic leanings.

The first of these is addressed by a building which very obviously fits into its Herefordshire vernacular context – the local medieval churches (and secular buildings such as barns) with their broad thatched roofs (Lethaby used thatch for its insulation not for its picturesqueness) and muscular, squat, stone structures. The issue of technology is addressed by the building's construction which consists of mass concrete vaulting with the marks of the form-work left proudly on show between the subtly curving triangular arches (derived from the same source as Prior's structures) which spring from low in the building's thick walls so that the building encloses the congregation like a great tent – the fabric of the canopy of the sky.

With this symbolic gesture Lethaby begins to address the third of the issues – that of symbolism. Perhaps most obviously the building is composed of a series of Platonic solids which come together like universal building blocks. The stumpy tower is formed by the stacking of two cubes crowned by a pyramid, all recurring forms which Lethaby explores in *Architecture, Mysticism and Myth*, the square as the symbol of strength and of the world itself. The tower, too, forms a cube penetrating the roof while the triple lancet window at the east end uses more conventional Christian

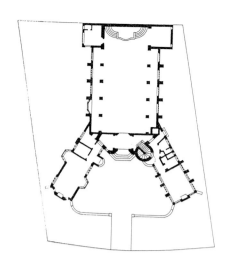

First Church of Christ Scientist, Manchester, 1909, E Wood

imagery – giving parity to all parts of the trinity and this is surmounted by a star, the symbol of Christ's birth and of the heavens themselves. A light fitting at the centre of the church (now removed) reinforced the cosmological theme as a visual representation of Lethaby's 'Jewel Bearing tree' or tree of light while a robust stone font is carved with a tree of life or a sacred vine. Other aspects of the building contain the same attention to detail and relation to universal cosmological archetypes and world models which would constitute a book in themselves.

Lethaby explored these themes in two other ecclesiastical schemes. One was his competition entry for Liverpool Cathedral (1903), a co-operative effort with Henry Wilson, Halsey Ricardo, F W Troup and R Weir Schultz. This was a remarkable entry which defies classification except to say that it is an embodiment of Lethaby's symbolic preoccupations which incorporates elements of Byzantine, Islamic vernacular and a bizarre Babel-like tower all intended to be executed in concrete. By far the most original of the entries and probably the least likely to win in view of the gothic brief, it remains nevertheless an enigmatic image from a route which may have generated a whole new architecture.

The final of Lethaby's ecclesiastical works mentioned here was in fact his first; the Chapel of St Colm and St Margaret at Melsetter House on Hoy in the Orkney Islands. Lethaby designed Melsetter House in 1898, a scheme which involved the conversion of an old laird's house and some outbuildings. In 1900 he built a remarkable chapel for the house which incorporated many of the ideas that he would later use at Brockhampton, including the use of the concrete roof (here covered in the local slate) and the triangular form of the structure. The font features a wavy relief symbolising the water, while sun, moon and cross adorn the keystone of the arched doorway in a simple display of

Lethaby's preoccupation with cosmic and universal symbol systems. Structurally and architecturally it was an advanced design which incorporated elements of the local vernacular, the local prehistoric stone monuments, and modern building technology; a very successful and thoughtful scheme which could have augured well for a new direction in church building.

Of the other entries for the Liverpool Cathedral competition, the most interesting was that of Charles Rennie Mackintosh. Unlike Lethaby's entry, Mackintosh's was in a gothic idiom and was a far less original design. It was, however, interesting in that it shed light on Mackintosh's regard for and skill at using the gothic language to inform his own individualistic style. The architect managed to inject the subtle feel of the Secession into the gently tapering buttresses and the fine, modernised gothic detail.

Mackintosh did in fact get a church built at Queen's Cross in Glasgow between 1897 and 1899. In this building can be seen the same respect for tradition and continuity that is apparent in his designs for the cathedral. Yet the design dates from a period when some of Mackintosh's greatest innovative masterpieces (hailed as precursors of modernism by a maverick genius) were behind him including the Glasgow School of Art. There are similarities between the art school and the church: both are plain and functional and relieved by thoughtful and exquisite detail. The modernity of Mackintosh's church lies in its simplicity and its bold, forthright structure. The church's tower is elegantly battered which gives an attenuated Art Nouveau feel to an otherwise plain gothic church although Mackintosh's fine detailing is in evidence throughout (including the extruded flying buttress). A simple vaulted roof defines the internal space while the walls are tied together with riveted steel I-beams and the unfussy nave has an uninterrupted view of the altar with few distractions within the building.

The roof bears great similarity to another fine church by a less known architect, the Unitarian Church, Middleton, by Edgar Wood designed in 1892. This building is more highly decorated than Mackintosh's with exquisite symbolic carvings; a tree of life on the organ screen and an idyllic agricultural mural engulfing the whole east end. This is very much a *fin-de-siècle* creation, unlike Wood's other important ecclesiastical commission, the First Church of Christ Scientist, Manchester (1903-9). Described by Pevsner as expressionist, the building is an eclectic blend of influences from the USA to Germany and Austria which probably found its way back to influence architects in all those countries in turn.

The building is defined by a Y-shaped plan which is reminiscent of the 'Butterfly' plan which was popular with Arts and Crafts architects working in the domestic field. The arms of the Y outstretch to embrace the outside world and gather the congregation into a basilica-shaped church. The building's exaggeratedly high gable amplifies the domestic message (that this is a house of God) while a Venetian window set into it defines a cross at its centre. This is mixed with a Richardsonian Romanesque entrance arch and a curious, fairy-tale turret set to one side. It is a building which would be at home next to the most avant-garde developments on the continent, and despite its curious vernacular idiom it remains bold, sculptural and modern.

Other churches which grew from the Arts and Crafts movement in Britain tended to be either spectacular bursts of fantasy which were never followed up or sober and worthy experiments which blended the muscular gothic which had garnered such a following with the functionalist simplicity of Morris and his followers. Examples of the latter can be found in W H Bidlake's St Agatha's Church, Sparkbrook (1899-1901) and in the stark, modern vernacular of Lethaby's pupil, Randall Wells, particularly at the Church of St Edward the Confessor, Kempley (1903) where he develops the language of the diagonal grid windows seen at All Saints, Brockhampton. Edwin Lutyens used a stylish but ephemeral mix of gothic and Arts and Crafts at St Jude's, Hampstead Garden Suburb (1909-13) in a pleasing piece of dramatic and picturesque folly, wholly appropriate to its garden city location.

The other category – the explosive and visually stunning

dead end of English Art Nouveau – is encapsulated in two spectacular churches both highlighted in Pevsner and Richards' book *The Anti-Rationalists* (1973). The first of these is Great Warley Church, by Charles Harrison Townsend (1904), architect of the Whitechapel Art Gallery, a seminal influence on European Art Nouveau. The church's rather unremarkable exterior gives way to an exuberant expression of the fecund organicism and swirling tendrils which define continental Art Nouveau but is usually only seen in a more restrained fashion in England. It is an embodiment of the symbolism of the tree of life executed with a lightness of touch which allows the church to breathe and remain a sacred space.

The tree of life and a less restrained palette of *fin-de-siècle* ornamentation has overgrown the other building's interior: the Watts Chapel, Compton (1896) by Mary Watts. Built as a memorial to her husband, the artist G F Watts, the chapel is a symbolist fantasy; every inch of its interior covered in relief gesso work, an interminably intricate pattern of organic overgrowth. Curved walls inside give the impression of a fully circular building and of being engulfed in a grotto with walls of jewels. It is the symbolism and poetry of Lethaby's writing tempered by none of the restraint and rationalism of his architecture. The memorial chapel of an artist, in retrospect it may as well be the epitaph of a beautiful few years in architecture which died away a few years later like the flame from a match but which set souls on fire in Europe in what would prove an unstoppable blaze.

III. SECESSION: Rationalism and Nationalism

After Nietzsche had declared God dead, the most eloquent epitaph was executed by Otto Wagner. His Catholic Church of St Leopold am Steinhof in Vienna of 1907 (illustrated overleaf) is a functionalist response to a brief which has become the generator of the building. The building was begun in the year Einstein published his special theory of relativity; it was a time of unprecedented rational and scientific questioning, of fundamental concepts being upturned, and new perceptions of time, space, God and man's place in the universe were emerging. Wagner had lost his own faith in God slowly over the preceding years;

> Up to my fifty-fifth year I believed in an unknown
> God. Later this God was forced to yield to an
> implacable fate until eventually the idea matured in
> me that man can have no faith and that after death

his body simply returns to the earth . . . There is something extremely distressing about my theory concerning life after death but my reason obliges me to adhere to it.[1]

Ironically it was that very lack of faith which enabled him to interpret the brief in a rational and objective manner and consequently make the great leap forward into the twentieth century. Church architecture had been shackled by the unquestioningly accepted language and clichés which were applied before the building's function had been seriously examined. With this detached analysis of the problems presented by the building of a rational church, Wagner the non-believer came closer to anticipating the reforms which swept continental church design in the twentieth century than did any of his contemporaries. It is perhaps all the more ironic that the capital which produced Freud, the figure who exposed the hypocrisy and the dark depths of the subconscious of *fin-de-siècle* Europe, would play host to this church – in the grounds of a mental asylum and sanatorium.

Nietzsche (who himself ended his days in just such an asylum) had argued in *The Use and Abuse of History*, (1873) that modern man was loaded down by the weight of history and that he was powerless to create or to express his individuality under this great burden. Otto Wagner was one of the first and possibly the most important architects to advocate the same abandonment of historicism in building:

The task of art, and therefore also of modern art, has remained what it has been in all times. Modern art must offer us modern forms that are created by us and that represent our abilities and actions . . . All modern creations must correspond to the new materials and demands of the present if they are to suit modern man.[2]

Wagner successfully moved away from the historicism which was so characteristic of Vienna (although he himself had worked for Ludwig Förster on Ringstrasse buildings) and transcended the raging stylistic debates to create a clean, 'Modern Architecture' the aims of which are proclaimed in his book of that name. The Church of St Leopold am Steinhof was among his most important designs and is roughly contemporary with his Post Office Savings Bank, a building revolutionary in its clarity, simplicity, the modernity of its elevations and its light, airy interior. The church is very much its ecclesiastical counterpart, a breath of fresh air among the formulaic gothic and baroque creations which dominated European church building at the time. This is a practical not a mystical church. J A Lux wrote in his biography of Wagner (1914): 'Whoever believes that the mystical-religious impulse is nurtured in the semi-darkness of a poorly ventilated, cold, damp interior is brilliantly contradicted by Wagner's building.'[3]

The church consists of a single central space defined by a Greek cross plan (with an extended vestibule), as did his earlier chapel in Währing (1895) and his plans for the conversion of a Capuchin church (1898). The structure is a single span crowned by a great cupola, which gives a volume free from structural interventions and distractions. All pews subsequently have a good view of the raised altar and the floor is very slightly raked to improve visual contact further. The pews are designed in rows of four so that any patients can be quickly removed in case of illness or fits. Male and female patients entered through separate doors on either side of the church and a first aid room and toilets were planned in the basement. A gallery allows relatives to attend mass segregated from the patients.

The space is light and white inside; Koloman Moser's stained glass provides much of the lighting and the presbytery is lit from the side to avoid glare. The holy water stoup takes the form of a fountain of running water as a device to stop the spread of infection in a gesture which is typical of the architect's approach to a hygienic building. The decoration is entirely integral to the building; mosaics, metalwork and chandeliers combine in a great Viennese *Gesamtkunstwerk*. An intricate copper baldachin highlights the altar while a profusion of angels in every media looks on. Outside, more angels are perched atop four columns which define the main entrance while above a gilded dome glitters, flanked by a pair of sculpted saints elevated on twin towers so that the effect of the church, which already stands upon a hilltop, is even more magnificent. The church achieves the monumental and the modern, beauty, practicality and even economy. Wagner calculated the costs of various church plans and thus came to the conclusion that the 'gasometer' design was the most economical in terms of visibility of the altar and construction cost. It was a conclusion that others would come to again later in the century.

Vienna was undoubtedly the heart of modernism at the turn of the century. Although the original impulse may have come from Britain, it had lost its way, shambling back into conservatism and only a few lonely

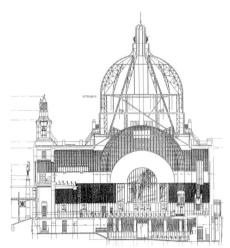

St Leopold am Steinhof, Vienna, 1907, O Wagner; section   St Francis of Assisi, Šiška, Ljubljana, 1930, J Plečnik

figures retained any semblance of innovation. Vienna's position at the hub of a cosmopolitan empire ensured a constant flow of talent into the capital and the best of these young architects gravitated to Wagner's progressive studio. Of these, by far the most original in terms of ecclesiastical design was a young Slovene, Josef Plečnik. Unlike the master, Plečnik retained his faith, to the extent that he devoted his life to God and architecture as if he were a monk. In fact he compared the role of an architect to that of a priest doing good work for the congregation.

Plečnik's first important church was a commission he obtained while still in Vienna in 1908. The Church of the Holy Spirit (1910-13) was to be a meeting place and chapel for Christian Socialists in a poor Vienna suburb. In plan, the church was not innovative: a standard rectangle with the altar at the far end, its section roughly that of a basilica, although the galleries are cantilevered rather than being supported on arcades creating the familiar aisles, but Plečnik's use of concrete was to prove highly influential.

The elevation is an abstracted Greek temple, the language of the columns has been further simplified into a blocky mass and the crypt is supported on angular columns which were to prove a pivotal influence in the development of the odd interlude of the emergence of a Cubist language in architecture in the Czech lands in the years before the First World War. (This itself was the impetus for a number of interesting church designs which, although resembling a form of expressionism, were mainly confined to elevational modelling exercises.) It was an important early use of concrete as a building material and an acknowledgement of its potential as a raw finish.

His next church, however, was a more complete project. He was called upon to build a church at Šiška in Ljubljana (1925-30), his home town. The building shows

a development of Plečnik's classical vocabulary which he used in such an intense and individual way that it cannot be called neo-classical or eclectic and certainly bears no relation to the facile wit of post-modernism, of which he has been hailed as one of the first proponents.

The Church of St Francis of Assisi is based on a square plan with no distracting side chapels and the altar reaches into the congregation to bring them closer to the celebration. The altar is raised in an echo of Wagner's functional preoccupation with view but there is none of the cold aloofness that is so apparent with Plečnik's old professor. Outside, the church is a curious blend of Palladio and a Slovenian mannerism which Plečnik was developing. His work at Prague Castle had shown his incredible talent with composition and detail; every facet of the building was treated with equal reverence resulting in an infinitely satisfying, organic whole. By the time the church was finished, Plečnik had almost completed his ecclesiastical masterpiece, the Church of the Sacred Heart in Prague (1922-33).

This building has an almost absurd presence on the Prague skyline. Its immense belfry protrudes like a looming headstone, a massive *memento mori* with an over-scaled clock at its heart counting away the seconds of our short lives, flanked by two attenuated metronomes.

The sheer brick walls are relieved only by a pattern of shadow caused by raised stones, apparently in an effort to mimic ermine, an emulation of the sacred robes and perhaps a nod to Gottfried Semper's symbolic typology of wall as textile or skin. Inside, the plain walls are relieved by tiny golden crosses which echo the patterns outside, yet do not distract from the monumental unity of the space. Here, too, the sanctuary and the altar are brought into the body of the church; the space that remains before them is a square. The walls of the church are plain brick while above, a row of windows is set into

Church of the Sacred Heart, Prague, 1933, J Plečnik

St Michael's, Barje, Ljubljana, 1938, J Plečnik

the frieze. The altars, too, are plain; veined pale marble articulated using Plečnik's favourite device, the column.

The altar itself is a slab of marble supported on those same columns and enclosed at the sides and back. The device of the columns as legs alludes to the altar's role as table (and the open space behind to its role of reliquary) while to Plečnik the column represented the body, the humanist notion of man as the mark of all things, so it is appropriate that the mensa is supported on columns; as Rudolf Schwarz pointed out, the altar used to be regarded as the body of Christ. Side altars are set diagonally into the corners, each supported on a single column placed at its centre – a recurring device of the architect (and his successor Otto Rothmayer) and one which symbolises his eccentric and distinctly anti-rational approach to the classical language. Another columned altar appears in the tunnel-like crypt, a space defined by one continuous vault creating both ceiling and walls, like the canopy of the encompassing sky.

These are Plečnik's most urbane churches. Those further from the city centres speak another architectural language, a pan-Slavic vernacular blended with his own quirky classicism. For Plečnik, architecture was a language which, like the spoken word, expresses the nature and character of the people. He was concerned to articulate a Slovenian artistic expression in his buildings and consequently referred to those influences which he saw as best defining the local character. His obsession with ionic columns derives from crude vernacular capitals which can be found on ancient Slovenian buildings which show an abstracted but instantly recognisable ionic order. This is blended with the characteristic steep pitched roofs and the mislead-ingly naive mix of classical and local vocabularies which forms the language of his work. This expression is exemplified by his Church of the Ascension, Bogojina

(1925-7), the 'gasometer' Byzantine of his St Anthony of Padua, Belgrade (1929-32), and exquisite interventions into existing structures including the Church of St Michael in the Marsh, Crna (1938-9).

Apart from these, one of the other works which stands out is the remarkable Church of St Michael, Barje (1937-8), a church planned so that it is much wider than it is long. The space has the intimacy of a log-cabin and the altar is placed at the heart of the congregation in a move which presages some of the changes which would be advocated two decades later. The church is approached by a symbolic, long stair and entered through an oddly punctured bell-tower of rough rubble. Lined with column/banisters the ascent is reminiscent of the processional route of the Via Appia in Rome, its culmination is the steps which rise to the altar.

Finally, mention must be made of Plečnik's necropolis. After having as much effect on a city (Ljubljana) as any one architect ever has, he created a city for the dead nearby. His remarkable necropolis can be read like a history of architecture and of entombment. It is a surreal realisation of Loos' contention in *Architecture* (1910) that: 'Only a very small part of architecture belongs to art – tombstones and monuments. Everything else that serves a particular purpose must be excluded from the realms of art'. In those terms this becomes an absurd art gallery, an anti-rational manifesto and a place of immense beauty and power.

Plečnik was not alone in his desire to create an architectural language which could encapsulate a national character. It was a fundamental concern of many architects across the continent at the turn of the century. Again, the impulse can be seen as having sprung from the Arts and Crafts movement in Britain with its incessant longing for a style which was both functional and derived from local conditions, traditions

*Zebegény Church, Hungary, 1909,
K Kós*

*Reformed Church, Budapest,
1912, A Árkay*

Högalid Church, Stockholm, 1923, I Tengbom

and materials. It can be seen as a rational development, one which relied on a Darwinian response to the environment. But often it was more a yearning for national expression and a defiance of a foreign authority. The achievements of these national romantic architects were often greatest where there was most to rebel against. Plečnik's example makes an ideal beginning; countries come little smaller than Slovenia. But many others had architects keen to develop a new national romantic vocabulary and while the movements produced much architecture that was whimsical and irrelevant, much was also created that was of lasting value and great innovation.

Like Plečnik, István Medgyaszay had worked in Otto Wagner's office. Also like Plečnik, he later strove to find an architectural expression of his people's existence. Medgyaszay was a Hungarian who made his life's mission the creation of an architectural language which was derived from the folk art of his nation but which used new techniques of construction to carve out a modern architectural genre. He had also worked in the offices of François Hennebique, the leading French advocate of reinforced concrete. Medgyaszay became an important (though largely forgotten) innovator in concrete design and specifically the use of prefabricated elements.

His church at Rárosmulyad (1909-10) – now Mul'a, Slovakia – is a masterpiece of modern church design. Built entirely from reinforced concrete and to an octagonal plan which ensures the full participation of the congregation, it is a remarkable and prophetic edifice. The tower evokes the image of the spires of the timber folk churches of the area while the shallow dome of the church (surrounded by sculpted angels) recalls Wagner's planned chapel at Währing of 1898. That same church was the inspiration for Vjekoslav Bastl's design for the Church of Saint Blaise at Zagreb of 1901,

although the design of Viktor Kovačič which was finally realised (1912) evokes a more Byzantine feel, perhaps closer to the intense Orthodox feeling of the period which saw the outbreak of the First World War in the Balkans.

Three other Hungarians made a significant impact on church design; Ödön Lechner, Károly Kós and Aladár Árkay. Lechner's churches at Kőbánya (Budapest, 1893-8) and Bratislava (Saint Elisabeth, 1907-13) are further explorations in his search for a Hungarian national style, comparable in their extravagance and originality to his contemporary Gaudí. The Church of Saint Elisabeth features an oval plan and a single impressive domed space with an eccentric strap-work belfry at its side. Kós worked in a national romantic genre which was inspired by the British Arts and Crafts movement and designed a subtle, folky church in Zebegény (1908-9) in a self-effacing vernacular; a handsome building. Árkay dealt in a more monumental national style very much influenced by Lars Sonck in Finland and developments towards a Byzantine modernism in the USA. Árkay's masterpiece, the Reformed Church in Budapest (1912) is a true *Gesamtkunstwerk* in the vein of Otto Wagner: a single great space with a domed roof, adorned with abstracted folk motifs centred firmly on a raised pulpit set into a recess beneath the organ. Every detail of the church is thoughtful and convincing.

The Finnish architect who was an inspiration to many of the Hungarians was at the forefront of the search for a national style along with his contemporary Eliel Saarinen. Lars Sonck's Tampere Cathedral (1902-7) is an abject essay in mass and material, a robust mountain of stone and a highly influential work while Saarinen was to come to prominence in church building later. Elsewhere in Scandinavia two buildings in Stockholm stirred much interest. L I Wahlman's Engelbrecht Church (1904-14) was a kind of ecclesiastical answer to

Grundtvig Church, Copenhagen, 1926, P V Jensen Klint

Berlage's modern handling of brick to contain monumental yet functional spaces which presaged the romantic yet rational work of Ostberg. Inside, huge parabolic brick vaults anticipate the forms of the expressionists in Germany. Its elegant tower is clearly based on northern European precedents yet its stark simplicity recalls the Arts and Crafts; a fine landmark building.

Ivar Tengbom's Högalid Church (1918-23) explores similar territory but with references to an attenuated brick baroque. Most remarkable of all the Scandinavian churches is undoubtedly the Grundtvig Church in Copenhagen. Designed by P V Jensen Klint in 1913 and built 1921-6 it spans the periods of Arts and Crafts, national romanticism and expressionism in a single, great stride. The rugged, stepped massing is derived from traditional Danish models but appears like a looming exaggerated organ. The building's sheer verticality and physical expression of the ascent towards the heavens is clearly gothic in emotion but not in style. The building becomes a kind of stylised mountain in an interesting parallel to the visions of the early expressionists and their obsession with crystal mountains as the palaces of a new society. It is a wonderful creation which bridges the centuries and augurs a new approach to mass, monumentality and form.

IV. GAUDÍ: A Rational Expressionism of Piety

Gaudí's incredible Expiatory Church of the Sagrada Familia in Barcelona combines the mysticism and structural rationalism which defined the gothic and an expressionism, piety and nationalism which was purely his own. Its genesis was as a neo-gothic church but, in the hands of Gaudí, it became the most remarkable monument to the turbulent cultural and intellectual upheaval that occurred at the turn of the century.

The church is very much in the tradition of the *Gesamtkunstwerk* from which Wagner's St Leopold am Steinhof also sprang but even closer to the impetus which spurred the construction of the great gothic cathedrals, not the rational, functional response of Wagner but a desire to create a monument reaching for heaven, a Bible in stone.

Gaudí, who took over the project in 1884, had been heavily influenced by the writings of Viollet-le-Duc and his quest for a reinterpretation of gothic forms using modern technology to overcome the structural problems which the medieval builders were unable to conquer because of the limitations of stone. In the Sagrada Familia he applied the principle of the parabolic arch as a successor to the flying buttress of the gothic; a superior form, one which was stronger and had an inherent strength and one which could be constructed with the skill of the stonemasons who Gaudí admired. But as well as the structural impetus, Gaudí was driven by an intense passion for God and for his Catalan nation. In this he stands close to Josef Plečnik who carved out a Slovenian architecture from his religious fervour and his monk-like devotion to his nationality. Thus, the Sagrada Familia has become a landmark and an icon which both defines and is defined by Barcelona.

The first religious building in which Gaudí's approach becomes clear is the Chapel at the Colonia Güell (1898-1914), a writhing mass of twisted stone in which each element is unique and sculpted according to its position in the overall scheme and the loads and stresses which are imposed on it. It acts like a great organism adjusting its body until it finds the most comfortable position and, as in an organism, each part fulfils a function, nothing is superfluous. The ideas reach fruition in the Sagrada Familia which mixes its metaphors between skeleton and forest temple. The structural elements appear like the

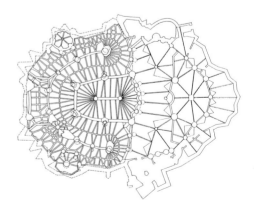

ABOVE AND CENTRE: Church of the Sagrada Familia, Barcelona, 1884-, A Gaudí; plan of the Sagrada Familia; BELOW: Colonia Güell Chapel, Barcelona, 1898-1914, plan of structural elements, A Gaudí

bones of the building while the columns of the nave lean in towards the centre like the canopy of trees in the romantic interpretation of the origin of the gothic arch. The church is a *Biblia Pauperum*, a whole language of symbolism fossilised in a stone which looks like it might burst forth into life at any moment. The twelve soaring spires represent the apostles, their twisting forms metamorphosing into trees, mitres and crucifixes *en route* to the heavens. Sculpture, text and organic decoration envelop every surface in a fantastic recreation of the gothic spirit.

It is an unprecedented construction which from some angles can look like the sticky mess of chewing gum on a shoe straining to stretch between the sole and the earth and from others like a cry of genius rising from the soul to the heavens. Its mere presence cannot but exert an influence on anyone who sees it and the ambition and wild expressionism which stem from a fanatical piety would have a lasting effect on architecture, from Le Corbusier to South America with the remarkable work of Candela and Dieste.

V. GERMAN EXPRESSIONISM
The Star and the Sacred Mountain

When Walter Gropius' Bauhaus manifesto appeared in 1919, Lyonel Feininger's *Cathedral of Socialism* adorned its cover; a fragmented, sparkling image of a gothic cathedral (see overleaf), the shining stars of the trinity burning brightly atop the three spires and emitting rays of light to illuminate the world. It was a metaphor for the enlightenment which was to be found in this new movement, this new school of thought.

The background against which this manifesto appeared is one of chaos and a crumbling society. Germany had lost a crippling war, had suffered a crushing blow to national pride, and its economy was spiralling out of control towards oblivion. There was a frantic search for a model, a utopia to be aspired to. Encouraged by the success of the Russian Revolution, socialism was gathering popularity as a response to a desperate situation. Artists began looking both at the alienation of the individual, the scream from within characterised by Munch's masterpiece and Kierkegaard's existentialism, and the coming together of individuals to create a society and an art which was greater than the sum of its parts; an achievement which would express the unity of mankind in a single, synchronised outburst of artistic creativity moulded into plastic form, an ambition embodied for some in the gothic cathedral.

Just as Pugin had envisaged his utopia on the frontispiece of his *Apology for the Revival of Christian Architecture* (1843) as a medieval city, an idealised urban landscape punctuated by a proliferation of spiky gothic towers, so the Bauhaus used the image of gothic architecture to personify their vision of a utopian ideal. It is a northern European ideal, a picture of the medieval society that created the gothic cathedrals as a high point of Western civilisation, free of the Machiavellian cynicism of the Renaissance and the notion of the artist as inspired demi-urge, a lone maverick genius. The gothic represents the ideal of art as a communal achievement; the individual subsumes his will into the work until it becomes one great collective cry of creativity.

The Bauhaus itself was created in the image of a medieval guild, partly inspired by the English model of the Guild of Handicrafts and Lethaby's Art Workers' Guild. (Lethaby, who we have already encountered here had said that 'No art that is only one man deep can be worth much'.)[1] The socialism of the pioneers of the Arts and Crafts Movement in Britain, from Morris to Lethaby himself, can also be seen as a direct influence on the emerging German idealists. The peculiar blend of gothic imagination and imagery which constitutes the expressionist language and the functionalist aesthetic that emerged from the Bauhaus and from the nascent European modern movement seems paradoxical but the two are inextricably linked.

There are two parallel strands which permeated German architecture around the period of the First World War and which would have resounding repercussions in the emergence of modernism. There was the rational architecture of Peter Behrens, whose workshop was a breeding ground for some of the most forward-thinking young architects (including Le Corbusier), which, despite its popular associations with functionalism, was perhaps more closely related to Schinkel's classicism than to Lethaby. This was an *architecture parlante* in the vein of the French revolutionary architects; it could evoke power when needed, or strength and reliability, or the rational process of a factory production line.

The other vein was a plastic expressionism. This approach generally had little affinity with functionalism and, as a concrete proposition, it is perhaps best exemplified by the work of Hans Poelzig. His was an architecture close to the expressionism of the artist's canvas, architecture as experience, a sculptural and emotional response. What is surprising is that the two approaches met in a brief union. What is perhaps more surprising is that the arena in which they met most fruitfully was sacred architecture.

We have seen that the image of the church, or more precisely the cathedral, was one which helped to define the early expressionism of modernism. The image can be seen in its expressionist manifestation at the heart of Fritz Lang's film *Metropolis* (1926): a nightmare society is saved from doom through co-operation of workers and bosses brought about by love and basic human contact. Technology and rationalism brought to their extremes by a wicked overlord constitute the enemy. Redemption is found through a heroine who preaches from an underground chapel; the finale takes place on the roof of the great gothic cathedral, image of the city itself (see Victor Hugo, p10), while reconciliation takes place outside its doors.

The genesis of this vision of gothic and the centrality of the cathedral to man's mystical yearnings can be traced back in artistic terms to the romanticism of Caspar David Friedrich. His painting *Cross and Cathedral in the Mountains* (1813) shows an image in sympathy with the prevalent mysticism of German expressionism. Nature, the landscape, the trees and the soaring gothic spire combine in an image which is both overtly Christian and dubiously pantheistic.

In *Abbey under Oak Trees* the gothic in question is a ruin, a single lancet window standing as a testament to a lost civilisation and to the permanence of God as a fragment in the landscape, at once within it and part of it. Like Plečnik's rogue single columns (like the cross, the column represents the figure of man, a humanist reaction to Wagner's rationalism), the image is always centred, the cross, the spire always define the focus, just as the spire dominates the centre of the Feininger's woodcut *The Cathedral of Socialism*. This is an expression both of the centrality of the church as a binding force in a society which finds itself increasingly de-centred and alienated and as a reinforcement of the idea of a mysticism at the centre of creation, an unknowable force.

This mysticism included elements from Indian cults and from the highly influential cult of theosophy. The oriental ideal of an architecture which embodied a fusion between the inner yearnings of the soul and the form of the building, an existential sculpture, was particularly attractive to the expressionists. Also

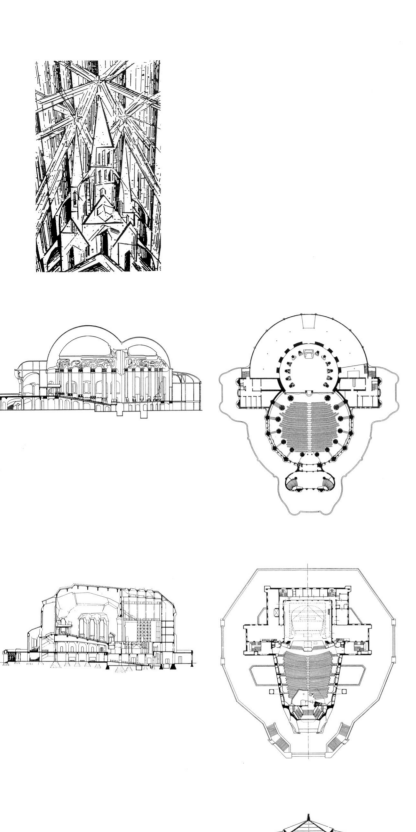

FROM ABOVE: Cathedral of Socialism, *1919, L Feininger; first Goetheanum, Dornach, 1920, R Steiner; second Goetheanum, Dornach, 1928; Sternkirche project, 1922, O Bartning*

attractive to them was an oriental spiritualism which was woven into Rudolf Steiner's cult of anthroposophy, a development of theosophy. The aim of Steiner's cult was in essence to allow man to discover new levels of spirituality and to open up new worlds beyond the physical plane through adherence to the principles of anthroposophy. Steiner was not himself an architect but he nevertheless designed two buildings which would have a lasting influence on both ecclesiastical and secular architecture. The buildings took the form of temples dedicated to Goethe, who was seen as a spiritual father of the cult.

The first of these (Dornach, 1913-20) was a timber building of two great domes on a concrete structure, the columns and elements of which featured variations in form on a pattern attributed to Goethe's theories of metamorphosis. The walls are created in such a way that they dissolve into the whole and cease to be barriers. The plan-form of the circle was adopted because of its symbolic representation of the whole and of complete-ness and the second circle was added to interlock with the first and create a resolved directionality which would avoid the tensions inherent in straight-sided forms, or the incessant revolution implied by the unbroken circle. His experiments with the circular form would have an influence on other architects who began to address the problem of the plan-form of a building to express both spirituality and community.

The first building succumbed to fire and a second Goetheanum was erected, also at Dornach, between 1924 and 1928. Radically different in conception from the first building, this was a sculptural creation in reinforced concrete. Steiner used to mould clay with his hands to create models and the appearance of the building is precisely as if it had been formed in such a way. It is an organic architecture in that each piece relates to the others and the orthogonal; the straight-sided and any trace of angularity have been banished. It is a remarkable display of what can be achieved in the medium of concrete and an immensely powerful building which has exerted an effect on architecture comparable to the curiously organic effect of its elephantine mass on the landscape. Steiner claimed his architecture was an illustration of 'the spiritual evolution of mankind'. It was this evocation, the expression of an inner spirituality, which would have such a far-reaching influence.

Steiner's structures derive from the same impetus as the early visionary sketches of the expressionists. At the centre of these visions is a single structure, usually of crystalline or vaguely gothic form, the function of which is often unclear. The one type of building which crops up in these sketches most frequently is the church. As a building type it has a mysticism and an elemental quality which was an attractive image. But these early pioneers saw the task as deeper than one of merely using the church as a convenient and universal archetype. It was used as a metaphor for the community, a single building which would express the will of the people. It is a Platonic vision of the cathedral as a representation of a higher order, the collective will. It also conveys a pure Platonic beauty, the embodiment of a detached, ethereal ideal. As Taut wrote in *Alpine Architecture* (1919):

> The cathedral and its side aisles are filled with cool daylight. At night, however, its light shines forth into the Mountains and the Heavens . . . The purpose of the Cathedral? None – if prayer in the midst of beauty is not sufficient.[2]

One of the first and most successful architects to translate these disparate and often incohesive ideas into a body of work which contributed significantly to the development of ecclesiastical architecture was Otto Bartning. In the same year as the Bauhaus manifesto appeared, Bartning wrote that a pious person found his way to church out of:

> a conscious or unconscious need to immerse his ego in the great melting pot of the community – in the hope, not only to unite his voice with a thousand other voices in the same words but to lend his outcry from the depths of despair a thousand tongues and a thousand mouths.[3]

Thus the mysticism (the faith in an unknown and unknowable force), the socialism (the immersion of the individual into the greater being of the community) and the visionary new form of architecture with which to express the new ideals in the new shapes and materials (the glass architecture of Scheerbart and Taut and the crystalline cathedrals which litter the sketchbooks of expressionists) come together in the form of the church.

This collective expression of the communal ideal as an architectural generator coincided with increasing interest in the liturgical movement in Germany, the aims of which were fundamentally in sympathy with the move towards architecture as an expression of unity. For a slightly fuller examination of the liturgical movement we can wait for the next chapter; here it will suffice to say that it was a movement from within the Church towards a different kind of worship space; one which would increase the participation of the congregation in the mass and decrease the alienation of the laity from the clergy. While this movement primarily came from within the Catholic Church, architects like Bartning who was a Protestant were coming to similar conclusions and a notion of 'unanimous space'. The gothic was again the model (in idealistic and societal if not liturgical terms) as it seemed the result of a community working in harmony towards a common ideal (in contrast to the bitter fragmented contemporary German society which had been torn apart by war and poverty). But the architecture which sprang from the German debates was far from the historicism of the nineteenth century. It was a genuinely new expression created through a slowly emerging understanding of the capabilities of new materials, a sculptural and emotional approach to space, and the re-examination of the nature of worship and ritual.

Otto Bartning's churches developed from the same impulses which inspired Bruno Taut and the crystalline fantasies of Paul Scheerbart. Taut's Glashaus pavilion for the Deutsche Werkbund in 1914 was illustrated in the accompanying pamphlet, captioned with the phrase 'The Gothic cathedral is the prelude to glass architecture'. The building was one of the first manifestations of the crystal mountain which appears in Taut's own drawings and those of his contemporaries. Until then, these fantasies had been confined to paper, more symbolic images than concrete proposals. Bartning was one of the first to develop them into three dimensions and to visualise them as buildings with functions: churches.

Whereas the Taut brothers, Wenzel Hablik, Wassili Luckhardt and the others had given these glass mountains spurious names, or simply labelled them 'monuments', Bartning saw that this vision could be translated into a functioning type, a church which would inspire and unite, achieving the lofty ideals of the expressionists while steering clear of the rational, materialist, positivist approach of the functionalists. His project for a stellar church (*Sternkirche*) in 1922 is a remarkable example to begin with. Constructed of a series of shells formed around a circular plan, this is one of the most visionary church designs of the century. Its conception can perhaps be seen in the prose of Bruno Taut. An article which appeared in the expressionist magazine *Frühlicht* (edited by Taut himself, 1920-22)[4] contains the following extract:

> The visitor will be filled with the joy of architecture, which will drain all human elements from his soul and

Circumstantes project, 1923, D Böhm

Church of Christ the King, Mainz-Bischofsheim, 1926, D Böhm

make it a receptacle for the divine. Building is the reflection and the greeting of the stars: its plan is stelliform, the holy numbers 3 and 7 combine in it to form a unity . . . the illumination comes from between the interior and exterior glass shell . . . it shines from afar like a star. And it rings like a bell.

Bartning used the star shape with which Taut was also enamoured to create the structure for his church. The points on the plan are defined by structural ribs which support the shell, which could be described as resembling the articulated back of an armadillo with glazing between the joints. Steps push outwards from the form like ripples in water and elevate the building until its image becomes familiar as the embodiment of the crystal mountain from the sketches. The mystical obsession with the magic power of numbers referred to in the text is here applied to the building's structure; seven bays create the internal space while the sanctuary is supported by three piers in a bay which departs from that unit seen elsewhere. The design is the personification of Johannes van Acken's vision: 'Now trigger the process off by adding Christ, which must be a clear and purposive liturgical awareness of Christ, and the whole will grow into the new and powerful crystal unity'.[5]

Although it is a beautiful and visionary structure, the true significance of the design lies at its heart: the altar. The plan is centralised and symmetrical and the altar is at its centre in a radical departure from the orthodoxy. From the *Cathedral of Socialism* is derived the socialist cathedral. This is a building in which the congregation surrounds the altar, the church is brought to the people; the crystal mountain has come to Mohammed.

The other revolutionary feature at the heart of the building is the pulpit. One of the long-standing problems of Protestant church architecture had been the positioning of the pulpit relative to the altar. Bartning's

remarkable solution was to create two scenarios within the same building. In one variation the congregation would face the pulpit at its centre while the altar stood above. The move to an altar-centred space was achieved by the worshippers physically moving around so that the altar dominates while the pulpit is lowered away so as not to interfere and, thus, the crowd partakes in a symbolic journey or pilgrimage around the space. The floor dips towards the pulpit in a rake (the symbolic valley) and rises around the altar, a metaphor for the mountain: altar as extension of the earth while the canopy of the sky and the forest of vaults and columns form the covering. Some of these remarkable ideas were later realised at Bartning's Church of the Resurrection at Essen.

Although the *Sternkirche* remained a paper project its influence was felt strongly and some of the innovations inherent in the scheme were realised by the other towering figure of expressionist and modern church design in Germany, Dominikus Böhm. In the same year as Bartning's proposal, Böhm designed a scheme which was sadly also destined to remain a sketch; the *Circumstantes*. This was an elliptical church with the altar where you would expect the stage to be in a theatre. The structural piers all point towards the altar, as if defining some mystical energy emanating from the heart of the building. An arched baldachino surmounts and emphasises the altar in the midst of the cavernous space while in elevation the building is almost reminiscent of the Tower of Babel.

A number of other buildings which were executed display a remarkable expressionism. Böhm's St John the Baptist, Neu-Ulm (1926), is executed in a brooding, powerful gothic expressionism with a wonderfully mystical cave of a baptistry. The interiors of his Church of Christ the King in Mainz-Bischofsheim (1925-6) and the Parish Church at Freilingsdorf (1926-7) are defined

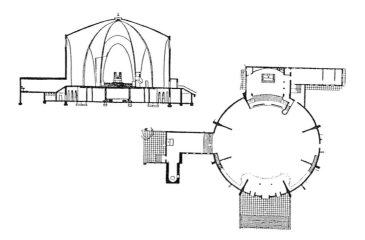

Church of St Engelbert, Riehl, 1930, D Böhm

by curious triangular gothic pointed arches which spring from floor level. These vaults are in fact of concrete on an iron-mesh framework which is itself suspended from the steel structure; theatricality was a greater concern than functionalism. Wolfgang Pehnt has compared the shape of these vaults to Lethaby's All Saints Church in Brockhampton and, while the structural integrity and honesty which obsessed Lethaby is wholly missing, there is no mistaking the shape or the concerns about mystical archetypes which the architects obviously shared. Böhm's sketch for Christ the King, Kuppersteig of 1928 also presents a powerful vision of a great, single parabolic vault covering an undeniably impressive, cavernous space.

The parabolic vault which replaced the almost triangular vault in Böhm's work reached its apex in his design for the Church of St Engelbert, Riehl (1930). In one of the most influential buildings of its era, Böhm created a perfectly circular church; the first modern Catholic church freed from the tyranny of the rectangular plan. The points of Bartning's *Sternkirche* have evolved into great arches, almost disappearing as thin piers on plan. The body of the church is left free for corporate worship; the ancillary functions including baptism and the campanile are banished to the side for the sake of clarity while other rooms are housed beneath the building (there is also a community centre beneath; this was a popular facility at the time in Germany and a reflection of the ideal of the church's role as *Volkshaus*). The uninterrupted space leaves the congregation free to concentrate on the service without distraction while the circular plan brings them into a closer and less hierarchical union with the altar. The altar, however, is set in a small sanctuary in a recess from the main circle and is reached by a series of steps; thus Böhm deliberately retains the directionality of the

building, the idea of ritual procession and progression towards the altar while maintaining the unity of the congregation.

This is fundamentally a church belonging to the modernist tradition but its form is so spectacular that it merits its place with the expressionists, as do many of Böhm's other designs. Huge parabolic arches of reinforced concrete meet to form a structure which is as remarkable as that of a perpendicular church. The structural ribs converge on the building's apex – like segments of an orange from the inside – where an unseen lantern spreads light around the roof, like the halo around the sun in an eclipse. The effects of the shadows and the remarkable natural lighting which models the curves and arches so boldly would have found its place on most expressionist film sets. It is a remarkable and powerful space which achieves the effect of gothic monumentality in an unsentimental manner. There is no question of historicism, this is a purely modern structure, using the latest technology and materials.

The form of the parabolic arch had been used in factories, hangars and engineering projects (as well as notably by Gaudí) and its effect remains almost shockingly modern. From without the building is a mass of bricks, almost unrelieved but for a few small details – the round windows beneath the apex of the arches and the ends of the concrete beams which support the choir and organ gallery protruding through the wall above the door, which form a kind of visual canopy to attract attention to the main entrance. Again, approached up steps, the whole has the effect of a great mountain rising from the mud of the earth towards the heavens.

Böhm was also responsible for a series of monumental churches which, while not exactly expressionist, speak a language of monumentalism which belongs more to the *architecture parlante* of the expressionists than to his later, profoundly modern work. Among these, the Church of St Joseph, Hindenburg (now Zabrze, Poland) of 1938 is a haunting composition of arches and brick bulk. It has the brash engineering power of a Roman aqueduct and a rational solidity which make it enigmatic. It can be seen as a forerunner of some of the curiously sterile monumental works constructed under fascism in both Germany and Italy, particularly the EUR buildings and later the rationalists.

The Church of St Adalbert, Berlin (1931-3) by C Holzmeister uses a similar archetypal architectonic language successfully in a tight urban setting and Böhm's Church of St Elisabeth, Cologne (1932) and St Engelbert's Church, Essen (1935) also belong to the same genre (if rather more muted in ambition and reference to the vernacular), while his Church of the Holy Cross, Dulmen (1939), is a fine example of his later crisp modernism, exquisitely articulated, beautifully lit and liturgically functional, a very high level of architecture indeed.

Other architects were also creating astonishing expressionist designs through the 1920s. Max Taut's Marble Church of 1919 was a pioneering vision of the church as a pilgrimage way ascending into a crystalline paradise while Otto Kohtz's project for a cathedral as far back as 1905 (published in *Gedanken über Architektur*, 1909) seems to presage the Taut brothers' geological inspiration. The designs of the Czech cubists may also be linked into expressionism although their concerns were rather with the creation of a new national mode of expression and a geometric configuring of space as the tectonic answer to the revolution in the depiction of planes in cubist painting. Jiři Kroha's design for a church at Vinohrady (1919) and the sketches of Bedrich Feuerstein and Josef Štepánek, however, create an interesting parallel over the common border.

Hubert Pinand's St Marien's Church in Limburg an der Lahn (1927) featured the altar in an apse of parabolic vaults and crescent-shaped windows in a surreal vision of what appears to be a melting morass of structure and light. Hans Poelzig himself, the great expressionist master, made his contribution in model form with a remarkable design for a pilgrimage chapel reminiscent of a huge, ordered stalagmite formation, the form of the gothic church lingering below the surface. Fritz Höger's Wilmersdorf Church in Berlin (1932) blends an almost Art Deco modernism with expressionist devices and a triangular gothic entrance to build a dramatic church with an attenuated belfry, constituting one of the most distinctive buildings to come out of the era.

By the end of the 1920s the focus had shifted towards a more rational response to an increasingly defined liturgical brief. Bartning and Böhm are the two key figures who stand astride both expressionism and the next phase. Their pioneering work formed the foundation of a powerful new modernism born not of aesthetic whim but of solid, underlying liturgical and theological reform. The centre of progress remained in Germany but we need to move to France and back a few years to pick up the thread of the narrative.

VI. AUGUSTE PERRET
Prophet of the Modern Church

With the building of one particular church by Auguste Perret, the focus of innovation in ecclesiastical architecture shifts momentarily from Germany and back to France. The last mention of France came with Anatole de Baudot's St Jean de Montmartre of 1894. Pevsner names this church as the first non-industrial building to 'use reinforced concrete systematically'.[1] Equally importantly, the architect has abandoned the historicist vocabulary and the church's interior is light and simple, the structural ribs providing the form and definition of the space and the articulation of the structure itself; they are left exposed and proud of it.

By the time St Jean was finished in 1902, another structural innovator, Auguste Perret, had designed an apartment block in the Rue Franklin in Paris with a concrete skeleton, a staple building in books on the origins of modern architecture. It was to be Perret who would single-handedly shift the focus of innovation back to France twenty years later with the Church of Notre Dame du Raincy in Paris.

The Church of Notre Dame du Raincy was completed in 1923, the year which saw the publication of Le Corbusier's *Vers une Architecture*. The influence which it exerted and the effect which it had on twentieth-century church architecture is easily comparable to that of Le Corbusier's most famous book on secular building and planning. At a stroke, Perret demonstrated the worth of the liberation of church building from the straitjacket of historicism; as Gropius states in *Scope of Total Architecture* (1943) he 'succeeded in freeing architecture from its ponderous monumentalism'.[2]

Perret had been commissioned to design the church

largely because other architects had submitted proposals which were far too expensive. He had never designed a church before, which makes it all the more remarkable that at Le Raincy he created such a visionary and insightful masterpiece. Using reinforced concrete, Perret was able to create a new type of space, a single great hall reminiscent of the basilica form in which the early Christians worshipped and a space which presages the great 'single-space' (*Einraumkirche*) churches which German architects would later develop and which became common currency in the post-war period.

As well as freeing the internal space, the use of reinforced concrete negated the walls' structural function thereby allowing the expansive fenestration which gives the church its character and its intense quality of light. G E Kidder Smith compares the revelation of the liberating effects of structural concrete to the effects of Abbé Suger's order to 'open up' the walls of St Denis to allow the light to flood into the church,[3] and there are indeed similarities with the gothic. The invention of the flying buttress was a similar leap forward in gothic structure, which allowed a greater freedom of expression in the windows as a metaphor for the light of God in structural acrobatics which finally led to the perpendicular style, in which the wall as solid element almost disappears.

Perret's church is also reminiscent of the gothic in its massing, its form culminating in a slender, reeded spire tapering to open-work fins surmounted by a crucifix. But it would be superficial to dwell on these interpretations. The church is a remarkably innovative structure, not only for its daring use of exposed concrete (the marks of the shuttering are left exposed throughout and there is no effort expended to cover up the nature and texture of the concrete), but also for its plan.

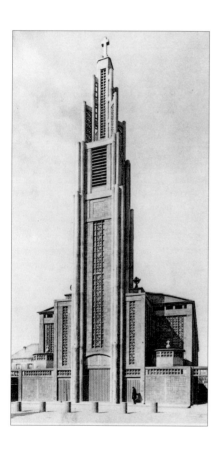

Although there may seem nothing particularly innovative about the single long rectangle which constitutes the building's interior, on closer inspection, it becomes apparent that Perret has done away with the choir and consequently with the marked separation of the altar and the congregation in a move which is, in fact, the very antithesis of the gothic plan. The relative strength of the concrete means that the arcades which broke the space of the gothic interior up into nave and side aisles have been reduced to spindly columns which barely demarcate a separation so that the whole space melts into one and the congregation feels as one great body. In an extension of this breaking down of the

ABOVE: Wilmersdorf Church, Berlin, 1932, F Höger; CENTRE AND BELOW: Church of Notre Dame du Raincy, Paris, 1923, A Perret

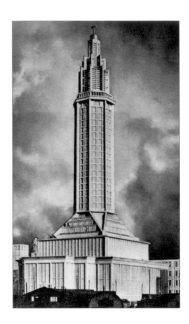

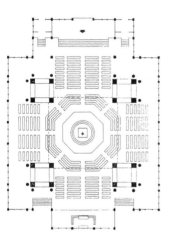

demarcation of solid and void and interior and exterior, Perret replaces the walls with concrete lattices which seem to deny the weight of the structure and open it out to the light so that the walls disappear into an abstract pattern of light and colour: the physical structure of the church is reduced so that the emphasis is on the single collective body of the congregation; the mass shifts from the building as the House of God to the worshippers as the Body of Christ.

The church is flooded with light; a remarkable spectrum of colour follows the ritual progression from entrance to altar. The glass nearest the entrance is yellow in colour and, going east, it changes through orange, red and violet until the shallow curve of the apse wall bathes the altar in a mysterious deep blue light. Other innovative touches in Perret's church include a floor which falls slightly towards the raised altar in an effort to achieve better visual contact in what is in fact a large building, designed for a capacity of 2,000, and the placing of the vestry and sacristies beneath the raised chancel so that the purity and simplicity of the single space is retained from within and without.

It should also be noted that this was a design with economy in mind. The building elements were designed to be cast as simply as possible and with the minimum of different forms. The columns are repetitive as are the lattices which make up the walls so that the whole could be constructed with the minimum fuss and labour. Far from leading to a poor space, this repetition introduces a sublime simplicity: the use of the curtain wall adds to the metaphor of the church as 'God's tent', as if the walls have disappeared into a tarpaulin of exotically coloured fabric. It is a prophetic metaphor and one which would recur later in church design.

Perret executed one more church commission soon after the completion of Notre Dame du Raincy, at Montmagny, near Paris, with his Church of St Thérèse (1925). The building is similar but less powerful than his earlier masterpiece and continues with the same concerns and devices while not taking them any further and without the effortless elegance of his church at Raincy. He further developed and articulated his architectural language with a design for St Benedict's Church, Carmaux in 1939, a design which shows a refinement of his vocabulary to a monumental classical language closely related to his work at the Musée des Travaux Publics of 1937. But the design he submitted for a competition in 1926 to build a cathedral to Joan of

ABOVE: Church of St Thérèse, Montmagny, 1925, A Perret; BELOW: Church of St Joseph, Le Havre, 1959, A Perret

Arc was a remarkable reassertion of his genius. In the design, Perret developed his ecclesiastical architectural language one stage further. He proposed a huge tower which was to have been open much of its absurd height and would have flooded the interior with an extraordinary light.

This was a monumental proposal with less in common with the simple aims of the liturgical movement than his other churches; a building with perhaps too big an ego, but architecturally it would have been a *coup*. It had something of the New York skyscraper in its stepped forms and the monumental nature more of a ziggurat than a cathedral, but it was not chosen and lost out to a dull entry; a sad loss to the history of church building. The consolation is that Perret was given a chance to try out some of the ideas of the failed scheme in his capacity as architect and planner for the French town of Le Havre, which he helped to rebuild after the destruction it suffered in the war.

At the Church of St Joseph, a square plan is surmounted by a huge tower which, like its predecessor on paper, is open throughout and lets a shaft of brilliant light down to illuminate the altar which is placed centrally beneath. The body of the church is simple and does not distract from the service which is conducted in a progressive fashion, with seating surrounding the altar on all sides. The effect of the light above the altar is almost mesmeric; the same use of colour is employed as at Le Raincy, noting the liturgical importance of the colours and relating this to their position in the architecture.

From without the church is a symbol, a great spiritual lighthouse, its tower a looming beacon for the harbour. In it can be felt an echo of St Andrew's, Roker where Prior was also aware of the church's spiritual and physical significance in its dockside location. The similarity between two architects who were concerned to create powerful and simple forms as houses for worshippers and to abandon trivial aesthetic considerations is not a superficial comparison.

By the time St Joseph's was completed in 1959, Perret was dead. In the time that had elapsed between the genesis of the ideas which formed the basis of his submission for the Joan of Arc competition and their realisation at Le Havre, the momentum in the world of modernism in church building had shifted back to Germany again after the brief flirtation with France due almost entirely to Perret's genius.

VII. MODERNISM AND LITURGICAL REFORM
A Brief Background

The word 'liturgy' is derived from the Greek words 'leiton' (people, the same root as 'laity') and 'ergon' (work). The liturgical movement was, in essence, a re-examination of the roots of the word.

To outline the situation at the turn of the century, it is necessary to go back to the Middle Ages, and before. There had been a gradual erosion of the participatory nature of the early Christian celebration so that by the Middle Ages, the laity was virtually excluded from the ritual. The mass was celebrated in Latin, which was understood by few across Europe. Primitive and illiterate peoples and tribes had followed their leaders into Christianity and understood little about its nature; their exclusion from the Eucharist became almost inevitable. The priest celebrated mass with his back to the congregation whilst he mumbled away in meaningless tones. The Church itself treasured and protected its privileged position as the sole guardian of knowledge, education, enlightenment and mystical powers.

Architecturally the effects of the change are embodied in the gothic cathedral when seen against the early Christian church form, the basilica or the simple room in a domestic house. The chancel, originally an area for worshippers, came to exclusively house the clergy and grew in length as their self-importance and pride increased. The area became increasingly separated physically from the rest of the church with the advent of rood screens and other devices so that the laity became alienated from the clergy and the ritual. The Reformation had reacted to both these circumstances and an increasingly corrupt and powerful clergy, and in Protestant architecture, the focus was generally shifted to the pulpit, as the sermon and the Bible itself (spoken in the vernacular) became the underpinning element of the service, along with private prayer and a personal relationship with God, without the brokers.

The Counter Reformation followed with a massive effort to draw people back with gold and angels and a new, sumptuous plasticity in architecture (after the humanist experiments of the Renaissance which were seen as pagan-based and part of the reason for the decline in the Church's authority). The nineteenth century saw a return to a blind admiration of the medieval forms and the Latin mass which affected many Protestant countries (a short account of which occurs in the first chapter). Thus, the situation at the beginning of the twentieth century was comparable in many places to the Middle Ages. Architecture had ceased to be a living response to changes and developments in theology and had become a historicist exercise concerned with the minutiae of detailing and style; even within the gothic camp there were debates about what period of gothic to copy. Architecture had become fossilised and largely irrelevant.

The historical styles which were the mainstay of church building had been appropriated by secular buildings. A gothic building was as likely to have been a town hall or a station; domes and towers could be found on concert halls and pumping stations. The symbolic significance of building elements had been diluted and meaning became fuzzy around the edges. As well as this, the Church had been gradually losing its central position in an increasingly materialist and rationalist society, its fundamental precepts being eaten away by theories of evolution, positivism and political ideology on the left and right but particularly by the rise of Marxism.

This situation led a handful of reformers from across the Church to reassess the Church's role in society and its most important manifestation, the liturgy. The early moves towards this analysis and rethinking emanated from Belgium towards the end of the nineteenth century and spread through The Netherlands, Germany, France and beyond. The real boost came at the beginning of the twentieth century from Pope Pius X who encouraged the reforms throughout his papacy (1903-14). The pope died at the beginning of a war which would change the political landscape of Europe and see a revolution in Russia. The war was devastating and left behind it a trail of disillusionment with the *status quo* which gave an added momentum to the urgency of the reforms if the Church was to retain its vitality as an institution.

The objectives of the reformers were succinctly described by Anton Henze in his book *Contemporary Church Art:*

> The aim of the liturgical movement was to transform the faithful from 'silent onlookers' (Pius XI) to active participators in the offering; the individual worshippers were to join with the priest to form one community united by sacrifice. It was the task of church architecture to conform to this developing community of the altar, confirming and strengthening it and providing it with an environment in which each person should be in contact with each, and all with the altar, participating visually and orally, unhindered, in the sacrifice of the mass.[1]

Henze begins to outline the implications of this fundamental reform on ecclesiastical architecture by stressing the central importance of the altar. This was a return to the conception of the altar as the table of the Last Supper, around which people gather; a very different notion to that of the high altar which is seen as exclusive and separate from the people, the preserve of the clergy. The Protestants had already experimented with moving the altar during the Reformation when the traditional stone altar was replaced by a table of wood. This had the effect of making the communion table moveable and it could be set up in a forward position in the chancel or actually among the congregation in the nave. The wooden table constituted a return to the symbolism of the supper, and of the participation in the meal of the congregation. It also meant that the celebrant could face the congregation across the table and not with his back to them. But as the focus in Protestant churches tended to be the pulpit and the 'Word', the significance of this move was sometimes lost. The change in priorities also led to the demand for all to be able to see and hear and, ultimately and inevitably, in the reduction of the size of churches.

For these reasons, the elemental shift in liturgical thinking which has occurred during the twentieth century can almost be seen as a new reformation and the effect that it had on architecture was as drastic as that of the Reformation itself. The architecture of the Reformation was a reaction to a group of gothic buildings which had become an anachronism, no longer relevant to the new situation, and generally adopted a stripped, austere classical vocabulary with light, simple spaces which was seen as the most modern architecture at the time.

Similarly, the liturgical movement in the twentieth century responded to a debased historicist vocabulary and a set of buildings which had nothing to do with the new liturgical perception by using the most modern architecture available to them. The aims of this were broadly in line with those of the Reformation: light, humane spaces; the aim of which was not to intimidate or instill with awe, but to facilitate communion, participation and a sense of the congregation itself as the House of God and the Body of Christ. The function of the building was not to be in itself a representation of some paradise, or a trailer for the forthcoming attraction of heaven (the spirit in which the gothic was conceived). Instead, the aim of the architecture was to promote community and (here we return to the expressionist vision of the submission of the will of the individual to the crowd), in the words of Otto Bartning, to encourage 'active contribution of the individual's emotion as expanded into and absorbed by the collective emotion of the foregathered community'.[2]

What made the period so fascinating from an architectural point of view was that it coincided exactly with the birth of modernism and in many ways the objectives of both the liturgical movement and the modernists coincided. Both were a rejection of the hypocrisy of a prevailing situation which was characterised in both fields by complacency and a lack of understanding of the brief or the fundamental roots of space and the liturgy. In *The Church Incarnate* (1938) Rudolf Schwarz, the great prophet of modern liturgical design wrote:

> We cannot return to the early cathedrals and take up their interrupted discipline once more. This was the error of the Historicists. Even the tools, our 'technology' would fail us. It would of course be possible to copy the deep doorways and the mighty pillars of the Romanesque or the pointed arches of the Gothic. But it would not be true. For us the wall is no longer heavy masonry but rather a taut membrane, we know the great tensile strength of steel and with it we have conquered the vault. For us the building materials are something different from what they were to the old masters. We know their inner structure, the positions of their atoms, the course of their inner tensions. And we build in the knowledge of all this – it is irrevocable. The old, heavy forms would turn into theatrical trappings in our hands and the people would see that they were an empty wrapping. They would draw premature conclusions about the matter which is served by these empty forms.[3]

That part of the modern movement which was concerned with functionalism, the inheritors of Lethaby rather than the builders of white villas which adopted only the functionalist aesthetic, was concerned principally with a rational examination of the brief. When this approach was applied to ecclesiastical architecture, architects did not have the clear brief that a factory, hospital or house could provide. They had to return to the fundamentals of worship, another move which ran parallel to the aims of the liturgical movement. Simply an application of modern technology and forms to the problem of ecclesiastical design was an inadequate

solution and would have been a betrayal of modernist ideals. Schwarz summed up:

> . . . it does not suffice to work honestly with the means and forms of our own time. It is only out of sacred reality that sacred building can grow. What begets sacred works is not the life of the world but the life of faith – the faith, however, of our own time . . . that sacred substance out of which churches can be built must be alive and real to us.[4]

VIII. THE CHURCH INCARNATE
Modernism and the Church

Perret's Notre Dame du Raincy constituted a fundamental turning point in Ecclesiastical architecture. It illustrated that modern materials could be used in a modern idiom to create an architecture which was both sacred and relevant to an industrial age. It was a result of a change in liturgical thinking allied with a grasp of modern technology and construction; in effect, the first modern church. What Perret achieved in concrete, Otto Bartning was to achieve in steel.

Bartning (whose experiments in modern church architecture were referred to in chapter V and were among the most advanced) dismissed the mysticism and sentimentality to which church architecture had been bound (and which, it has to be said, was not entirely absent in his own earlier expressionistic designs) to transcend stylistic arguments and create an architecture which was fundamentally of its time: an architecture which took the liturgy as its heart and which developed its expression from the inside out. Thus he was closer to the spirit of investigation associated with the functionalism which was developing in contemporary Germany. He wrote: 'It is wrong to believe that by using modern materials and building techniques we secularize church construction. There is a spiritual quality in any material. It is our task to find this spirit and put it into the service of religion.'[1] In so doing he freed church architecture from the constrictions to which it had been subjected and was able to undertake an experiment in steel which became one of the foundations of modern ecclesiastical architecture.

The *Stahlkirche* (steel church) was built for an exhibition at Cologne in 1928 and was later re-erected in 1929 in Essen. As Perret had done, Bartning used the structural strength of the material to free the walls from their load-bearing responsibility. This allowed him to break down the sense of enclosure through fully glazed walls which 'close us in and at the same time open up the inside to the outside and hold us in the magic spell of the changing light of day and night'.[2] The concrete grille framework of Perret's church has here given way to a butterfly-wing effect, the frame is like lace and the whole church is light itself. The columns of the structure stand out against the glass as expressions of the aspirationally vertical.

The plan of the church was also a departure from Perret's basilica form: it is roughly parabolic, its apex being the curved apse of the sanctuary. The seating fans out slightly to place the congregation closer to the centre of the celebration. As the walls melt into one continuous membrane, what is left of the hierarchical division is expressed through the floor. The altar and pulpit are granted equal emphasis by their position on the central axis although the altar sits on a raised dais giving it extra importance in the composition as a natural culmination to a plan which is focused entirely upon it. Just as the altar is raised to express its sacred nature, so the whole building sits above ground level and is entered via a ritual procession heavenward. Below the church are accommodated all the ancillary facilities so that the single worship space is kept pure and unhindered.

The church was erected using very simple constructional techniques so that it could be easily dismantled and rebuilt. The building presages prefabrication and is a model of the mass production ethic of the Bauhaus, genuinely cheap and mobile (in a dramatic nod to the metaphor of the church as tabernacle, 'God's tent'), utilising the standard elements of engineering construction, notably the humble I-beam which forms the basis of its construction. Bartning used a solid foundation, a plinth of reinforced concrete which contrasted with the delicacy of the glass and the building was massed in such a way that it rose to the church above, from the massive to the light. This also meant that at night, when lit within, the building appeared to be a floating crystal of light in what was both a reflection of the form of the gothic cathedral with its broad, curved apse and the expressionist obsession with transparency and light. Yet the picturesque preoccupations of expressionism have been expelled and the gothic sentimentality which survived in Perret's spires has been replaced by a rational response; the tower remains, but as a blocky mass to house the bells and signify the entrance. This is a tough church for an industrial age and an industrial area. It revels in the local technology of steel and sits comfortably in the industrial landscape of northern Germany. If Notre Dame du Raincy was the first modern church, the *Stahlkirche* was the first modernist church.

Another of Bartning's highly original designs was the Gustav-Adolf Church, Berlin-Charlottenburg (1934), where he explored another plan form, that of the fan, which can be seen as a variation on the parabolic plan of his *Stahlkirche*. The fan is a segment of the circle, thus the perfection of that form is implied but with a clear directionality which is lost in the often aimless circular plan, the focus of both space and structure (the concrete beams of the roof) being firmly fixed on the altar.

Bartning's earlier buildings appeared in the expressionist section along with those of Dominikus Böhm, although the works of both men could simultaneously appear in the modernist section as pioneering and experimental, but the buildings which I included in that section retain a whiff of the picturesque and the deliberately mystical. Böhm's great Church of St Engelbert, Riehl (see p27), was the first building to exploit the perfect circle as a plan for a democratic church, a body for truly corporate action, the circle being the traditional symbol of togetherness and wholeness, of God himself.

It was consequently one of the most influential of twentieth-century church designs but Böhm was in fact preceded by his contemporary, Bartning, with a circular church which embodied a harder approach than his slightly self-consciously elegant parabolic forms. The Round Church, also in Essen (the final destination of the *Stahlkirche* until it was destroyed by bombing), is an example of the 'gasometer' design propounded by Otto Wagner. Stacked circles form a subtle pagoda effect, executed in stark materials; brick, concrete, glass and metal. The interior is light and functional and highly centralised although, curiously, focused on the font rather than the altar.

Maguire and Murray in their book on modern churches (1965)[3] compare the form itself to the traditional form of the baptistry and specifically to a baptistery designed by Bartning in Berlin in 1927, where a simple circular space reminds us of Bruno Taut's pavilion at the Cologne Werkbund exhibition. There is an element of the courtroom about the church and the organisation is definitively democratic but it is a curious building and, although more modern in its language than Böhm's church at Riehl, it is perhaps a less successful church, though a highly influential scheme.

The other German church of the same period which had a similar impact on modern ecclesiastical architecture was Rudolf Schwarz's Corpus Christi in Aachen built in 1928-30. Like Bartning's *Stahlkirche* this was an architecture of functionalism but it was derived not from superficial aesthetic concerns and the 'white' architecture of the International Style but from a deep understanding of the liturgical renewal. It is a modernism which has developed from the functional requirements of the changing liturgy and not imposed as a stylistic vocabulary. It is the embodiment of Walter Gropius' assertion in *Scope of Total Architecture* (1943) that 'Modern architecture is not a few branches of an old tree – it is new growth coming right from the roots' where those roots are the liturgy and a re-examination of the spirit and meaning of the Eucharist. The building is a starkly plain mass, unrelenting in its purity. At the time it was referred to in a derogatory fashion as 'the factory' due to its uncompromising functionality.

The church consists of a single cubic volume and another rectangle at right angles to it which contains the ancillary accommodation and is divorced from the worship space. A tall white campanile rises beside the building like the chimney of a great power station. The interior of the church culminates in a chancel raised seven steps above the floor. Below the eaves is set a series of small square windows. The black marble altar contrasts harshly with the dazzling white of the interior. The pulpit is wrapped around a long pier which is similarly of black marble and which divides the eucharistic space from the lower ceilinged aisle to its side which runs the length of the church. Thus the twin foci of the church are highlighted by material and elevation alone. The only other relief to the interior is that of light: both the simply punctured openings and the pendant light wires which fall like a shower of stars from the ceiling. These innovative fittings could be switched in such a way as to change the pattern and intensity of light; they serve to fill the austere emptiness which surrounds the congregation.

The idea of emptiness is considered and deliberate. Schwarz was at the heart of the liturgical movement and close to one of its key figures, the theologian Romano Guardini. When Guardini visited the Church of Corpus Christi he spoke of the 'silence' of its interior. This arose partly from Schwarz's studies of oriental thought and form and is close to the intense spiritual contemplation

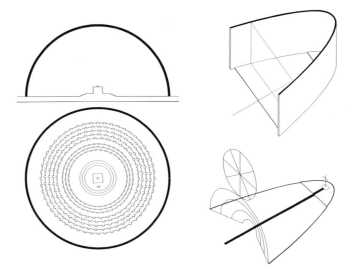

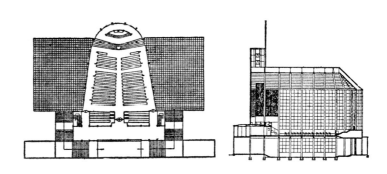

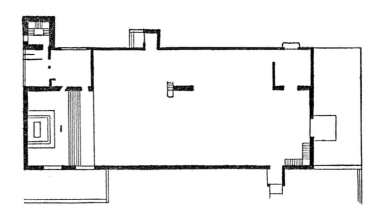

ABOVE L TO R: 'The Ring' and 'The Sacred Cast' – illustrations from The Church Incarnate *(1938), R Schwarz; CENTRE: Stahlkirche, Cologne, 1928; BELOW: Church of Corpus Christi, Aachen, R Schwarz, 1930*

of Zen in many ways. Just as Japanese students were taught to contemplate the form of a jug by attempting to visualise the space contained within and without and ignoring the vessel itself, Schwarz compares the act of worship with God's act of creation 'out of nothing'. Consequently, in *The Church Incarnate*, he argues that:

This creation [the corporate act of worship] should take place in living men, not in images and buildings – at the beginning the building should be simply the means of this creating and afterward the result of it.

Schwarz was perhaps the first architect to move on from the preoccupation with materials which informed Perret's concrete structures and Bartning's steel structure to a higher plane where the architecture is purely generated from the liturgy; from within, and is thus the clearest expression of the sacred.

Rudolf Schwarz had worked in the office of Dominikus Böhm and the two architects who, together, did perhaps more than anyone to revolutionise church architecture were friends. In *Moderne Bauformen* (1927), Schwarz wrote of Böhm that he laid the 'path to the hard simplicity of the single, great interior' and while Schwarz was building his church at Aachen, his master was at work on a building which occupied a parallel plane to Corpus Christi.

Built at the same time as St Engelbert, Riehl, Böhm's church in Nordeney of 1930 is a complete departure from his expressionist tendencies. Every bit as austere and rational as Schwarz's design, Böhm's church stands dazzling white against the surrounding houses. Its haunting open bell tower is engaged and casts great shadows on the white mass of the church as does the spindly black cross which stands in front of the building. A stair rises up towards the single exposed bell in an emphatic gesture of ascent so that the entrance to the church becomes a symbolic pilgrimage. There is something of the purity of suprematism in the composition; the great side wall of the church is relieved only by the single perforation of the stained glass window which illuminates the altar.

As in Schwarz's church the space is composed of a single long nave and a side aisle of lower height. The culmination is again a black marble altar, raised, but not aloof from the congregation. Columns are kept to a minimum and the space is kept pure and simple with no distractions. Böhm was also heavily involved with the liturgical movement and, like Schwarz's, his plans arose from the liturgical impetus whence they gain their great

spiritual power and boldness while his architectural language was that of the finest European modernists, a true ecclesiastical functionalism.

Böhm and Schwarz continued to build fine churches including many other important and influential designs which there is no space to dwell on here. But their work was made increasingly difficult by the rise to power of the Nazi party in the early 1930s and the subsequent return to anachronistic architecture. The impression should not be given, however, that the path of the liturgical reformers was ever easy or that the new architecture was universally accepted. It faced many obstacles among which simple conservatism was the greatest. Schwarz had written: 'Architecture is giving an example, but it shines on chaos; no-one understands it'.[4] Under the Nazis that conservatism became an even greater burden and although many architects continued pioneering work, the focus of innovation in ecclesiastical architecture shifted over the border to the more receptive territory of Switzerland.

IX. SWITZERLAND
The Consolidation of Modernism

The new architecture which was the fruit that grew from the union of liturgical reform and modernism was largely attributable to the innovative work of Perret in France and the prolific German pioneers. The only other country which imposed its presence on innovative ecclesiastical architecture to a comparable extent was Switzerland. In 1927 Karl Moser built the Church of St Anthony at Basle. Leaning heavily on the achievements of Perret over the border in France, the church was not only a dramatic leap forward for ecclesiastical architecture in Switzerland but one of the first significant moments in the history of Swiss modernism, representing one of the first truly modern constructions in the country.

The building exhibits greater clarity in the relationship of its elevations to its plan – it is a starker, more stripped construction, closer to the pared down, almost industrial aesthetic of the later German churches. The interior is perhaps more raw than Perret's, with chunkier, squarer columns and a great vaulted nave of rational, waffled concrete. The wall reappears here as a structural element as opposed to Perret's net curtain walls, although Moser, too, creates a space which is defined by the quality and quantity of light. The most notable presence of the wall comes behind the altar where it serves to bring it down to the structure and the level of the congregation, whereas Perret exalted the altar at Le Raincy in a shroud of light. On the elevations the mass of the wall is emphasised by a cavernous entrance, like the gate to a tomb from a lost civilisation which casts ziggurat shadows on the raw concrete. Anton Henze has grouped together Moser's church and its ancestor, Perret's at Raincy with Böhm's St Engelbert's at Riehl and Schwarz's Church of the Blessed Sacrament at Aachen as the foundation stones on which all further development in modern ecclesiastical architecture would be built.

The rise to power of the Nazi party in Germany meant that the initiative in ecclesiastical design fell across the Alps to Switzerland and a creative surge was set in motion which presents the most homogenous vision of a developing church architecture intimately interconnected with liturgical renewal. In his book *Liturgy and Architecture* (1960) Peter Hammond states:

> Switzerland was the only country in western Christendom which, by the late thirties, had created a living tradition of church architecture. There is still no other country where modern churches of real quality take their place so naturally among the best secular buildings of their day . . . The Church has learned how to speak in the language of the living.[1]

As well as Moser, there were three other architects adding to the country's stock of fine modern Catholic churches (Protestant Churches were slower to take up modernism but had begun to do so by the mid-1930s): Fritz Metzger and two former pupils of Moser himself, Hermann Baur and Otto Dreyer.

Metzger's Church of St Charles in Lucerne (1933-4) is one of the most exquisite buildings to come out of liturgical reform and a key monument. The church stands like a gleaming modernist jewel on the banks of the River Reuss; the clean lines of its belfry, a beacon of purity against the verdant hills. The plan is clear and simple, its single space wraps around the altar in a sweeping curve. A continuous band of window generously illuminates the space while the structure is supported on columns which define the aisles. The curve and the uniform treatment of the apse and the body of the church have the effect of drawing the space, the communion table and the congregation together. The elevations are clearly defined and elegant, the lower 'deck' containing ancillary functions while a terrace above the river is sheltered by an expansive overhang; the building is inviting and unambiguous.

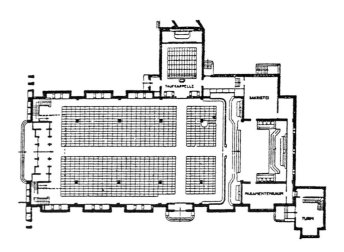

ABOVE: Church in Nordeney, 1930, D Böhm; CENTRE AND BELOW: Church of St Anthony, Basle, 1927, K Moser

Church of St Thérèse de l'enfant Jesu, 1928, P Tournon

Church of St Wenceslas, Hradec Králové, 1927, J Gočár

Metzger's Church of Our Lady of Lourdes (1935) shares many characteristics of this earlier building including the clarity and the pared down belfry with its clock (typically Swiss) and pure modern architectonic language. The same language defines Werner M Moser's church (the son of Karl) at Zurich-Altstetten of 1941, which also incorporates a super-modern belfry and clock. What sets Werner Moser's church apart, however, is its unusual asymmetrical interior which aims to separately emphasise each aspect of the life of the church: font, pulpit and communion table. The building also contains a considerable amount of social facilities.

The original church was kept on the site as a chapel while Moser's building became the main church. The asymmetry which defines the scheme was part of the architect's solution to the retention of the old building, not wanting to smother it, and also led to a more self-effacing modernism. Moser's background of having worked for both Mies van der Rohe and Frank Lloyd Wright resulted in an effective grasp of spatial composition and a simple clarity of expression which led to this church, a highly influential structure. More than the other modernist churches (which could often be seen as generic architectural solutions), this was a site specific solution which took into account the old church and its vernacular surroundings. Moser writes:

> To create a relation between the new and the old building without compromise for the new – just by careful proportions – was a special aim. It resulted in an asymmetrical shape, which was very individually fitted and just only to this solution.[2]

The open-work tower of St Johannes Church in the same city, by Burckhardt and Egender (1936), gives an idea of the building's almost high-tech interior, a celebration of the steel structure and glass wall in a simple and effective space: the first modernist church in

Switzerland built for a Protestant congregation. These few churches illustrate adequately both the varied architecture which emanated from Switzerland and the uniform high standard of so many of the works, all partaking in a living theological and spatial experiment at an almost unprecedented time of exploration.

X. EUROPE BETWEEN THE WARS

Germany provided the early impetus for the new architecture and Switzerland took over the mantle. France had not responded to Perret's genius and remained largely conservative. There were however notable exceptions; Paul Tournon's Church of St Thérèse de l'enfant Jesu (1928) is an almost freakish experiment in plasticity, blending Perret's approach to structure and the dissolution of the wall into a geometric grille of light and a gothic attitude to the stylised statuary which cloaks the west front. The interior is liturgically advanced; a single space focuses on the altar while a blocky pulpit protrudes into the nave from a column. Although individual and brilliant, the building belongs more to the modern, sculptural expressionism of Gaudí than to the modern movement. The same architect's Church of the Holy Spirit (1928) in Paris is a monumental mass of concrete with an interior worthy of the power of Byzantine architecture, dramatic and theatrical in a positive and a negative sense but a stunning work nevertheless.

There were isolated incidents of innovation throughout Europe but nowhere was a momentum built up. Josef Gočár's little Church of St Wenceslas at Hradec Králové of 1926-7 is a remarkably advanced work of functionalism within a modernist urban setting and an early example of a trapezoid plan, illustrating the progressive search for new forms which grew out of one of the centres of European modernism. The little

Interior of St Wenceslas

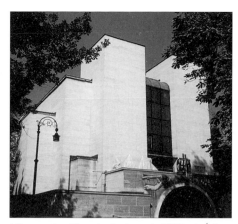

Városmajor Church, Budapest, 1933, A Árkay

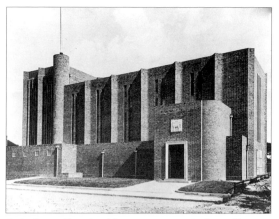

St Saviour's Church, Eltham, 1934, N F Cachemaille-Day

church's interior is stunning in its simplicity and its curved apse and converging walls bring the congregation into the heart of the liturgy. Its sculptural stepped roof serves to illuminate the building brilliantly while the tall windows of the apse curve around above the altar to introduce an intense purity and brilliance. It is one of the few churches which matches the clarity of the Swiss examples which followed a few years later although very different to Plečnik's great work of the same period.

Elsewhere in Central Europe there was entrenched conservatism. Two fine modern churches were built in Budapest: Városmajor Church (1932-3) by Aladár Árkay – a fine, elemental, blocky modernism of a very white kind – and Pasarét (1934) by Gyula Rimanóczy – Italian influenced modernism; but neither advanced the cause of the functional re-analysis of the interior although both are wonderful works of art. Poland was yet more conservative, nevertheless, Jan Witkiewicz-Koszczyc's competition design for the Church of the Holy Providence of 1930 is a fascinatingly bizarre mix of expressionism and New York skyscraper, while Oskar Sosnowski's Church of St Roch (Bialystok 1927-46) is a strange modern gothic creation, beautifully massed and utterly anachronistic.

In Italy, L G Daneri's Church of San Marcellino in Genoa (1931) provides us with an example of a circular plan, built a year later than Böhm's seminal St Engelbert, Riehl, although Peter Hammond reminds us that its precedent (with its apses containing side altars around its plan) could be baroque as easily as modern. I Gardella's chapel in the Sanatorio di Allessandra is an early example of Italian modernism applied to ecclesiastical design in a rational manner. There were other examples of modern, rational and expressionist oeuvres in Italian church building although here, too, much of the action was dominated by historicism.

Great Britain was also stuck in the backwaters of conservatism. The few bright sparks had little effect but nevertheless created some interesting works. Eric Gill was one of the first to realise and utilise the consequences of liturgical reform; his Church of St Peter, Gorleston-on-Sea presented a centralised worship space but little else. N F Cachemaille-Day was probably the most adventurous and consequently interesting architect on the British scene. His Church of St Michael and All Angels (1937) uses a plan of two intersecting squares, one rotated through 45 degrees to create a space capable of successfully involving the congregation in the celebration, which he combined with a clean modernish architectural style which is almost close to that of Baudot four decades earlier.

The same architect's St Saviour's Church at Eltham (1934) is another of the few good examples of inter-war church architecture in Britain. With its rugged brick detailing and robust shell it seems a mixture of the earthen solidity and curving forms of the Amsterdam school and the municipal style of the country's councils. Its close relative, St Barnabas, Tuffley (1939), displays similar, if perhaps more gothicising characteristics, while St Nicholas' Church, Burnage (1932), is a streamlined Art Deco construction with a finely modelled and light interior.

Many architects were using the 'moderne' style without applying the investigation of the brief which characterised much continental building, the modernism of the Odeon rather than the Bauhaus. Other architects were still working firmly within the historicist camp including J Ninian Comper who, despite his anachronistic vocabulary, was among the first to respond to liturgical change in generous, light interiors which began to resemble the 'one room plan' advocated by Pope Pius X.

A Randall Wells continued the line and symbolism of his master Lethaby; one of his most interesting achievements being the Church of St Wilfrid, Leeds (1938), an odd, eclectic blend of an eccentric nature. Another great eccentric was H S Goodhart-Rendel who created some of the most interesting British churches using an architectural language which was both monumental and highly individualistic and in which he continued working until the post-war years. His greatest achievement perhaps came with the massive brick pile of the Church of the Most Holy Trinity in Southwark (1957-60) which is almost Roman in its sheer power and force.

One character who made a considerable impact on ecclesiastical architecture in Europe at this time was Dom Paul Bellot. A monk and an architect, Bellot was a central figure in the move towards the realisation of the architectural implications of liturgical renewal. His architecture was a fantastic cabaret of devices which could place him as easily among the expressionists as it could among the historicists or the early modern movement. His work has something of the intensity of Plečnik and the remarkable organic conception of the sculptural qualities of brick, which defined the approach of the Amsterdam school and expressionism, glued together with a passion for a modern gothic idiom which stemmed directly from the tradition of Viollet-le-Duc. If this sounds an eclectic mix, then it has succeeded in giving an inkling of one of the most interesting of twentieth-century architects.

Standing outside the formal language of modernism, Bellot has, like Plečnik, only recently come to attract wider attention and it is impossible to outline his œuvre in this short introduction. But for some of the best examples of his work one can look to the simple, beautiful brick-encased spaces of Saint-Paul d'Oosterhout (1906-20) in The Netherlands, Quarr Abbey, Isle of Wight (1907-14), the polychromatic Art Deco blue-burst of the Church of Saint-Chrysole in Commines, France (1922-33), the expressionist structural lines of the Church of the Immaculate Conception, Audincourt, France (1928-33), and the remarkable, almost Deco moderne of the interior of another Church of the Immaculate Conception in Porto (1938-47) among many other masterpieces.

All these interiors were liturgically advanced but never starkly modern like those of contemporary Swiss and German churches. They delight the eye and the spirit, a fine testament to a man who believed that to create good Christian art, a man must be a good Christian; the intensity of his faith and love for God are finely expressed in an incredible collection of works.

XI. POST-WAR DEVELOPMENTS
Theology and Architecture

The liturgical movement, which began in Belgium at the beginning of the twentieth century, given impetus by the Benedictine Lambert Beauduin and the monks of the Abbey of Maria Laach in Germany, slowly gained momentum over the course of the century and it proved a living impetus for architectural innovation in Germany between the wars. Its effect was felt little elsewhere in Europe but in the last years of the Second World War and immediately afterwards it gained a powerful foothold in France, where architects could build on the foundations laid by Auguste Perret in the 1920s and ignored ever since.

In 1947 the Papal encyclical *Mediator Dei* was issued and constitutes a formal recognition of the advances made by the German liturgical movement. After this date liturgical renewal spread throughout the Catholic world at differing rates. Although the movement began in the Roman Church, the fundamental upheavals and changes in thinking had a profound effect on other Churches, many of which began to move in similar directions, which had the effect of drawing the Churches closer together. A decade after the *Mediator Dei* the bishop of the Roman Catholic Diocese of Superior, Wisconsin, set up a commission which issued a set of directives for church building in the same year which contained far more detailed recommendations for church architecture. It begins with the words: 'The primary purpose of the church is to serve the sacred liturgy.'

The widespread acceptance of the imperatives of the liturgical movement, however, dates from the convening of the Second Vatican Council (Vatican II) in 1960 and the coming into force of its *Constitution on the Sacred Liturgy* in 1964. This embodied the principles of bringing the clergy closer to the laity through the celebration of the mass in the vernacular and a physical closeness brought about by a proximity of the altar to the congregation, whether physically within them, 'in the round' – to use a theatrical analogy – or at least to not separate the chancel from them by the use of physical or symbolic barriers.

The architectural implications were enormous and the expression of these ideals was highly varied. It allowed great experimentation with new plan forms and structures; some of which are merely architects playing at creating a building which 'looks like a church' or is supposed to instill some vague, abstract notion of sacredness, others which are genuine expressions stemming from deep understanding of the liturgy and the role of the church in both spiritual and secular life.

The reforms also coincided with a period of rebuilding in Europe and the Americas and led to a great deal of experimentation with forms, materials and space. Some are brilliant, others are irrelevant and others are irrelevant and yet still brilliant. Le Corbusier's church (see chapter XIII) is one of the latter. There is not room here for a comprehensive overview of the church architecture of the second half of the twentieth century. I have attempted to select a few buildings to complement those in the latter half of the book to give a brief context for those works.

XII. POST-WAR GERMANY
A Church Meant for our own Time

> The art of building . . . is the creation of living form, and the church . . . is not merely a walled shelter, but everything together; building and people, body and soul, the human beings and Christ, a whole spiritual universe – a universe, indeed, which must ever be brought into reality anew.
>
> . . . This holy work is comparable to no other. It cannot be derived from contemporary art and its fashionable motifs nor from the aesthetic doctrines nor from social theories nor from cosmic myths. Rather is church building a work in its own right, bound strictly to its own meaning and with it exhausted . . . a church must be developed wholly and in all its parts out of its own inner meaning, that is, out of prayer – this is to us the meaning of sacred objectivity.
>
> *Rudolf Schwarz,* The Church Incarnate, *1938*

> The exterior of a church should not attempt to imitate contemporary secular buildings either in its proportions, its structure, or its decoration. Nor should it try to catch the attention of the passer-by with the architectural equivalent of the cries of the market place. The aim should rather be to announce in a manner which is both dignified and eloquent the totally different nature of what lies within the church – totally different because belonging to another world – and yet at the same time to allow the building to take its place harmoniously in its surroundings.

> *Point three of the* Guiding principles for the design of churches according to the spirit of the Roman liturgy *Issued by the German Liturgical Commission, 1947.*

In between these two quotations lies less than a decade but it was a decade which saw Germany launch Europe into the most devastating war in its history. Schwarz was writing under the difficult conditions of the Nazi state, what Mies van der Rohe called 'Germany's darkest hour'. Mies wrote the foreword to the English language version of *The Church Incarnate*, published in 1958. He wrote:

> Rudolf Schwarz, the great German church builder, is one of the most profound thinkers of our time . . . [The Church Incarnate] is not only a great book on architecture, indeed, it is one of the truly great books – one of those which have the power to transform our thinking.

National Socialism interrupted the advance of ecclesiastical architecture on its most fruitful territory and the mantle of progress passed to Switzerland. The war virtually stopped building throughout Europe in its later stages. In 1945 Germany found itself again in the wake of a terrible and devastating war and, again, this created a great impetus for rebuilding and rethinking. The war had left many German cities flattened and many churches destroyed and there was an urgent need for rebuilding. More than any other nation except perhaps France, the Germans launched themselves into the task with a rare combination of thoughtfulness and enthusiasm.

The period saw a consolidation of the aims of the liturgical movement (set in stone by the work of the German Liturgical Commission and the publication of their report in 1947) and a reassessment and reinterpretation of the expressionist vision which had followed the first world war. It once more proved a fertile blend of vision and function and the range of church buildings which rose from the ground in the post-war period is staggering. The weightiest presence was exerted by the old masters Rudolf Schwarz and Dominikus Böhm and by Böhm's son, Gottfried, who developed the expressionist aesthetic to a higher plane and built on the remarkable achievements of his father's œuvre.

Both Schwarz and Böhm senior moved from their functionalist application of minimal design to the sole service of the liturgy to reintroduce elements of symbolism and monumentality. The Church of St Michael in Frankfurt (1954) is based on a frankly phallic plan (which is related to the ovoid shapes of the German

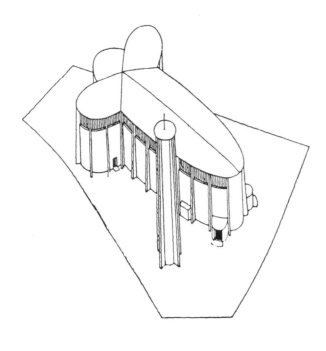

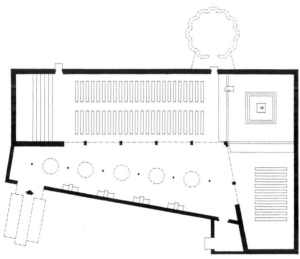

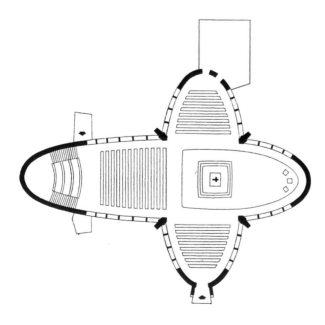

ABOVE: Church of St Michael, Frankfurt, 1954, R Schwarz;
CENTRE: Church of St Anna, Düren, 1956, R Schwarz;
BELOW: Church of Maria Königin, Saarbrücken, 1959, R Schwarz

Baroque), a long ellipse forming the eucharistic space, two apses which serve as choir and chapel and a free-standing campanile. It is a realisation of Schwarz's concept of the 'open-ring'; a restful space which does not confine but embraces and which opens up to the infinite at its apex in the altar. This is expressed by the culmination in the apses and in the different articulation of the east wall which is free of the strip window which otherwise runs around the church below the roof. The building achieves both weighty presence from the exterior and an inner peace, an austere and calm interior which was rarely equalled.

The Church of St Anna, however, built two years later (1956), is closer to Schwarz's notion of the 'sacred journey', based on a long rectangular space with an arm which branches off to create a more intimate worship space for the parish sharing the same square altar. The church rises like a phoenix from the flames which engulfed the city; it is built from the rubble which the urban fabric of Cologne was almost totally reduced to. Its walls are sheer cliffs of stone and it is a serious and imposing structure both inside and out. Entry is through an aisle or pilgrimage wing which runs the length of the church and links the side chapel into the main space, then through arcades to a confrontation with the awesome bareness of the great stone wall.

The church is illuminated by massive windows which constitute the whole wall over the arcades, above which a pattern of diagonal beams relieves the elemental concrete ceiling. Behind the altar a 'Tree of Life' pattern emerges from the stone, rippling through the coursing and illuminated by fruit as little roundels (like Lethaby's 'Jewel Bearing Tree' in *Architecture, Mysticism and Myth*, a reference to a tradition of mythical burning trees, Moses' burning bush, for example, and the Jewish Menorah candle-holder); one of the boldest and most genuinely impressive works of sacred architecture in the twentieth century: expressionism without whimsicality.

The same architect's Holy Cross church at Bottrop (1957) is the embodiment of another of Schwarz's ideas, the 'Sacred Cast; The Dark Chalice' (illustrated on p35). In *The Church Incarnate* of 1938 he writes:

> The structure is simply open roundedness . . . it is that roundedness which is end and shelter, the simple presence of joy, the awaiting light – that into which the people finally surrender themselves as if into an open hand.

The parabolic plan culminates in the blocky stone altar with its chunky legs which is very much a representation of the table of the last supper. The curved wall of brick effectively embraces the congregation without enclosing them or constricting them. The light comes from the decidedly odd west wall and is filtered through a swirling pattern of coloured opaque glass (meant to represent infinity), which seems to presage the spirals of Hundertwasser a couple of decades later, while a positively disconcerting eye of God design in the window above the altar looks down on the congregation.

1959 saw the return of Schwarz's attention to the plan explored in St Michael's, tempered with the parabola of the Holy Cross with the design of the Church of Maria Königin in Saarbrücken. Here a cruciform plan is united by the altar at its crossing and brilliant illumination emanates from four huge windows of translucent glass which are carved out of the mass of stone which forms the church's bastion-like walls. Schwarz skilfully manipulated the forms to eliminate glare – so the altar is nearly always seen against a background of plain wall, yet the space is light and airy. The building stands like a great castle among the trees, an immensely powerful work which evokes the force and strength of medieval building while utilising the most liturgically advanced of plans and a modern architectonic language.

Schwarz's other, smaller works also spread their influence wide and were impeccably skilful examples of their genre. These include the Heilige Familie, Oberhausen (1956-8), which consists of a perfectly square plan and a successfully urban setting with a peaceful forecourt and separate courtyard, its walls broken down by a repetitive and consistent pattern of glazing; and St Christphorus, Cologne-Riehl (1950), his last church: an interpretation of the small missionary church.

Dominikus Böhm's great contribution to German post-war church design is the Church of Maria Königin in Marianburg, built in 1954, a year before his death. It is an exquisite and intimate work of pure modernism. The plain worship space focuses on an altar in a curved apse and is illuminated by a wall of stained glass of the architect's design. This wall opens up between the seating and the chancel to a shrinking corridor of glass which leads into a small, delicate baptistry, also highly glazed. There is a feeling of rebirth as one enters the space through the false perspective of the passage, a beautiful sanctuary among the trees; a subtle building to end a magnificent career. His son was at hand to

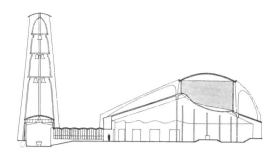

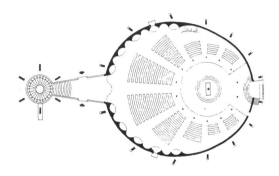

ABOVE: St Albert, Saarbrücken, 1955, G Böhm; CENTRE: Church of Neviges, 1968, G Böhm; BELOW: Christ Church, Bochum, 1957, D Oesterlen

continue the tradition of church building at its height of creativity and response to liturgical requirements.

Gottfried Böhm's Church of St Albert in Saarbrücken (1955) is reminiscent of a monstrous spider about to engulf its prey; but the expressionist imagery of the exterior gives way to a more sensitive interior. The sanctuary is enclosed in a ring of columns within the egg-shape of the church as a whole. This is both an expression of Rudolf Schwarz's idea of the 'sacred ring' form of church plan and a clear demarcation of the altar and the most holy space from the church which is never, however, separated from it visually or physically. A symbolic demonstration of the transition – 'The altar is the border between time and eternity' ('Threshold' Rudolf Schwarz) – the altar is raised on a plinth at the epicentre. Seating radiates outward from the altar which is set at the narrow end of the egg and almost entirely surrounded by the congregation.

There is a curious lack of structural expression on the inside as these duties are undertaken by the external concrete framework (the spider's legs) which lends an ethereal feel to the space, enhanced by the ovoid opening in the roof which illuminates the altar. The altar itself seems a reversal of the building's structure; the mensa is supported on a sculptural form reminiscent of the fingers of a hand outstretched. If it is the form in microcosm then the mensa would represent the earth to which the structure is anchored and the altar is seen as the earth reaching up towards heaven. The baptistry is related in form to that at his father's church, Maria Königin; a pure circle at the end of a glazed, reducing corridor.

The remarkable Church of St Gertrude in Cologne (1964-5) illustrates a return to the sculptural approach of expressionism with its craggy concrete roof simulating a hard, jagged landscape, a literal analogy of the rock of the Church. The ideas which he began to explore at St Gertrude's reached their climax at Böhm junior's most complete and fulfilling ecclesiastical building, the pilgrimage Church of Neviges (1966-8).

Here he comes very close to a realisation of the early idealism of expressionism, the notion of the sacred mountain. Böhm describes the pilgrimage as 'the expression of a living, continually moving church'[1] and his idea of the pilgrimage church as the culmination of a great route justifies a gesture which he might see as inappropriate for a parish church but wholly fitting as a climax of the great sacred way. A landscape of brick terraces builds up and climbs past the pilgrims' lodgings to the inevitable crest of a jagged mass of angular concrete forms which is the church. The interior is like a great cave carved out of the mountain; rugged and irregular prismatic planes of concrete build up into an interior landscape broken into light and shadow.

The structure is one of the very few amongst modern buildings which have the power and monumentality to answer Rudolf Steiner's Goetheanum. Its presence is immense and it dominates the town's skyline just as did the ancient cathedrals and, like the medieval cathedrals, its interior is as much an urban gesture as a sacred space; it embodies a town square, a centre for the community and the gathered pilgrims. It has been forgotten that the cathedral was at the heart of the town; that people ate and drank within its walls, that they conducted their business there and escaped from their tiny constricted dwellings. Böhm is one of the few architects to recapture the essence of the cathedral as the spiritual and physical centre, both the culmination of the sacred way and the focal point of urban life; the expressionist dream of the sacred mountain and *Volkshaus* in one great, unified gesture.

Elsewhere Dieter Oesterlen's Christ Church, Bochum (1957) imposes a wonderful prismatically sculptured roof on to an angular plan which avoids glare by its dogtooth arrangement with windows set into the blind side of the serrations in another building which realises elements of the expressionist vocabulary. Sep Ruf's Church of St Johan von Capistran, Munich (1960), presents a new slant on the early expressionist round churches in a close counter to Schwarz's recommendations on the circular plan-form in an impressively sparse and non-monumental modern style. Egon Eiermann's Kaiser Wilhelm Memorial Church rises next to the old bombed out tower which was left as a symbol of the destruction wrought by the war. A simple refuge, bathed in the coloured light of its wholly perforated walls, it became a symbol of Berlin's resilience, an urban monument and the gesture of a new generation of architects. Paul Schneider Esleben's St Rochus, Düsseldorf (1955) is defined by a parabolic dome rising like an absurd bishop's mitre but not competing with the neo-romanesque tower which stands next to it, another fragment of the legacy of war.

Hans Schedel's Church of St Joseph, Hasloch-am-Main (1958), uses a spartan set of white walls which ingeniously interlock to embrace a calm interior expanding from the altar which is mysteriously lit from an unseen window formed at the junction of two wall elements – a building with some similarity to Richard England's Manikata Church of a few years later. The Paul Gerhardt Church, Mannheim (1961), by Gerhard Schlegel and Reinhold Kargel presages a kind of early high-tech unusual in ecclesiastical work with a wonderfully simple barn of an interior, characteristics also of Joachim Schurmann's St Pius, Cologne (1961).

Another architect of great ability was Emil Steffann. His intervention into the ruins of a Franciscan church in Cologne is a masterpiece of the re-use of a shell and the reconfiguration of space to modern liturgical demands with the simplest altar and pulpit creating a very pure chancel area. The superb bell tower rises like a rationalised ghost of the romanesque from its side. The same architect's Maria in den Benden, Düsseldorf (1956-8), is described by Peter Hammond as a 'house for the local church' in which the spaces, secular and sacred, are arranged in a building like a Roman villa around the atrium which was prescribed by the German Liturgical Commission. Steffann's Church of St Lawrence, Munich (1955), presents a stripped, elemental interior and the same curved apse as at Düsseldorf.

Taken as a whole (and including many other buildings for which there is not space here) the German contribution to church building after the war is as monumental as that of the pre-war period; a final realisation of the experimentation and theorising of the earlier generation and a fruition of the pioneering work of Böhm and Schwarz; certainly the most significant contribution of a single nation.

XIII. THE CHURCH BUILDING AS ART
Le Corbusier and the Mediterranean

When Le Corbusier was asked by a reporter from the *Chicago Tribune* whether he thought it necessary to be a Catholic to design his chapel at Ronchamp, he famously replied 'Foutez-moi le camp' (roughly translated as 'leave me alone'). The gulf between Schwarz and Le Corbusier could hardly have been greater even though they were both working within the same tradition of modernism. Schwarz believed in an architecture that was solely generated from the liturgy, the requirements of the mass; what he termed 'Sacred Objectivity'. Ronchamp on the other hand is the fundamental turning point of the modern movement; the point at which a kind of expressionism, a sculptural approach to architecture found its way back into the fold and, like the prodigal

son, was greeted with both mistrust and much rejoicing.

Some modernists saw the Chapel of Notre Dame du Haut, Ronchamp (1952-5) as an affront to the functionalism which its architect had been instrumental in creating; a wilful exercise in plastic massing and a lack of truthfulness to structure and material (the building is sculpted using concrete sprayed on to mesh). On the other hand it was greeted with a wild enthusiasm by those architects who felt they had been constrained by the rational logic of functionalism; the master had moved on, the building had become a gesture of sculptural expression, wilful symbolism was about to become acceptable again. Le Corbusier's chapel of Notre Dame du Haut is at once one of the greatest moments in twentieth-century architecture and a virtual disaster for ecclesiastical design from the liturgical point of view; it led to a spate of idiotic 'gestures', buildings symbolising anything from praying hands to doves; buildings emanating from a single, bland idea, justified in the name of the new modernism.

It may seem odd that Le Corbusier was chosen for such a commission. But he had the support of Father Couturier, editor of the influential journal *L'Art Sacré*, who believed that the Church should actively commission works from those artists who were the greatest in their field, only thus could a great sacred art emerge again. It is the precise opposite of the view of Dom Bellot who believed that good Christian art could come only from a good Christian. Couturier's influence later led to great works being commissioned by the church from Matisse, Cocteau, Léger and others.

Le Corbusier himself saw the building's sacrality coming from a vague mysticism of the type that had been condemned by the German modernists. He turned to the mythical sacredness of the hill on which the church was built, a tradition which stretched back beyond Christianity as a kind of universal expression of the sacred, and stated boldly that: 'The requirements of religion have had little effect on the design, the form was an answer to the psychophysiology of the feelings.'[1] He saw the chapel as a form of sanctuary at the culmination of an eternal pilgrimage. He explained in his dedication speech:

> In building this chapel I wanted to create a place of silence, of prayer, of peace and of internal joy. The feeling of the sacred animated us. Some things are sacred, others not, irrespective of whether or not they are religious.

The chapel is built on a pilgrimage site among rolling,

verdant hills. Its brilliant whiteness stands out like a beacon against the landscape. The building is covered by the canopy of a huge roof which billows out like a reference to 'God's tent' and seems almost weightless as it is lifted from the structure, a gap being left between the walls and roof so that a crack of light can penetrate. It is entered via two bastions which curl inwards to invite the pilgrim who, on entry, is confronted with a huge battered wall perforated in an abstract composition of openings (Charles Jencks is prompted to ask, '"Swiss cheese" facade or "cotton candy"?')[2] which has become an icon of modern architecture. The deep, coloured glass-filled holes illustrate the massive thickness of the wall and create an exquisite play of light and colour within the building. As well as the altar within, another altar sits outside under the shelter of the great sweeping roof and a pulpit is built on to the huge concrete column which supports the roof above at a single, tiny point. This is a place for commune with the landscape, a pantheistic celebration of the mystical presence of the object within the hills; close to the Greek temple in conception.

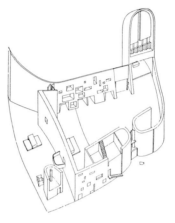

Christian Norberg-Schulz cites the church as a 'symptom of renewed interest in basic existential meanings' and continues to state that:

> Le Corbusier has succeeded in recovering the basic properties of the Christian sanctuary. His building is receptacle and giver, fortress and poetic vision of otherness. Above all he has managed to recreate the interiority of the early churches with means which are simultaneously new and old, making the interior . . . a space which simultaneously protects and liberates. It is a cave, open to the essential meanings of human existence, and supporting Heidegger's equation that 'on earth' means 'under the Heavens'.[3]

In his book *New Churches of Europe* (1964) G E Kidder Smith ends the Ronchamp entry by stating that it is 'to many the most impressive church of the last 500 years'. Maguire and Murray's comments in *Modern Churches of the World* (1965) are altogether different: 'seen as a folly it is outstanding; but in the development of church building, it is a blind alley.' These comments define the poles; that the building is still capable of arousing more comment than almost any other modernist work is a testament to the power of Le Corbusier's art.

If Ronchamp was one of the critical moments in modern architecture it was partly because of the intensity of the architect's conviction to a vision. It can

ABOVE: Chapel of Notre Dame du Haut, Ronchamp, 1955, Le Corbusier – axonometric, interior; BELOW: Monastery of Ste Marie-de-la-Tourette, Eveux-sur-l'Arbresle, 1960, Le Corbusier

be said that the vision of the artist has almost replaced religion in a secular age, that art galleries are the new temples, and the works of art treated like holy relics. The reverence for the artist (which comes out of the Renaissance humanist tradition) and his works provides us with one extreme attitude, the liturgically driven functionalist provides the other; for him architecture can only be generated from within the faith. This polarisation remains as two threads which run through contemporary church architecture.

In his other famous scheme for the Church, the monastery at La Tourette (1957-60), Le Corbusier makes a return to the more humanist approach of his Unité d'Habitation. When working to a more specific brief, i.e. the housing of monks and a complete environment for their needs, Corbusier seemed to return to the rational style which was more familiar in his work. He wrote:

I tried to make a place of meditation, research and prayer . . . The brief was to house monks while trying to give them what people of today need more than anything: silence and peace. Monks, in silence, find a place for God . . . It is the interior which lives. The essential goes on in the interior.[4]

The work is closer to that of an architect working for a functional sacred architecture and it evokes the interesting parallel of the artist himself as a monk in a cell creating true beauty from a mystical source; finding his God in contemplation of the darkness and the landscape.

The other great French architect who defined modern church building, Auguste Perret, made a reappearance when he was called in to supervise the building of a tiny chapel in Vence – its designer was Henri Matisse. The Chapel of the Rosary (1952) is a temple to colour, a *Gesamtkunstwerk* in which the artist created the whole vision, from the chasubles to the windows. The building itself is a simple canvas of white Mediterranean vernacular, it is the art which is applied to it which makes it a pivotal work. Matisse wrote, 'my chief aim was to balance a surface of light and colour against a solid white wall covered with drawings.'[5]

The chapel was the apex of the concept of church as canvas, art itself as the expression of the sacred, pure, inner soul. Its influence was to be out of all proportion to its size. It was a notion which was reinforced by Jean Cocteau in his designs for the Chapel of St Pierre, Villefranche-sur-Mer. He explains, 'As an artist I wanted to create a chapel in which the poet, without losing any of his prerogatives, would become immediately accessi-

ble to fishermen and simple people'.[6] His surreal style created hypnotic and highly successful representations of biblical stories, a new interpretation of the symbolism of the bible as a link between the Freudian analyses of the subconscious in surrealism and the Catholic notion of the soul, two existential visions brought together.

Other artists were also brought in on a kind of crusade to reinstate the Church as a pivotal patron. Fernand Léger designed windows for the Church of the Sacred Heart, Audincourt, and the Church of Courfavre, Switzerland, while he also collaborated with almost all the most important French artists of the time on the Church of Notre Dame de Toute Grace in Assy (1950). This project was the ultimate result of Father Couturier's efforts. Its architecture was merely a piece of Alpine vernacular interpreted in a modern manner but its importance is as an art gallery. It brought together the talents of Léger, Chagall, Braque, Rouault, Lurçat, Matisse and others in a cornucopia of modern art. It is an emotional achievement which attained the expressiveness of ancient religious art in a way that had been unprecedented in modern times, a final realisation of Father Couturier's assertion that 'it was our duty to procure for God and our faith the best art of the present'.

The Church of St Thérèse in Hem by Hermann Baur is another fine example of the church as a total work of art which makes full use of the French technique of Betonglas – rough chunks of coloured glass set into a concrete frame – designed by Alfred Manessier and a tapestry by Georges Rouault.

There was an increasing consensus in France that the qualities of modern art which sought to depict an other than figural world, to reveal a reality which is not physically visible, was 'more suited to the expression of what is sacred' (Father Couturier, 1949) of which the surrealism of Cocteau born of the Freudian subconscious is the finest example. The Church in France had been generally conservative and had not followed up on the progress made by Perret in the 1920s but this began to change during the war and the pace of reform dramatically increased in the post-war years until France took its place at the forefront of a radical new ecclesiastical architecture, an approach characterised by a deep understanding of both the structural possibilities of new materials and technologies and of the demands of the changes in liturgy.

One of the most spectacular churches to appear was that of Notre Dame in Royan by Guillaume Gillet (1958).

In conjunction with engineer Bernard Laffaille, the architect created a spectacular church which is a reinterpretation of some of the concerns of the expressionists; a building which expresses the heavenward thrust of the gothic and imposes its monumental presence on the town as a kind of man-made mountain of concrete. A jagged canopy defines the entrance while exquisite spiral stairs rise to either side to give access to the galleries from which one enters the building's impressive concrete structural rib-cage, an expressive landscape of raw concrete prisms. The interior is less satisfactory despite its useful horse-shoe shape plan which focuses naturally on the altar. It is a cavernous space dominated by the bright light which emanates from the great east windows, dazzling the congregation and impairing the clear view of the altar; nevertheless a wonderful monument.

Another structural masterpiece built in the same year imposes a less monumental presence in the landscape at Lourdes. Pierre Vago's St Pius X Basilica (brilliantly engineered by Eugène Freyssinet, virtual inventor of pre-stressed concrete) lies underground in an effort to limit the impact on the landscape of this vast arena, which encloses a space approaching that of St Peter's in Rome. The building is designed to cope with the huge flow of people who flock to Lourdes (it is designed to shelter up to 22,000 pilgrims) and Vago came to the conclusion that the best and most practical solution to the plan would be the form of the ellipse in consideration of the vast structural spans involved.

A dished floor and a central altar raised on steps creates the best possible proximity to and view of the celebration for the gathered masses. The interior is austere and plain, the concrete structure left bare. Vago specified a lack of decoration and the result is a brilliantly theatrical space which converges solely on the altar. The space is surrounded by the structure – a huge ring of braces – so that the feeling is almost of a great clearing in the woods, the archetypal temple. Vago had also been responsible for a very fine church in Arles-Trinquetaille (1950), an elegant response to liturgical reform in a crisp, clearly articulated modernist shell, and later designed the Church at Salies-du-Salat (1962), a simple egg-shaped space with only the most minimal distractions from the altar, a pleasing and functional result of the liturgical movement.

As an antidote to the monumental scale of these buildings it is worth mentioning Rainer Senn's tiny

ABOVE: Church of Notre Dame, Royan, 1958, G Gillet and B Laffaille; CENTRE AND BELOW: Basilica of St Pius X, Lourdes, 1958, P Vago and E Freyssinet

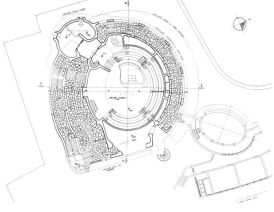

ABOVE AND CENTRE: Baranzate Church, Milan, 1958, A Mangiarotti and A Morassutti; BELOW: Church at Lungarone, 1975, G Michelucci

Church of St André at Nice. This tiny elemental church was built out of logs by the architect himself for a small community. A square plan topped with a pyramidal roof and braces which emerge from under the eaves like tent poles, it is the personification of the mobility of the tabernacle. The church represents the notion that the building itself is a meeting place only, that the House of God is the congregation itself. An abject lesson in humility, and an influence which belies its tiny size.

Ecclesiastical architecture in Italy had not fully responded to modernism in the years between the wars. The seeds of visionary modernism sown by Sant'Elia, and later Terragni, did not seem to land on fertile ground. Terragni's remarkable plan for the Danteum could have been a blueprint for a new sacred architecture which stemmed from a source outside Christianity in the way in which Steiner's Goetheanum had done. Both were conceived as monuments to great humanist thinkers and interestingly it was to be Steiner's architecture which would seem to have created the deeper impression on the Italians.

The architecture which emerged in the Italian church was often based on a remarkable expressionism inspired by the malleable, plastic qualities of concrete. But there was another tradition, that which remains familiar to us in Italian design – the tradition of the beautifully designed object; a clarity and a simplicity which is unmistakably Italian and which showed through in a number of designs. Perhaps it can be seen most clearly in the exquisite Baranzate Church in the heartland of Italian design, Milan, designed by A Mangiarotti and A Morassutti (1958). If Abbé Suger's aim was to achieve a total dissolution of the walls into light, then this is the final realisation of his vision.

From without, the church appears as a harsh, almost industrial box of a building. The walls are articulated in rectangular panels crowned with a roof structure of which the ends of the beams are exposed, half a dozen X-sections emerging from the eaves. Steps lead up to the church (which is raised because of the high water table) and the simplest of wooden crosses defines the threshold of street to church. Once inside the walls glow with a delicate translucence. The effect is achieved using a sheet of translucent plastic sandwiched between two sheets of glass while the structural role is fulfilled by four sturdy columns which also subtly delineate aisles, chancel and nave. The usual criticism of dazzling glare is thus avoided and the evenness of the light across the whole interior is a brilliant solution to a perennial problem.

The effect is reminiscent of Japanese paper walls and the building's elegant and articulate minimalism would exert a significant influence across the world, from Ireland to Japan. Beneath the church a solid and dark crypt creates a complete contrast of feel and spirit, lit only by a row of openings directly under the ceiling to create another hauntingly simple space.

A harsher, more industrial aesthetic is exhibited at Figini and Pollini's Church of the Madonna of the Poor (1952) also in Milan. These architects were among the most advanced in Italy having developed their brand of modernism between the wars. Here the chancel appears like a stage inside the church, separated from the nave by a geometrically perforated concrete beam like a proscenium arch. It is lit from an unseen source above, brilliant in comparison to the semi-darkness of the nave; a powerful, almost brutal design which captures something of the elemental nature of sacred space.

The other approach, the expressionist way, is exemplified in a number of Italian churches including Nicola Mosso's SS Redentore (1957) in Turin. Apparently directly inspired by the dome of Guarini's nearby baroque Sindone Chapel the church is very much defined by its dramatic roof – a concrete vault of triangular coffers and diamond shaped openings which sparkle in the bright light like gems. The elevations are treated in a similar crystalline stack of geometrics, the small hexagonal chapel is a mini version of the chancel itself. The composition seems a strong reference to the angular, geological forms of the expressionists.

An exponent of the more sculptural side of an Italian neo-expressionism appeared in Giovanni Michelucci. Le Corbusier had shown the way with the sculptural expressionism of Ronchamp and Michelucci took the forms in a more organic direction a decade later with his remarkable Church of San Giovanni (1960-3) on the Autostrada del Sole near Florence. There is something of the existential angst of twentieth-century man in the design, a dramatic turnaround for an architect who had been a leading member of the rationalist movement in the 1930s, very much as Corbusier himself had reacted when his functionalist approach was confronted with the notion of building a church.

Michelucci used an organic blend of materials and forms to create a highly plastic composition which has affinities with organicism in the USA and with a kind of emergent post-modernism – the billboard school of architecture, or an attempt to create new, dramatic forms for a car-based culture where everything is seen in glimpses which then have to encapsulate an idea or a specific vision. It also evokes the spirit of the roadside camp or tent. The interiors become theatrical sets, scenes of the heightened dramatic tension of the celebration.

His church at Lungarone (1966-75) embodies a womb-like sanctuary, in response to Vatican II, which encloses and hugs the congregation in an embrace of concrete. The sculptural organicism is reminiscent of Steiner's Goetheanum, particularly in the bold use of flowing concrete as an expression of both the structural and spiritual forces acting on the building. The roof is sculpted as an auditorium for services, a great amphitheatre with the background of the powerful, rocky hills; an answer to the pantheism of Greek architecture. The building is as close to modern theatre as the mass has come; the idea of the Eucharist as catharsis, as the congregation becomes closely involved with the action unfolding on the theatrical altar on its stage at the centre of the galleried interior. The Chapel of Vergine della Consolazione in San Marino (1961-7) becomes an actual manifestation of an expressionist set, a disturbing internal expression of an uncertain world.

Also worthy of mention here is Giuseppe Vaccaro's Church of St Anthony the Abbot (begun 1949) in Recoaro. His design embraces elements and characteristics of all the great architectures from early Christian to Renaissance and modernism. The church features an archetypal and timeless vaulted space and a facade which is richly appreciative of Italy's urban tradition.

The competent weaving of references from the historical context into a thoroughly modern composition is one which has characterised much Italian architecture and is a thread which still runs through some of the fine churches being created, including the exquisite and thoughtful work of Burelli and Gennaro. Vaccaro has said:

The Catholic Church, within its long history, has maintained within very different styles, some essential characteristics, both liturgical and psychological. I have tried to express these characteristics without, however, reproducing the building forms and systems of the past. Personally, and without reservation, I believe that religious architecture should be modern architecture. However, I feel that the Church would be wise to reject all formalized style, which is destined to lose its validity in a very short time. Rather than an anxious search after style, architecture should seek to be a sincere and lively expression of contemporary life and techniques of building. Such always were the greatest architectonic creations of past time.[7]

These are the beginnings of the questioning of a rigidly imposed functionalism as the only acceptable way of working. They would be developed over the years into branches stemming from the broad trunk of modernism. One of these branches has been termed contemporary regionalism and one of its earliest exponents was Richard England. England's master, Gio Ponti, had already questioned the tenets and the narrowness of functionalism before the war. His own cathedral at Taranto (1964-71) is an impressive piece of sculptural design which echoes a kind of late gothic with its attenuated, pointed openings yet, like his exquisite little chapel at the convent in San Remo, its modernism is never in doubt. However, England's church at Manikata in Malta was a more seminal work and an indicator of a new era which was increasingly conscious of the context and of local tradition but which still carried with it the investigative exploration of modernism. England's church (described pp108-113) takes the liturgical reforms as its kernel and pre-empts the changes of Vatican II in a subtle and sculptural design which also presages a move away from the formal language of modernism while retaining its fundamental conceptions and, in some cases, a reassertion of the importance of the liturgy over the sculptural play of masses for the personal artistic expression of the architect. As Gio Ponti once told Richard England, 'Religious architecture is not a matter of architecture but a matter of religion.'[8]

XIV. UNITED STATES OF AMERICA
'For the Worship of God and the Service of Man'

The words which form the sub-heading of this chapter are inscribed above the entrance to the building which brought American ecclesiastical architecture into the modern age: the Unity Temple in Oak Park, Illinois. Its architect was Frank Lloyd Wright, one of the figures responsible for instigating and inspiring a new approach to architecture both in the USA and in Europe and here responsible for what can probably safely be called the world's first modern church.

Wright's approach to space and to the brief for the temple was prophetic and highly advanced. In a lecture given at the Art Institute of Chicago in 1931, he said of the Unity Temple that it represented:

An entirely new sense of architecture, a higher conception of architecture; architecture not alone as form following function, but conceived as space enclosed. The enclosed space itself might now be seen as the reality of the building. The sense of the 'within' or of the room itself, or the rooms themselves, I now saw as the great thing to be expressed as *architecture*.

The bold, angular forms of the building are not seen as style but as the expression of space and as the expression of the building's function. Just as Gaudí's intense Catholic piety found expression in the ecstatic Sagrada Familia, Wright's liberal Unitarian background found expression in the rational, democratic solidity of the Unity Temple. He abandoned the traditional symbols and elements of ecclesiastical architecture, the spire in particular. In his autobiography he wrote of Unity Temple:

Why not, then, build a temple, not to God in that way – more sentimental than sense – but build a temple to man, appropriate to his uses as a meeting place, in which to study man for himself for his God's sake? A modern meeting house and a good time place . . . What would such a building be like? They said they could imagine no such thing.

'That's what you came to me for,' I ventured I can imagine it and I will help you create it.[1]

And lo, he did create it. Wright's rational approach led to a revolutionary new building: a solid mass of concrete; no effort was made to disguise the nature of a material which was widely regarded as only useful for a structure which would later be clad, and certainly not worthy of a church. Perret did the same in Europe nearly two decades later. The simplicity of the blocky exterior expresses the clarity of the interior. The building is entered through a space which connects the auditorium with the social hall, both elements are clearly and separately expressed in plan (it seems possible that Wright was influenced in the form of the building's plan by his experiences of Japanese temple architecture and their sublime and eternal simplicity of repose).

The auditorium is a galleried cubic space crowned by a coffered ceiling in which the recesses are glazed to complement the light from the high windows to make 'a creation of interior space in light'. The podium projects into the central space and is surrounded by and pushed into the congregation. It is an expression of the democracy of Wright's vision, both in the auditorium and the equal disposition of the building's sacred and secular parts which carries a deep sympathy with the aims of the liturgical movement, although it is a coincidental affinity.

The Unity Temple has to be seen against a background of a United States architectural scene dominated by historicism. The building's austerity and plainness must have been a great surprise. As in much of Europe ecclesiastical building was particularly in the grip of the gothic revival. Grace Church (1843-6) and St Patrick's Cathedral in New York (1858-79) both by James Renwick Jr. helped to set the pace of the gothic revival in that city while even the Cathedral of St John the Divine (begun 1892) which had started life as romanesque metamorphosed over its construction into a gothic structure. Others also operated in a gothic vein, Ralph Adams Cram and H C Pelton and C Collens taking the revivalism deep into the twentieth century. Perhaps the most significant structure in terms of an American architecture had been H H Richardson's Trinity Church in Boston (1872-7) which shows the architect's mastery of an original romanesque solidity in carving out a modern idiom. It is a powerful building which exerted an effect on European as well as American architects, notably in Scandinavia.

Little had prepared the States for Wright's masterpiece and only Bernard Maybeck's First Church of Christ Scientist, Berkeley, California (1910-12) caused a comparable wave in the conservative church scene. He created (with Greene and Greene and others) a modern idiom using the reference of West Coast vernacular and some of the same Japanese influences that had affected Wright, armed with a similar enthusiasm for modern materials. Maybeck remained attached umbilically to his Beaux-Arts training which shows in the axial planning of the church and although the building is one of the earliest encapsulations of the 'California Style' it does not possess the revolutionary qualities of Wright's work.

Other churches would also emanate from Wright's office over his mighty career. Among these was the Unitarian Church in Shorewood Hills, Wisconsin (1947). This expressive triangular structure is often compared with that of a ship or an ark ploughing its way through the landscape, an analogy which would have the pastor placed at the building's helm. It is a slightly freakish building from a stage in the architect's career where he seems to have forgotten the lessons which he taught with the sublime clarity of the Unity Temple. The plan is

ABOVE: Unity Temple, Oak Park, Illinois, 1907, F Lloyd Wright; BELOW: First Church of Christ Scientist, Berkeley, California, 1912, B Maybeck

unsatisfactory, with much of the seating facing away from the pastor due to the awkward triangular form. Yet the image is undeniably powerful and this kind of extravagant symbolism (at the expense of functionality) became common throughout the world in the years following this scheme. Interestingly the Beth Shalom synagogue in Pennsylvania (1954), which uses a similarly expressionistic, form encases a more successful space.

His son, Lloyd Wright's Wayfarers' Chapel of 1951, built for the Swedenborgians in Palos Verdes, California, is a beautiful little structure with an organic relationship to the landscape and the sea. Delicate and intimate, it is a fine continuation of the mantle of organic architecture and is a precursor of Fay Jones' Thorncrown chapel.

Wright's final building and legacy was another church, the Annunciation Greek Orthodox Church, Wisconsin (1956). It is a great UFO of a building which attempts to evoke the architectural language of the Byzantine Church in an effort to encapsulate the spirit of the Orthodox Church in a kind of successor to an *architecture parlante*. Wright created a huge shallow, gilded dome to crown the building, possibly influenced by his love for the Hagia Sophia. The building inside is more Las Vegas than Istanbul, focusing a curiously tacky sanctuary of souvenir icons, gold and lightbulbs.

Wright made a terrific impact on the US architectural scene and his followers began to develop individual approaches which led to some of the country's most eccentric but most original buildings: Charles Warren Callister designed the First Church of Christ Scientist, Belvedere, California (1954) in an extension of the style which Maybeck set under way. Callister's opinion was that 'Architecture evolves from faith'.[2] His approach was more unified than was Maybeck's and the result was a fine little building of timber with a delicate spiky spire and wall subtly broken down to admit light through slots of leaded windows.

The building echoes the prow metaphor of Wright's Unitarian Church but the interior here is far more thoughtful and successful; its intimate scale and layout brings the congregation close to the altar. The feel is deliberately that of a log cabin – the structure which this church replaced but which the congregation had become sentimentally attached to – so the architect used that most archetypal American form as a point of reference in this friendly structure.

Another architect from the same background, Bruce Goff, was creating some of the most interesting designs.

His 1927 plan for a cathedral design was remarkably similar to Bartning's *Sternkirche* while the sketch elevations bear a marked German expressionist influence. His Methodist-Episcopal Church in Tulsa, Oklahoma (1926) was a fascinating design which reflected both his expressionist interests and contemporary Art Deco stylings. The stepped, ziggurat form of the skyscraper had usurped the role of the church spire as urban marker and Goff's church is an acknowledgement of this, an exercise in spire-scraping. It is a soaring design capped in copper and glass fins to reflect the light. The church consists of a round auditorium and numerous social facilities reflecting the concerns of the expressionist ideal of the palace of the people. Goff came even closer to a realisation of the dreams of Taut and Scheerbart with his Crystal Chapel design (1949), a dramatic vision of the crystal mountain sheltering a non-denominational chapel.

Goff's interest in transposing expressionism to an American idiom was shared by Barry Byrne. Byrne, who started off in the Prairie School and travelled to Germany to meet the expressionist masters (Böhm, Poelzig, Feininger and the others) went on to create some of the most interesting and advanced church designs anywhere. His writings echo closely those of the liturgical movement architects in Europe. In *The Western Architect* (October, 1929) Byrne states his principles:

> The way of architecture is from the ground up; from the general to the particular.
> Function is first; Building second.
> In a Catholic church, then, what are the functions? First, the altar. It is primary. The church building exists to house it, the celebrants at it and the people who come before it.
> The building structure surrounds these with walls, covers them with the span of a roof. This is a church. The people come to worship and to participate in worship. The liturgy of the mass is not for the few, it is for all to follow, as intimately as they can. The altar and the worshippers then must be as one, or as much so as space and a large number of worshippers permits. The modern church is for the people who build it and of the day that produces it. It fulfils the functions and its use of its structure, it is a church in the truest sense of that word.

This text appeared with the designs for the Church of Christ King, Cork, Ireland, a scheme which closely reflects expressionist experiments in its stepped plan and its ziggurat form; a very powerful design which blends the aspirational climb of the gothic with the populist modernism of Art Deco, yet transcends easy classification. The seating begins to curl around the sanctuary in a presentiment of liturgical reform and the shape of the plan brings the whole congregation together very much as a single unit. The church was finally built in 1937, as Ireland's first modern church – a remarkable achievement in a conservative country.

Byrne went on to design a number of churches in a less dramatic but nevertheless highly modern style. The Church of St Columba in St Paul, Minnesota is a sleek, streamlined piece of modernism which nevertheless retains a kind of gothic massing. Its less fortunate aspect is that its plan is apparently based on the shape of the fish as a reference to the symbol of Christ; these gestures are at best spurious and usually futile, no matter how well intentioned. Among his other churches was the innovative Church of Saints Peter and Paul in Pierre, South Dakota, with a fine plan based on two converging rectangles which meet at the focus of the altar.

Frank Lloyd Wright had spent his life trying to create an American architecture and he greatly resented the awe in which the European expatriates (Tom Wolfe's 'White Gods') were held and the way in which they had dominated the US architectural scene. But despite Wright's influence on their own early work, it was these European modernists who set the agenda for American architecture over the next decades.

While Wright was experimenting with increasingly eccentric forms, Mies van der Rohe was paring down the elements of architecture to a minimum and out of this impetus came the chapel at the Illinois Institute of Technology in Chicago (1952). It was a remarkably simple building: if less was more, then this was the most. A load-bearing brick structure, a glass wall at the front, a single, solid block of travertine for the altar and a silk hanging to separate the sacred space from the utility rooms at the back; there is little innovation, but a striking clarity. Philip Johnson once said that 'What makes Mies such a great influence . . . is that he is so easy to copy.' Mies' buildings may have been masterpieces traceable back to Schinkel's universal classicism but in the hands of others, the vocabulary was used too often to cover up a lack of skill and thoughtful design.

Mies' minimalism did not stem from the same spirit which drove Schwarz or Böhm. Theirs was a modernism which combined with a zealous passion and a heartfelt

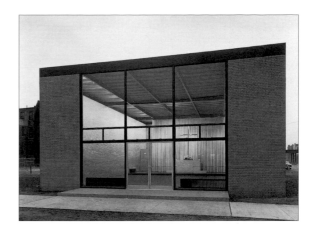

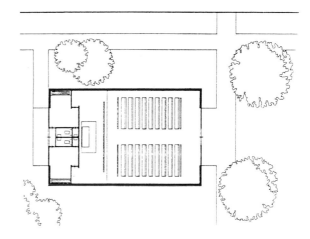

Chapel at the Illinois Institute of Technology, Chicago, 1952, Mies van der Rohe

connection with liturgy to create a purity which came from the soul, even when their forms hinted at an odd mysticism or expressionism. Mies was interested not in the specific solution for the church or the forms that would facilitate changes in liturgical practice, but in the universal form; an architecture which could accommodate any function which would have been anathema to his contemporaries in the German liturgical movement despite their often common roots in early expressionism.

Yet Mies' minimalism gave rise also to positive trends. The architecture of the Sirens in Finland can be seen to be deeply connected to Mies' minimalism and his architecture did have the benefit of stripping away the superfluous paraphernalia which had accumulated around ecclesiastical architecture, to make a fresh start.

Another recent European immigrant from the Bauhaus created one of the most important US schemes of the century: Marcel Breuer. Breuer was a Hungarian who had come to prominence at the Bauhaus largely as a furniture designer (he designed the famous tubular chair). In the USA he was given the chance to practise architecture on a huge scale as the partner of Walter Gropius.

In the 1950s he was commissioned by the monks of the Benedictine Abbey of St John the Baptist in Collegeville, Minnesota, to design them a new church. It was an unusually enlightened community and one which was keen to promote the ideals of the liturgical movement; one of the first to do so in the USA. Breuer's architectural place is exactly between Mies and Wright. He clearly rejected the notion of an organic architecture but he was also wary of the over-rationalisation of Mies.

The church was to be the focus of a large community, as well as being a parish church and a scene of great procession during holy events. As such it was decided that the church needed a certain monumental presence and, as he had recently designed the Paris Headquarters for UNESCO, Breuer was felt to be an appropriate choice. He carried his large-scale civic vision through to St John's where the church was placed at the entrance to the community with its great bell tower forming a physical gate to the internalised world of the monastery.

The sound of the bells and the striking of hours is an essential part of the lives of the monks while the towers used to guard the monastery from intruders and became a symbol of the insulated monastic world, so it is entirely appropriate that this becomes the building's visual identity. The entrance sequence shows an acute awareness of symbolism and the history of the Church as

well as its regard for the liturgical movement of which this church was possibly the most complete expression.

A baptistry is placed as the first element in the progression after passing under the bell tower. It serves to fulfil the function of the atrium recommended by the German Liturgical Commission, a preparatory space for the church, and it makes manifest the importance of baptism as the entrance rite to the faith; the font is on axis with the altar and accorded due significance in plan and not shoved into a corner. The plan of the baptistry is derived from the trapezoid and is a microcosm of the space of the church itself, a shape which is expressed first in the form of the stone slab which surmounts the bell tower. The plan form allows for smaller services in the horse-shoe shaped enclosure at the rear of the plan and larger services for the whole parish and on holidays to be accommodated in the seating which fans out from the sanctuary.

A simple altar with a separate slab mensa forms the focus for whatever arrangement is adopted. It is raised on four steps and emphasised in the vast interior space by a canopy suspended by wires which appear like rays emanating from the centre. The huge space is uninterrupted by columns or structure and the architect achieved the great unity and oneness which was such a critical aim of liturgical reform. It is one of the most successful churches of its era both as symbolic gesture and as a practical response to a complicated brief.

Another Central European immigrant was responsible for two influential churches: Richard Neutra. The Viennese architect was in the vanguard of a pure modern architecture and his chapel at Miramar, La Jolla, California (1957), is an exquisite exposition of his art. The building is perched by an artificial lake in which the slender cross which defines it as a chapel is reflected next to the delicate stair which rises in a symbolic gesture of ascent into the light of the interior. Its purity marks it out as a predecessor of Tadao Ando's little Church on the Water. The interior is a simple, single space with elegant curved fins supporting the walls; well-lit and clear, a simple and impressive statement.

His later church at Garden Grove, California is another building of great clarity. Here the symbolic ascent is fulfilled by a glazed stair tower on the skyscraper belfry culminating in the imposing cross which surmounts the tower. The church is light and clear: a simple long hall. Again there is the relationship with the water, the implications of baptism, the reflection of another world and a return to the waters. It also includes the innovation of a drive-in church arranged in a fan shape inspired by the drive-in movies.

While these functionalist monuments to light and clarity were being erected, the form of the swooping triangle, the pyramid and the teepee as already seen in Wright's work, was becoming a very widespread symbol for ecclesiastical architects often unsure of how to achieve a monumental presence using modern forms. Skidmore, Owings and Merrill's US Air Force Academy Chapel in Colorado Springs (1962) is a good example of the genre and an undoubtedly impressive structure against the mountains which form its backdrop; the church evokes the spectre of the spiky visions of expressionism, but it is a single, simplistic statement based on a dramatic form.

The same could be said of the swooping form of Victor A Lundy's First Unitarian Church at Westport, Connecticut (1960), and his Church of St Paul, Sarasota, Florida, with its swept-up curved front. Eero Saarinen's North Christian Church, Columbus, Indiana (1959-63), also features a penetrating needle of a spire directly over a central altar, while a sweeping roof encompasses all the building's functions under its generous eaves, creating a fine building based around the octagonal form of the church at its heart.

Perhaps most impressive of all in the tent/triangle category was the church designed by Wallace K Harrison. Not an architect much associated with church buildings, his First Presbyterian Church in Stamford, Connecticut (1958), is a remarkable crystalline structure. Harrison asked his biographer, Victoria Newhouse: 'Have you ever thought what it would be like to live inside a giant sapphire?' At this church he did his best to supply the answer to his own question with an interior which glows with a crystal sparkle which Taut and Scheerbart would have undoubtedly approved of. From without the church's exterior is simple and rugged with only the fractal formations of the glazing giving any inkling of the luminous quality of the interior. From within, the interior truly resembles a great tent with walls of jewels. It is not a ground-breaking building and is liturgically rather backward but it is a stunning evocation of the tent of God.

Pietro Belluschi practised an altogether more restrained architecture, a simple and homely effect in which he used laminated timber to create sympathetic and human churches. His Church of St Thomas More, Portland, Oregon (1938), and the Zion Lutheran Church (also

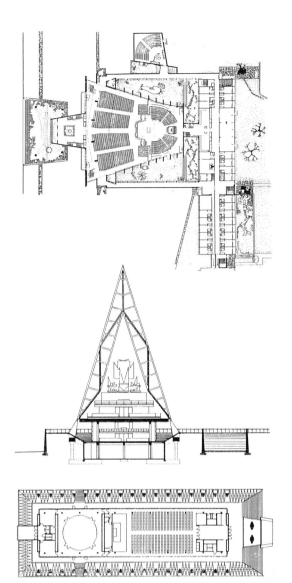

ABOVE: Church of St John the Baptist, Collegeville, Minnesota, 1961, M Breuer; CENTRE: US Air Force Academy Chapel, Colorado, 1962, SOM; BELOW: First Presbyterian Church, Stamford, Connecticut, 1958, W Harrison

Chapel of St Francis of Assisi, Pampúlha, Brazil, 1943, O Niemeyer

Portland, 1949-50) show off the effect, while the Church of the Redeemer, Baltimore, Maryland (1958), is church as barn, the simplest vernacular space given a gothic feel by the pointed arches of the structure while remaining simple and modern. His First Presbyterian Church, Cottage Grove, Oregon, is an example of a return to the Japanese influences of Wright and Maybeck, a beautifully clear and elegant space articulated in simple, refined forms.

A similar simplicity, but expressed in brick, can be seen at Eliel and Eero Saarinen's Christ Evangelical Church, Minneapolis (1949), where architects usually associated with expressive forms and extravagant structures created a church of unusual clarity. Its tall, elegant belfry, with its grid perforation and slender cross, allied with the light airy space contained within, evoke the calm simplicity achieved in the Swiss churches. Its older brother, the First Christian Church, Columbus, Indiana (1942) designed by the same architects, is a similarly exemplary modern church of great clarity and one of the first such structures to be erected in the USA and indeed, the first modern building in the city.

Despite the quantity and quality of some of the churches in the USA, many of the most impressive achievements in post-war American church building came from below the borders, from the Latin cultures and lyrical sensibilities of South America.

XV. SOUTH AMERICA

If there are many equally varied technical solutions to a problem, the one which offers the user a message of beauty and emotion, that one is architecture.
Luis Barragán

Ecclesiastical architecture in South America grew from a combination of a poetic Borgesian world of fantastic forms and fantasy, and an application of structural innovation and a rational approach to the practical problems of building. The result was some of the most fascinating church architecture of the century which sprang from the deep well of a faithful people.

Perhaps the first manifestation of a new church architecture was seen at Oscar Niemeyer's church in Pampúlha (1943). Here, the architect took a slab of concrete and folded it into parabolic forms to create a sheltering, wavy roof which defines the building. The walls are decorated with a bright mural in *azulejo* tiles reflecting the colonial influence of the Portuguese. A simple, flared belfry stands by the church, its angularity emphasised by the curves of the church, and the whole composition is distorted even further in the image it creates in the artificial lake on the banks of which it stands. The curves are Niemeyer's homage to the undulating Brazilian landscape which he loved: 'The whole universe is made of curves.'

It was a powerful reaction to the rigidity of orthodox modernism and it is a building which prefigures Le Corbusier's plastic treatment of concrete and canopy at Ronchamp in the next decade (rather than the landscape, Corbusier used a crab's shell as the inspiration for his roof). Yet Niemeyer's building has not adopted the expressionism which defined Corbusier's dramatic departure from the functionalist aesthetic. Gaudí had used the parabolic arch not because of its expressive qualities but because it was a superior structural solution; it negated the need for ungainly flying buttresses. But its very perfection made it for him a symbol of God and it became a manifestation of his faith. The adoption of curved structures was a rational rather than an expressive decision just as it was with Niemeyer.

But just as a powerful neo-expressionism had affected church architecture in Germany and Italy during the

Church of La Virgen Milagrosa, Mexico City, 1955, F Candela

post-war period, so it struck many of the architects in South America. Less constricted by history and tradition than the Europeans, many South American architects approached problems of church building with a freshness and originality which was often stunning.

Eladio Dieste used brick at his Church at Atlanida in Uruguay (1958) in a way in which perhaps only Gaudí could have prophesied; as a rational solution creating a wild expressivity as its by-product. A fantastic wavy wall undulates like clay collapsing on a potter's wheel. The vaults of the roof are similarly wavy. Dieste was enamoured with the skill of the bricklayer and determined that it should not be lost to an invasion of industrial building techniques merely for the sake of the modern. The church is the apex of his search for forms which were revolutionary, structurally logical and expressively beautiful.

In Mexico, Felix Candela was also exploiting a language of forms which seemed to owe something to Gaudí. The Church of La Virgen Milagrosa in Mexico City (1954-5) seems to be a development of the dramatic, organic forms of the later phases of the Sagrada Familia. As with Gaudí, the forms are guided by a sharp appreciation of the lines of force and stress and the inherent qualities of the materials and are not the purely visual expressionism which they might seem.

Candela was an engineer and mathematician as well as architect and, in a way, his structures reflect the engineering genius of his forebear Perret and his contemporary Pier Luigi Nervi, both of whom took the art of reinforced concrete to new peaks of creativity. His great feat at the La Virgen Milagrosa is his unification of structure and enclosing membrane. The whole fabric is working in unity to create an effect which sends the building soaring skyward in a single, angelic thrust. It is a true realisation of the verticality and vaulting as the earthly representation of the heavens

to which the gothic cathedral builders aspired.

The structure is light and ingenious and yet at the same time the shadows cast by the hyperbolic paraboloids and the spiky, angular form of some of the elements recalls a cubist approach to space, leaving mystical patches of darkness and an ambiguity of planes. Both the extreme thinness of the concrete structure and its triangular form conspire to evoke the image of the tent, a canopy seemingly held aloft on faith alone.

Candela's other masterpiece was carried out in conjunction with architect Enrique de la Mora y Palomar; the Chapel of Nuestra Señora de la Soledad in Coyoacán, Mexico (also 1955). Although it does not feature the structural bravado of his other church (still not bad though) it does embody one of the most liturgically advanced and innovative plans of the period. The seating is arranged on three sides of the altar in the church's triangular plan. The seats in front of the altar are on a slight curve to begin to surround the celebrant. This allows a versatility of use including the seating of a large choir around the altar. The swooping roof is based on a hyperbolic paraboloid which sweeps up at the sides and the whole roof lifts towards the welcoming entrance.

The most influential design to come out of South America was, however, undoubtedly Oscar Niemeyer's new cathedral for Brasilia (1970). After Le Corbusier's Ronchamp this is perhaps the most iconic church of the century, full of the optimism and hope of the modern spirit. The cathedral as a type was made almost anachronistic by liturgical reform. Although it has a clear function, the idea of a church to house a city full of people does not seem compatible with the increasingly accepted notions of the intimacy of the Eucharist and the desirability of the closeness of the celebrant and congregation. The great cathedral poses a serious barrier

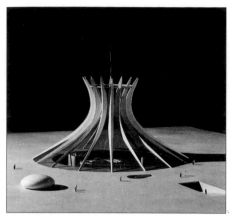

Model of Cathedral, Brasilia, 1970, O Niemeyer

Chapel at the President's Palace, Brasilia, 1958, O Niemeyer

to these theological aims. Niemeyer used the circular plan to achieve optimum closeness to and involvement in the celebration. The cathedral seems to be the continuation of the great urban plaza, swept up to an apex and flowering out at its crown. It is entered via a ramp from the square which descends into the subterranean darkness so that the emergence into the expansive and light world of the cathedral's interior is symbolic of the passage of birth and rebirth into the Christian Church, a metaphor which is made more explicit in the adjacent baptistry which is wholly unlit by windows like a stalkless mushroom in the plaza.

The structure of the church could barely be simpler. Huge reinforced concrete struts rise to form the framework which is filled by coloured glass to reduce the glare. The building works like a cooling tower so that the hot air from within rises and is released at the top. The struts continue once they have fulfilled their functional role and blossom out in a symbolic gesture of metamorphosis. They cast a spiky shadow on the ground which moves around and dominates the great urban space like a huge crown of thorns.

The altar, pulpit and seating within the cathedral are grouped together around the centre so that there is close proximity of worshippers and celebrant and even when the church is full there is good visual and aural contact. The cathedral's transparency opens it up to the city while its soaring presence is a symbol of hope and a grand urban gesture; a new conception in design, monumentality superimposed on the city at a human scale recalling the cathedral's organic presence in the heart of the medieval city.

The cathedral's antithesis in scale, but not beauty, is the chapel at the president's palace in Brasilia (1958). Its form is based around an unfolding shell, a sketch of a spiral brought into solid and void. It is one of the simplest sacred spaces with an intimacy and intensity which remain almost unparalleled. It is designed as part of a built dialogue with the palace; its enclosing concrete wall a private, meditative answer to the open glass structure of the public nature of the palace.

The chapter opened with Luis Barragán's definition of architecture. What this means in physical terms can be seen at his chapel in Colonia Tlalpan in Mexico City (1952-5). It is a small space, an intervention into an existing convent, but one which sparkles like a gem and illuminates the complex from its centre. There is little innovative about the chapel other than its beauty and simplicity. A golden altar shines against a glowing sunset background of pink and orange. One of the walls is replaced by a looming cross which acts as space divider between the sacred and the profane areas while the motif is echoed on the outside wall which is divided into quarters by a sculpted cross in relief casting its great, distorted shadow across the building.

It is the equatorial answer to the Nordic purity of Asplund's Stockholm Cemetery. God is expressed in its clarity and simplicity; it is, like so much South American church architecture, the solution which offers the message of beauty and emotion.

XVI. SCANDINAVIA
Modernism: The Organic and the Rational

The Scandinavian countries accepted modernism far more comprehensively than most other European countries. The design which emanated from the area exerted a growing influence throughout Europe in the years following the Second World War and two distinct streams emerged in architecture which largely defined the Scandinavian contribution to twentieth-century ecclesiastical architecture.

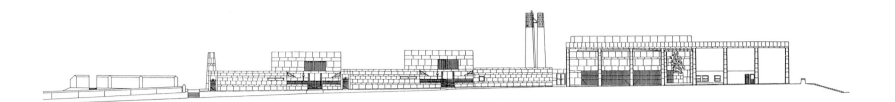

Crematorium, South Stockholm Cemetery, 1940, E G Asplund

The first of these is a Nordic classicism which treads the fine line between a traditional architectonic language and modernism exemplified by Gunnar Asplund, the second is an organic approach which softened the dogmatic harshness of Bauhaus-type modernism and which responded more closely to the landscape and the body, this form was embodied by Alvar Aalto. Both have had a lasting effect and, although less revolutionary than the developments in Germany, have continued to influence the architecture coming out of Scandinavia and elsewhere, largely for the better.

In Scandinavia, as in much of Europe, the Arts and Crafts influenced national romanticism which defined the desire for independence after the turn of the century gave way to a conservative neo-classicism in the years before and after the First World War. The Swedish architect Erik Gunnar Asplund was one of the few architects who were able to impart a touch of genius to the genre through a blend of spatial manipulation, materials and reference to tradition in a modern manner.

His Woodland Chapel in the South Stockholm Cemetery (1918-20) was a reinterpretation of the Abbé Laugier's primitive hut, the archetypal shelter of columns and roof executed in a self-effacing vernacular. However, his triumph is the crematorium chapel in the South Stockholm Cemetery, 1935-40. Franco Borsi writes lyrically about it:

> Asplund succeeded in combining the blood-curdling yet romantic howl of the wind in the virgin forest and over the great meadows, a rarefied classicism with marble cross and open portico, and the aggressive functionality of the crematorium, where even the mouths of the furnaces are exactly shaped to fit a coffin. Thus he succeeds in giving to each part, each functional element, not only its own shape, but also its own essential symbolic form, so that nature is nature, the cross is cross without a base or any other

architecture but itself, meadow is meadow, the wood is wood, and everything in the austere solemnity of the place exudes an impression of finality and proclaims indeed a final symbolic message.[1]

The austere portico stands in relationship to the wooded landscape like a Greek temple, rigid and eternal as is the simple, self-referential stone cross which stands in front of it. The vision recalls again the tradition of Caspar David Friedrich and a northern romanticism, an almost pantheistic position; in nature and with it, yet outlined against it. The interior of the chapel sees the cold perfection of the elevation give way to a more humane enclosure. Gently curved walls embrace the mourners and the stripped modern vocabulary is replaced by murals and rounded columns with capitals. Outside a suspended clock acts as *memento mori*. It should be seen as a seminal influence on the work of Kaija and Heikki Siren who were to refine a minimal version of a similar language which is able to embrace pantheism, a classic modernism and a minimal, archetypal architectonic language.

A similar softened classicism can be found in a building of the same period, the Resurrection Funerary Chapel in Turku, Finland (1938-41). Its architect, Erik Bryggman, had departed from his harsher, rational modernism (seen in Parainen Cemetery Chapel of 1930) to produce a humane synthesis of pure modernism and elements of a formal, archetypal classical language tinged with an elegant romanticism. The altar takes its place in a bright arched apse while the chapel is entered through an arcade of columns which gives on to extensive views of the greenery. In the early photos ivy intrudes on to the wall of the chancel as if nature had not yet given up its claim on the space: light, airy and exquisite. His Mortuary Chapel, Pargas, is an even purer paragon of simplicity; a single space lit by one tall window which

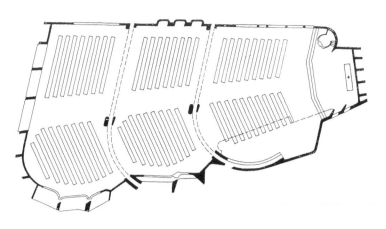

ABOVE: Vuoksenniska Church, Imatra, 1959, A Aalto; CENTRE: Church in Riola di Vergato, 1968, A Aalto; BELOW: Church in Hyvinkää, 1961, A Ruusuvuori

sheds light on the funeral bier. Light, airy and exquisite.

These words could also be used of much of the architecture of Alvar Aalto, who in the 1920s had worked with Bryggman. Aalto's church at Vuoksenniska (1956-9) is an odd but intriguing building and encloses a magnificent space. It consists of three segments designed to be used separately or as one; each can be divided by a screen to form a complete room for secular use. It is perhaps more auditorium in feel than church, but this is partly due to its protestant lineage and partly to its practical use. The church seems to waft away from the altar like a cloud, the soft curves of the walls billowing outwards. The metal roof allows the building to settle quietly into the landscape and the low eaves give it an eminently human scale while its presence is denoted by a slender belfry. It is by no means a revolutionary church, indeed its liturgical form does not respond to the new ideas, yet it is a seminal building with a decency and humanity which is rare, and an adaptability which is almost unprecedented.

Aalto's church at Riola in Italy (1966-8) is another highly influential scheme: a wavy roofscape of north-lights rests on a series of ribs which look like the bent plywood of his furniture to give an airy, irregular interior. His concept sketch recalls the expressionistic curves of Erich Mendelsohn while the plan has a jagged irregularity which looks remarkably modern, a deconstructed version of his earlier church at Seinajoki (1958-60), which also possesses an impeccably elegant modernist campanile. Aalto's work continues to exert an inestimable influence on the benign modernism of Reima Pietilä and many others practising today.

Elsewhere in Scandinavia a mini fashion for pointed and pyramidal forms was perhaps partly inspired by the local stave churches and partly by the experiments of Frank Lloyd Wright, as well as by a penchant for their expressionistic forms in a mountainous landscape. Magnus Poulsson's church at Gravberget (1956) is an example of a reinterpretation of the vernacular belfry while Aarno Ruusuvuori's church at Hyvinkää (1961) is a modern tent of God, a dynamic prism containing an impressive space.

Otherwise Scandinavian design was often sober and functional, Peter Celsing's St Thomas, Vallingby (1960) constitutes a serious urban gesture as well as a fine church and Sigurd Lewerentz's Markus Church in Malmovag (also 1960) is a timeless and understated work of great skill in handling the brick and containing the magically simple space. That Lewerentz had worked with Asplund on the nearby Woodland Crematorium is no surprise seeing the elemental clarity of this little structure. Lewerentz continued to produce some fine ecclesiastical work over the following years.

There is a consistency which runs throughout Scandinavian church architecture which was rarely equalled; an inherent humanising of the language of modernism which continues in some of the finest of today's designs.

XVII. ELSEWHERE IN EUROPE

Britain was among the slowest European countries to react to liturgical change and for much of the century ecclesiastical architecture was stuck in a vaguely historicist mode with minor concessions to modernism. After the war a tremendous amount of church building took place to cope with swelling populations, new suburbs and damage inflicted during the war. However, unlike France and Germany the architecture was not related to a living liturgy and was thus itself largely anachronistic.

Many schemes adopted the modern aesthetic without its reasoning. Churches began to look modern but not to be modern. Unusual shapes were used for their own sake, or as experiments in personal expression by the architect. By the 1960s, however, some of the ideas of the liturgical movement began to be accepted by the Church and a handful of architects. Maguire and Murray were among the first to create a thoughtful church which responded to the changes. Other great opportunities were lost. Alison and Peter Smithson's fine design for the Coventry Cathedral competition (1951) was ignored in favour of Basil Spence's scheme; a powerful design and one which recognised new liturgical thinking was usurped by one which had progressed in little else but structure from the gothic.

The Smithsons wrote in the report which accompanied their entry that they hoped that:

the building of this cathedral will finally explode the fallacy that Modern Architecture is capable of expressing abstract ideas and will prove that *only* Modern Architecture is capable of creating a symbol of the dogmatic truths of the Christian faith.[1]

The scheme was based on a square plan on the diagonal, covered by a dramatic roof rising to the altar, a conception of space which did not enclose the church but

ABOVE: Coventry Cathedral, 1962, B Spence; CENTRE: St Paul's Church, Glenrothes New Town, 1957, GKC; BELOW: Church of St Bride's, E Kilbride, 1964, GKC

allowed the space and the elements within to speak. Spence's church is elegant (particularly in its concrete structure) but uninspiring despite the wealth of artistic talent which contributed to it. It proved, nevertheless, an influential scheme.

Of all the ecclesiastical work to come out of Britain, that of Gillespie, Kidd and Coia was probably the most coherent and interesting even if it fell below the standards of much European work. Their St Paul's Church at Glenrothes New Town (1956-7) is a simple and subtle insertion into the landscape, its whiteness and clarity a response to Böhm's church at Nordeney, but features an interesting and innovative wedge-shaped plan and a plain tower over the altar which illuminates the sacred space below with an unseen and wonderful light filtered from the cold Scottish skies. The Church of St Bride's in East Kilbride (1963-4) is a robust brick construction, a heavily internalised building which confronts the world with an almost medieval, forbidding harshness. Its plan is fairly traditional but there are good touches; the font is placed a few steps below the level of the church in a channel of light from above, a dramatic gesture, and the principal wall is a kind of reference to Corbusier's Ronchamp with its randomly carved out niches and windows.

Frederick Gibberd's Catholic Cathedral in Liverpool (1960-7) was a dramatic utilisation of a round plan, part of a tide of churches inspired by Niemeyer's masterpiece at Brasilia. Ireland, which saw its first modern church designed by the American Barry Byrne, was the venue for a number of good churches in the post-war period. Among these, perhaps the finest is Michael Scott's Church of Corpus Christi at Knockanure (1964).

This brilliantly simple church is of Miesian clarity, but a far more successful building than Mies' own chapel in Illinois. It stands on a podium like a Greek temple and its wholly transparent facade is made a huge picture frame for a huge stone relief which gives the facade its face. It is without doubt one of the purest pieces of modernism to come out of ecclesiastical architecture and one of the finest pieces outside Germany. The other Irish church of great interest is Corr and McCormick's St Aengus, Burt (1967), one of the best examples of a round church, with a roof which is dramatically swept up over the altar in a gesture which sits strongly against the powerful rural landscape.

Central Europe has more recently seen some fascinating developments. Wojciech Pietrzyk and Jan Grabacki's church in Nowa Huta-Bienczyce (1974) is a masterful piece of sculptural expressionism in the vein of Le Corbusier's Ronchamp, enclosing a bright modern worship space; while Tadeusz Gawtowski and Jan Grabacki's Church of the Good Shepherd (1965-76) is a jagged geometric assortment almost reminiscent of the fragmented forms of Frank Gehry. In Austria, the artist Hundertwasser transformed the Church of St Barbara in Bärnbach (1988) from a dull building into a splash of colour using tiles and ceramics and a golden onion dome in a heady blend of Gaudí and Klimt. The churches of Imre Makovecz in Hungary have attracted world-wide attention for their stunning creativity and an organicism which has struck a chord as an antidote to a dulled modernism, while György Csete's Church of St Elisabeth at Halásztelek (1976) is one of the few fine examples of a round church. It weaves archetypal imagery and clarity of form into an impressively simple work.

Liverpool Cathedral, 1967, F Gibberd

Church of St Elisabeth, Halásztelek, 1976, G Csete

MOVEMENTS OF THE SPIRIT

Iona Spens

Even after almost a century of reform, the 'modern' churches of today are less readily accepted than their traditional counterparts. To a great extent this is to do with association; indeed, for many the experience of church architecture has been dominated by the influx of pseudo-gothic churches generated by the influence of Pugin and his circle. It is telling that Gilbert Scott lamented the fact that before he had time to discover the defects of his first design not only its form but its errors would be repeated in at least six other churches. While much of our built fabric has been shaped by the spirit of the time, church architecture seems to have been cast under the spell of historicism. Ever present is the sublime image of the medieval cathedral; yet, this, we must not forget, was very much an expression of its age and was built using the materials and techniques of the day.

Goethe referred to gothic architecture as 'a petrified religion'. One could say that this is reinforced by the number of cathedrals and churches that have been reordered to serve the theological needs of today. Many of these buildings were sanctioned in terms of style (in the same way as law courts or prisons, for example, which are undeniably rhetorical) and the essence of the church as a 'house' of worship for the people of God was often eclipsed by a standard layout and precon-ceived image of the church.

As can be seen, however, the twentieth-century church has experienced significant developments in the wake of the liturgical movement which originated in Belgium at the turn of the century. While technical developments were boldly expressed in the work of Anatole de Baudot, Perret and others, architects such as Rudolf Schwarz actively sought to untangle the genuine requirements of the church, redressing the balance with profoundly simple constructions which have influenced generations of church architects since. There have of course been many unsuccessful church buildings, saddled with a wealth of stylistic trappings and purely cosmetic improvements. These constructions have misread the fundamental message of what a church is really for and what is needed now and in the future. Many failed to address the real needs of the local community or lacked adequate guidance and communication between the ecclesiastical authority and the architect.

With respect to the latter, it is interesting to recall a discussion which took place between Finnish architect Juhani Pallasmaa and a church official about church design. Pallasmaa relates how the church official stressed the importance of knowing about the liturgy, iconography and other internal rulings of the church, remarking:

> He seemed upset when I said that only a heathen can design a really expressive church. In my view the symbol of faith can only be turned into stone by someone who is being newly introduced to the dimensions of faith.[1]

While many would disagree with Pallasmaa here, the following words (which echo the sentiments of Rudolf Schwarz) strike a deeper chord: 'A person for whom the design of a church is merely the organisation of given forms can produce only empty sentimentality.'[2]

The work of architects closely involved with the church is perhaps worth touching upon at this stage. The approach of the French monk and architect Dom Paul Bellot (1876-1944) encourages comparison with that of Dom Hans van der Laan (1904-91), also an architect, whose combined efforts in the field span much of the twentieth century. Bellot's projects, while economically driven, rejoiced in the decorative potential of materials such as concrete or brick, producing inspirational interiors such as Quarr Abbey Church on the Isle of Wight, 1912. In contrast, Van der Laan's approach was more ascetic, exemplified by Vaals Abbey Church which was completed in 1968. He criticised Bellot's work for turning 'the liturgy into a spectacle rather than a collective action'; reacting to the 'long and narrow' layout of his churches.[3] Van der Laan in fact rejected the liturgy as a basis for church form. Lecturing in 1946 he stated:

> . . . I believe that to look for such indications in the liturgy points to a complete lack of insight into the intrinsic laws of architecture. Just as secular architecture has tried to escape from the real problems of design by taking refuge in material, technical and practical requirements, so ecclesiastical architecture has plunged into a sort of liturgical functionalism, the illusory nature of which we shall come to recognise.[4]

Around this time a Swiss priest was leaving his imprint on the Japanese landscape. The work of Karl Freuler is less well-known but also worthy of a mention. A missionary and an architect, Freuler became head of the building section of the Catholic Church in Japan after fleeing from China in 1948. He designed over a hundred chapels, churches and monasteries during his twenty year stay in the country – the most memorable being the Cathedral in Kyoto (1968) with its keel-shaped roof (built a few years after Kenzo Tange's dynamic St Mary's Cathedral, Tokyo). While Freuler's early churches retained the influence of Western architects such as Dominikus Böhm, his approach became more intuitive, evoking a conscious dialogue with indigenous Japanese culture: the Leprosy Chapel in Tokyo (1958) made use of tatami mats instead of pews and used sliding screens of rice paper to gently diffuse and filter light into the interior.[5]

Inevitably, any discussion of modern church architecture will converge on well-known buildings such as the Pilgrimage Chapel, Ronchamp, by Le Corbusier, the Unity Temple in Oak Park, Illinois, by Frank Lloyd Wright, or the Church of the Sagrada Familia, Barcelona, by Antoni Gaudí. These are well-covered elsewhere and therefore do not feature here in depth. They have of course spawned numerous disciples world-wide. Significantly, the valuable contribution to church architecture of Rudolf Schwarz, Otto Bartning and the Böhms in Germany, Alvar Aalto in Finland, Slovenian architect Josef Plečnik, and Pietro Belluschi in the USA has gained greater recognition in recent years, as attested by individual publications on their work. Lesser known but equally valid are the extremely simple and economical works by architects such as Rainer Senn in

France, highlighted by Peter Hammond in his seminal book *Towards a Church Architecture*. This title, which was published over thirty years ago, continues to offer relevant insights into the subject; likewise, *New Churches of Europe* by G E Kidder Smith, published in 1964.

The following pages bring together a selection of small- and large-scale projects for the Church from the mid-1950s up to the present day by living architects from a variety of countries. Not all of those included would be associated with being 'church builders' as such; indeed, for some architects the projects represent their first experience of ecclesiastical design. With more time, this may have been a different book, since the scope of the subject is vast. However, although we can only touch on a fraction of the developments that have occurred around the world it is hoped that the selection will give the reader some idea of the way in which the twentieth-century church has progressed and encourage further research into the subject.

The body of the church has gradually been restructured for today's congregation with a spatial framework that is less hierarchical and seeks greater participation of the laity. In addition to maintaining its role as a spiritual home and acting as a solid anchor for the community, the church of today is more likely to incorporate a greater variety of functions, in the same way as its predecessor in the Middle Ages. A considerable number of churches being built are planned as church centres which offer space for other activities: this strengthens the appeal of the church for society.

Many church architects seeking to express a sense of the spiritual, such as that purveyed by today's museums, will find that this is no longer a prerequisite. Greater collaboration between the architect, the ecclesiastical authority and the worshipping community, however, will help produce a space that is both functional and stimulating, and one that is more in tune with the spirit of the age. As many of the churches in this volume illustrate, careful articulation of spaces and skilful use of natural and artificial light can be highly effective in creating an appropriate environment: simplicity and flexibility go hand in hand, and the latter seems of increasing relevance to architecture at this point in time, particularly with regard to the glaring number of redundant buildings that exist, many of which are churches. These visible scars not only remind us of where we may have gone wrong but clearly suggest the extent to which we have changed.

MAGUIRE AND MURRAY

Since the 1950s, Robert Maguire has built at least a dozen churches in England, initially in partnership with Keith Murray and later as Maguire & Co. The first of these, St Paul's, Bow Common, a Protestant church in London, was built in 1956. It represents a progressive step in the field of postwar church building in the United Kingdom, evolving from an intuitive and analytical approach to the requirements of a modern church, rather than one based on reproduction. The building is shaped by the needs of the community and responds to the liturgical movement's concern for more active participation of the laity.

Within an almost square plan, the altar is brought forward and surrounded by pews on three sides, effectively engaging a more immediate relationship with the congregation. A sense of enclosure is conveyed by the encircling colonnade of slender white columns, yet this subtle demarcation does not exclude those seated in the surrounding area when the normal congregation is expanded. Portable seating allows up to 500 people to be accommodated with the use of the lower aisles. Flexibility is essential for not only does it remove the problem of a small assembly feeling

lost within a lofty space or being surrounded by a lot of empty seats, but it enables the building to be used for other functions and gatherings. The only fixed elements in St Paul's, Bow, are the altar and the font; the latter positioned traditionally near the entrance and passed by the congregation after it has come in through the octagonal porch in the north-west corner.

The problem of achieving a centralised space with an off-centre altar was resolved by placing the lantern geometrically above, thus detached structurally from the colonnade. The downpour of light from the glazed lantern provides the main source of illumination while giving the altar added emphasis, sealed by the later addition of a ciborium (illustrated overleaf). The architects considered two steps beneath the altar to be sufficient in signifying the holy hill, though this was, Maguire states, one less than both the Church of England and the Roman Catholic Church were stipulating at the time.

The sanctuary area is also enhanced by a hanging corona of black-painted rolled steel sections supporting candle sconces and a change in floor paving to white flint bricks for the

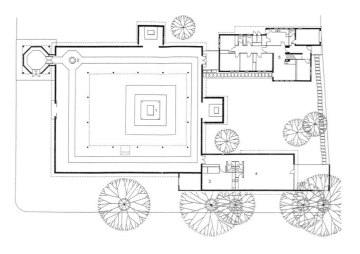

St Paul's Church, *Bow Common, London, 1956; ABOVE: Plan*

continuous processional path. To the north and east of the sanctuary lie the Lady chapel and a chapel for the reserved sacrament.

The exterior of the church is distinguished by Maguire and Murray's use of the bounding wall; a device that reoccurs in other churches by the practice, often in conjunction with the square form plan, encircling colonnade and exploitation of natural light from above. Aside from the practicalities of the project, their motive is to realise what Maguire referred to in a recent lecture[1] as the character of 'a set-apart place': the feeling of awe induced by the configuration of a place marked out for consecration and set apart from the world.

Through a gradual process of refinement, ways of 'marking' become more subtle, exemplified by the columns in the nave of All Saints' Church, Crewe, which are appropriately nautical in spirit. At St Mary's Abbey Church, West Malling in Kent – an exercise in reconciling modern architecture with buildings dating from the eleventh, thirteenth, eighteenth and nineteenth centuries (see perspective overleaf) – natural light supersedes columns as the primary force in unifying the internal space of the church, which is articulated with the utmost simplicity. In the St Matthew's Church, Perry Beeches, dramatic effects of light are occasionally cast into the interior; as a student, Maguire was impressed by John Soane's use of daylight.

In the United Kingdom many churches built after the war lacked proper guidance and an adequate liturgical brief. Some were more informed, such as the multi-functional church of St Philip and St James, Hodge Hill, Birmingham (1963-8), by Martin Purdy, which followed detailed surveys into the needs of the population and lectures on church architecture by the University of Birmingham. Maguire looked to the Continent for inspiration and acknowledges his debt to architects such as Rudolf Schwarz in reassessing the essential nature of what was required for contemporary worship. What is important is that Maguire scrutinised the traditional language of church architecture and

*FROM ABOVE: **St Paul's Church**, Bow Common, close-up of altar and ciborium; **St Matthew's**, Perry Beeches, Birmingham, view towards altar; OPPOSITE, FROM ABOVE: **All Saints' Church**, Crewe, interior; **St Mary's Abbey Church**, West Malling, interior*

grappled with the practicalities of each situation to find a solution that could work for the individual context.

In recent decades, the creation of relatively simple, low-key spaces has gained more ground in UK church architecture; evident in the work of architects such as Richard MacCormac, Inskip and Jenkins, Benson and Forsyth and Izi Metstein. Although notable precursors such as Coventry Cathedral (designed by Basil Spence, 1954-62), are considered 'modern' they often betray a spatial arrangement that is antithetical, albeit beautifully embroidered for posterity. Long due for reappraisal is Guildford Cathedral (1958) by Edward Maufe, which is historically concise and respectful of Anglican precepts, yet masterly in the precision of its minimalist brickwork. Devoid of the gesture and bombast of its Coventry contemporary, Guildford may well be viewed by posterity as the superior of the twentieth-century's post-war Anglican Cathedrals in Britain. Maguire and Murray carried out a well-related university residential scheme for Guildford University within the splendid context established by Maufe's masterpiece.

St Mary's Abbey Church, *West Malling, Kent*
OPPOSITE AND ABOVE. Views of exterior, LEFT. Plan;
BELOW: Section

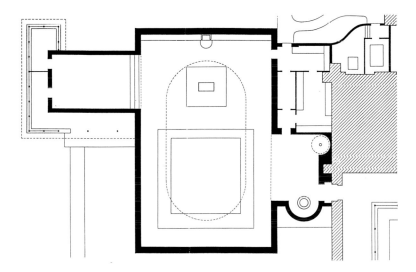

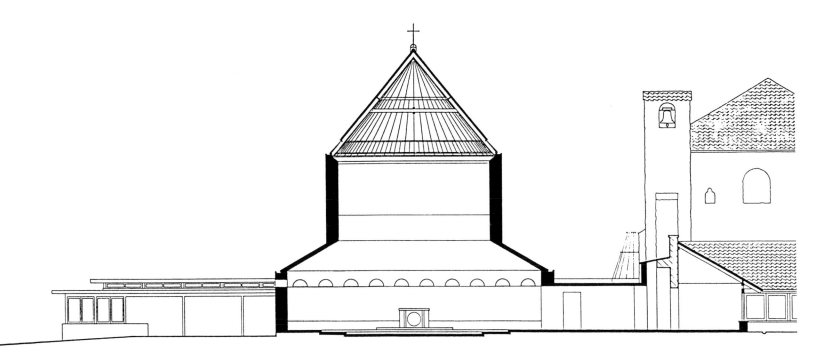

SIREN ARCHITECTS

The clarity and sensitivity associated with the work of Finnish architects Kaija and Heikki Siren is vividly expressed in the design of two churches: the chapel for the Technical University in Otaniemi (1957) and the village church in Orivesi (1961). Although modernism began to penetrate Finland in the late twenties it was not until the late thirties that churches were erected in the new style, exemplified by the work of Erkki Huttunen, Erik Bryggman and P E Blomsted. The style was to be given its most fluid and dynamic expression in the work of Alvar Aalto, establishing a unique tradition of Finnish modernism.

Much debate had centred on the appropriate character of new churches, reflected in the competition for Tehtaanpuisto Church in 1930. The influx of 'modern' entries prompted the jury to call for a second competition in 1932 in which they advocated the use of traditional church forms. In the first round the Turku modernists had won the three top prizes which stirred up a newspaper debate. The young architects accused the jury of summoning up the ghosts of history, while they in turn were informed that a church tower should not look like a factory chimney. A more conventional design by Lars Sonck was eventually built.[1]

Kaija and Heikki Siren's architecture assimilates the rudiments of Finnish modernism and the formal issues of the neo-classical style which preceded it (sealed by Johann Sigfrid Siren's new Parliament House of 1931) with a respect for anonymous indigenous architecture which they admire for its authenticity. This initiates a receptive approach to the environment, reflected in their design for the university chapel in Otaniemi.

Chapel in Otaniemi, *Espoo, Finland, 1957*
FROM ABOVE: Model; site plan; OPPOSITE: View of cross through glass altar wall

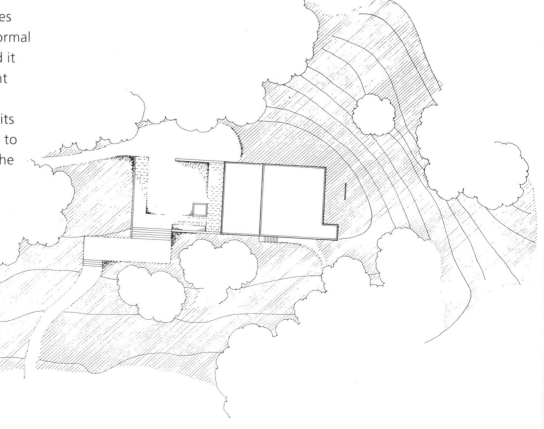

This building is strongly integrated into its forest setting, with which it immediately establishes an identifiable relationship. The intervention is softened by the partly fenced forecourt which makes use of natural wood rounds in a steel frame in conjunction with the projecting brick walls of the chapel. Wood rounds are also used for the belfry which further consolidates the effect.

By incorporating a forecourt into their design the architects reinstate an old tradition of Finnish church building, which is also reminiscent of traditional Japanese architecture. This transitional space represents the first stage of progressive movement towards the altar and is succeeded by a low entrance hall leading into the main chapel.

Chapel in Otaniemi
OPPOSITE: View of belfry and entrance to the chapel; FROM ABOVE: Rear of chapel with glass altar wall and sloping roof; a transitional space is provided by the partly fenced forecourt

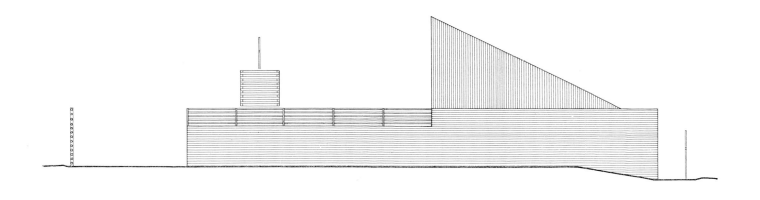

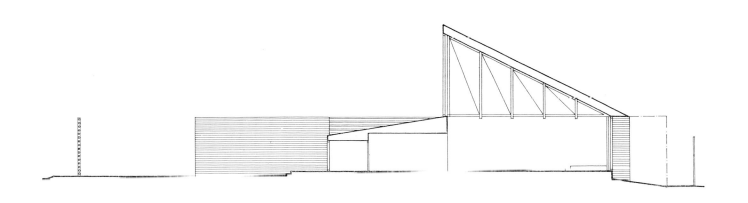

Chapel in Otaniemi
*OPPOSITE: View of interior;
FROM ABOVE: Elevation; sections*

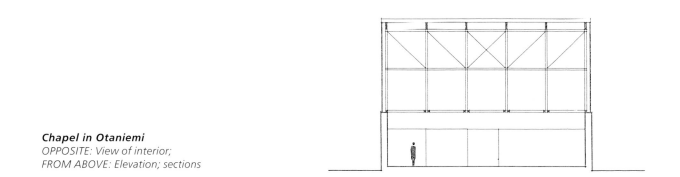

Inside the main chapel the worshipper is confronted with a magnificent altar wall of glass which affords a panoramic view of natural beauty. This aspect forms the basis of the overall design and effectively extends the spatial dimension to and beyond the large steel cross situated amidst the trees. The detached treatment of this motif reoccurs later in Tadao Ando's Church on the Water, completed in 1988 (see pages132-3) however, more immediately it recalls the isolated cross of Gunnar Asplund's Woodland Crematorium near Stockholm (1935-40) which signals the chapel beyond. At Otaniemi the treatment of this motif is pantheistic in spirit.

The sloping roof of the Otaniemi chapel is supported by open wood trusses with steel tension rods. The ends of the vertical truss members are fitted with artificial lights which are carefully designed not to reflect on to the glass wall. The Sirens also incorporated a window above the entrance to the nave to counteract the light admitted by the glass wall.

Constructed of simple materials such as brick and wood and with no need for ornamentation, the chapel in Otaniemi was very inexpensive to produce. It has been a source of inspiration for architects ever since.

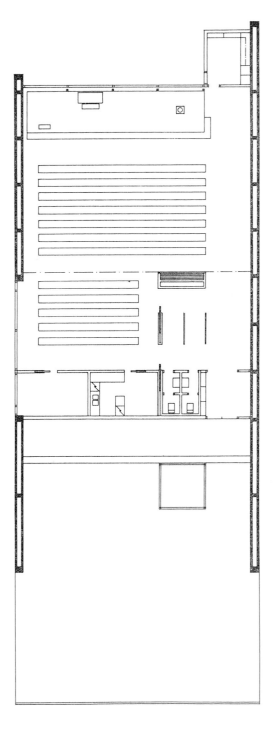

Chapel in Otaniemi
RIGHT: Plan; OPPOSITE: View of altar wall

Kaija and Heikki's church for the village of Orivesi is similarly restrained and equally focused. The building replaces a late eighteenth-century wooden church, of cruciform plan, which was destroyed by fire in the spring of 1958. The belfry is all that remains of the old church by Matti Åkerblom, a well-known church builder in Finland who was in practice with his nephew Matti Åkergren.

The new church is adjacent to the remaining belfry. It is composed of five freestanding, curved brick walls articulated to provide strong visual concentration on the altar. The fan-shaped arrangement of the curved, wooden pews offers an intimate space for worship in the main area, the balcony (which contains the choir and organ) and the parish hall extension.

Natural, glare-free light shines through windows above the curved walls and is filtered sideways through the vertical window slits; effectively enhancing curved surfaces and enunciating the formal arrangement of the ovoid.

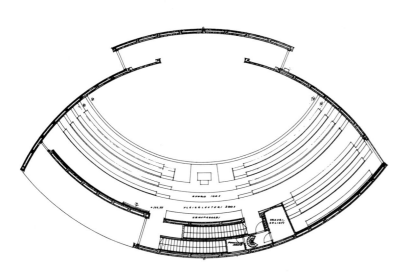

Orivesi Church, *Finland, 1961*
FROM ABOVE: Model; church beside remaining belfry of original building by Matti Åkerblom, 1791; gallery floor plan; ground floor plan; OPPOSITE: Views of entrance facade

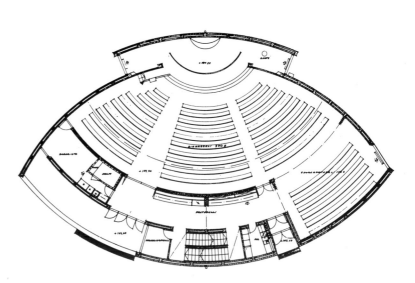

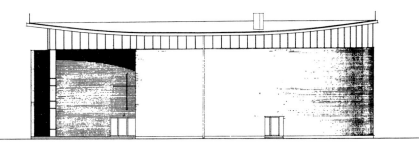

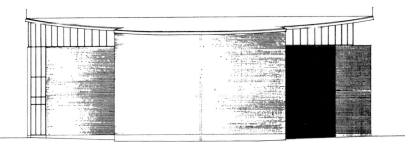

Light is skilfully manipulated to create a sacred atmosphere within the fluid space of the church. The altar is radiant with natural light from both sides which illuminates the carved wood relief on the sanctuary wall, depicting *The Hill of Golgotha* by Kain Tapper. Externally, the church complements Åkerbom's wooden bell tower; its sloping roof defers visually to the remains of its predecessor.

Both the chapel in Otaniemi and the church in Orivesi provide an intimate and authentic setting for worship. These buildings are progressive interpretations, infused with the spirit of the time but useful beyond it. They represent the quality of modern architecture that is often lacking: one that is modern in spirit rather than merely style.

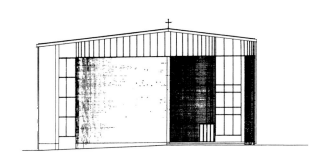

Orivesi Church
OPPOSITE: View of interior from gallery; FROM ABOVE: West elevation; east elevation; view from beneath gallery;
RIGHT: North elevation

JUSTUS DAHINDEN

Justus Dahinden has been designing churches since the early sixties. His first commissions were provided by the Catholic Church and encouraged further research into the subject, detailed in a book he published in 1968 entitled *New Trends in Church Architecture*. This stems from his experience of building in developing countries such as Africa. Dahinden has also built churches in his native Switzerland and in Germany, China and Italy. Although churches make up the bulk of his output, he has also designed private houses, holiday villages, hotels, multi-purpose buildings, bubble-system dwellings, trigon unit developments (based on a 50-metre-square triangular modular cell), and projects for floating structures reflecting the influence of Archigram and the Metabolist Group in Japan.

Dahinden seeks to develop space in all its diversity as a service to man which, he states, should be holistic:

> The treatment of space we deal with serves man for the fulfilment of his practical needs. This is the 'design function of space'. But space must furthermore generate openness (and preparedness)

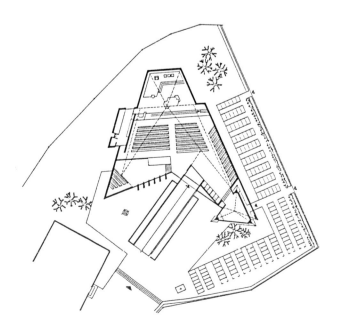

Church of St Francis, *Huttwilen, Switzerland, 1963*
ABOVE: Detail of tower; LEFT: Plan; OPPOSITE: Views of exterior and interior

and its use must be motivated through its appearance. This is its 'Gestalt' function. The total service of space finally lies in its capacity as a transformer of metaphysical relationships. This represents its 'spiritual function'.[1]

Early on in his career, Dahinden built the small parish church of St Francis in the small village of Huttwilen in north east Switzerland. This was erected in place of an existing building that was demolished and the structure therefore had to be relatively compact in response to the small area of the building site, which preserved the cemetery and presbytery.

The emphasis of St Francis is on the vertical, with a low slung roof culminating in a sliced pyramidal tower. The fracture draws light into the wood-panelled interior which offers an atmospheric, softly-lit space. The nave accommodates 220 worshippers in two blocks of pews which are stretched across the triangular plan within easy view of the altar.

The altar is located at the apex of the triangle which recalls the external form of the church and evokes the sheltered canopy of a tent – a recurrent

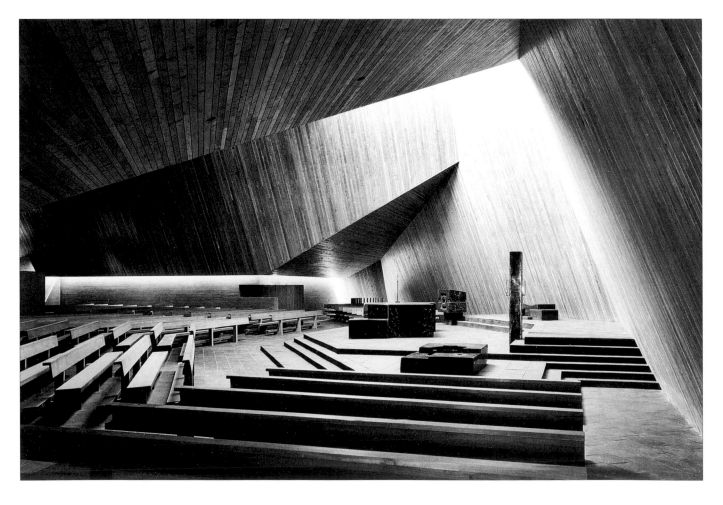

theme in Dahinden's church designs, similarly expressed in the Parish Church of St Mary's in Zürich-Witikon (1965). Access to the lower level of St Francis is gained by a covered vestibule. Here Dahinden has placed the community room, classroom, parish hall and cloakrooms.

A different approach informed Dahinden's design for the Church of St Anthony in Wildegg, Switzerland (1970), which is situated on a hilltop within view of the old castle of Wildegg. The church is characterised by the rhythmic geometry of its exterior form, which is entirely clad in copper, and by the spiral of movement generated by the plan.

The building is entered by way of a staircase which, passing under the bell tower, ends in a patio interior court closed on three sides. The path leads on from the entrance into the volume of the church, ending in a semi-circular space about the altar table. The wooden benches of Dahinden's earlier designs are superseded by movable chairs

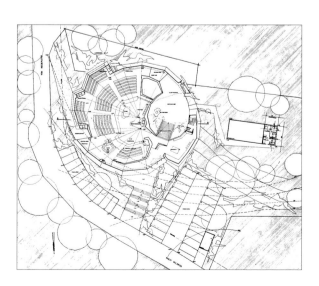

OPPOSITE: **St Mary's Church**, *Zürich-Witikon, Switzerland, 1965; Exterior and interior*

THIS PAGE: **Church of St Anthony**, *Wildegg, Switzerland, 1970; ABOVE: Sketch and bird's-eye view of church with belfry and atrium court; LEFT: Plan of ground floor*

to allow for more flexible seating arrangements. Even the altar – a simple wooden table – can be uprooted and relocated (to the chagrin of those who uphold that it should remain fixed). The confessionals are low niches adjoining the community rooms which are also accessible from the outside. A side chapel sheltering the glass tabernacle offers a place for private worship.

The simple interior of the church is characteristically enriched by wood panelling and hand-made red brick and floor tiles. The closed building envelope admits natural light through three glare-free skylights, supplemented by the constellation of artificial lights set into the ceiling.

Church of St Anthony, *Wildegg*
ABOVE: Views of church interior, RIGHT: Atrium court

Mityana Cathedral, Uganda, East Africa, 1972
ABOVE: Cathedral in harmony with nature; BELOW: Model of overall development

A more unusual departure is Dahinden's Mityana Cathedral, Uganda, East Africa, completed in 1972. This was built to commemorate the canonisation of three African martyrs, who are honoured by the three spherical segments of the design which represents an ancient Bantu building symbol. Within these segments Dahinden placed the baptistery (with space for the choir), a nuns' chapel with tabernacle, and a confessional, articulated around the central area.

The structure is conceived as the focus of an urban complex which includes a school, social centre, Carmelite convent, presbytery, parish hall and health centre. It can be opened to outer courts partially covered with tent-like roofs as a meeting place for the community.

The main entrance is signalled by a drum tower linking the inner and outer space of the church. The central, low volume of the building is covered by a flat roof with a skylight placed directly above the altar to emphasise its importance. The altar is simply constructed of brick which is also used for walls, floors and seating; complementing the mahogany-wood ceiling.

The structure of the spherical segments was prefabricated on site, followed by an outside cover of red dyed waterproofing plaster which was sprayed on to the surface. The unity of coloured architecture and earth reinforces the environmental integration of the building, which relates also to traditional African dwellings.

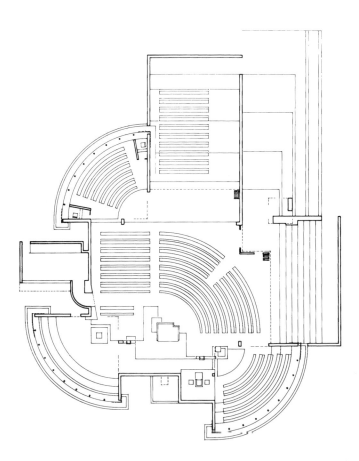

Mityana Cathedral
FROM ABOVE: African drum tower replaces traditional belfry; interior space with solid, backless seating; LEFT: Plan

FROM ABOVE, L TO R: Multi-purpose hall; sketch of exterior;
view of drum-tower, entrance and multi-purpose hall; traditional
African dwelling

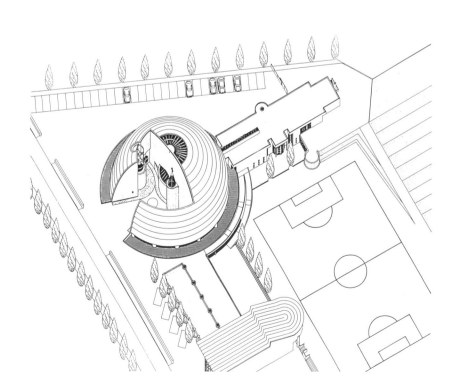

The distinctive form of Mityana is recalled in a recent project by Dahinden in the north Italian town of Varese. St Maximilian Kolbe, both a church and community centre, was completed in 1996. It is a much lighter interpretation of the theme, which in addition to liturgical functions, accommodates areas for cultural purposes, education and sport.

The domed exterior evokes archetypal associations with the mound, creating a spiritual bond with nature. The form appears in other projects by Dahinden, such as *Acro-Polis* (urban planning conceived in the form of terraced hill structures). Here it is sliced to create an open courtyard, shielding some of the noise of the Via Aguggari. On the left, a small chapel dedicated to St Maximilian Kolbe contains the baptismal font. A pond encircles and unifies the composition – the focal point of this is the altar inside the semi-circular church hall.

Within the hall, the structural woodwork is beautifully articulated, providing natural ornamentation for the interior. This is illuminated by natural light which is filtered through a variety of glazed openings, including garret and round windows and pointed skylights. The view upwards towards the daylight is uplifting and strengthens the

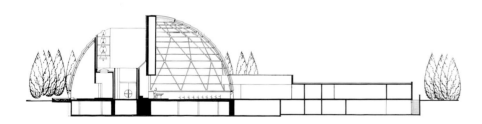

Church of St Maximilian Kolbe*, Varese, Italy, 1996*
OPPOSITE, FROM ABOVE L TO R: Main entrance to the church; axonometric; atrium court with belfry; LEFT, FROM ABOVE: Atrium court detail; section; elevation

introversion of the church space, as consistent with Dahinden's other churches.

The church hall seats 500 people in wooden benches which are curved in form and oriented towards the central altar. The priest approaches the altar by proceeding through the central area past the worshippers. The stele carrying the tabernacle stands in a top-lit tower structure; beside this a few seats are arranged for meditation.

The presbytery is placed in the axis of the church hall and protected against street noise and views from outside the compound. The confessional chapel with the sacristy behind it serves as a structural link between the presbytery and the church. In reference to the tradition of church building a Gothic spirelet is incorporated in the scheme; however, while Dahinden feels that tradition should be respected – recognising that church buildings have a dimension in the past at the same time as in the present – he is quick to acknowledge that 'the social aspect of the church is adaptable and dynamic'.[2]

Church of St Maximilian Kolbe
OPPOSITE: Wood construction of cupola; LEFT, FROM ABOVE: Gothic spirelet; church interior with altar in the foreground, aligned with processional route from sacristy through confessional chapel into church; BELOW: plan

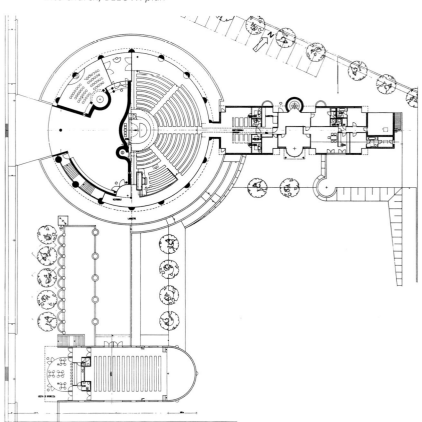

SUOMALAINEN ARCHITECTS

Not far from the centre of Helsinki lies Temppeliaukio Church, an underground church designed in 1961 by Finnish architects Timo and Tuomo Suomalainen. The structure, which was blasted into the rock of Temppeliaukio Square, was completed in 1969. The competition for the church dates back to the early thirties when it included entries by J S Siren and P E Blomstedt, who also proposed a circular, subterranean structure capped by a dome. Although this was unsuccessful it anticipated the form of the present church which won a competition in 1961.[1]

The Suomalainens' design was an innovative departure, particularly in its exploitation of natural light which reinforces the intrinsic nature of the structure. This is drawn into the underground interior through the concrete-ribbed window supporting the 24-metre, copper-lined dome.

The church is built into the rock as much as possible to preserve the open space of the square. In this densely populated area the rocky outcrop has long been a playground for children. An outer wall made from quarried stone (held together by steel bindings) shields the church from noise and people moving around on the rocks outside. The surrounding area is softened by the planting of bushes but maintains its relative austerity.

The total volume of the complex is 13,800m^3. The church itself accommodates up to 940 people – including the choir and orchestra – using a mixture of fixed pews (for 530) and movable chairs. The main area (11,000m^3) is designed as a flexible space which can be used as a concert hall. Inside, the walls of bedrock and quarried stone are left rough for acoustic and aesthetic reasons. Remaining drill marks were not removed artificially

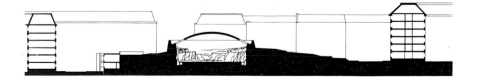

*Temppeliaukio Church, Helsinki, Finland, 1961-9
OPPOSITE: Night view of copper dome and entrance to the church; THIS PAGE: Sections*

Temppeliaukio Church

OPPOSITE: Interior with baptismal font in the foreground; FROM ABOVE: View of altar and supporting ribs of copper-lined dome; aerial perspective; RIGHT: Plan – 1 vestibule, 2 sacristy, 3 sanctuary, 4 connecting tunnel, 5 parish premises (upper floor), 6 technical premises, 8 rock park

but left unconcealed as a visible testimony of the working method. In keeping with the atavistic character of the place the font is formed of rough blocks of stone.

Parish premises on two levels are built into the side of the rock and connected by a tunnel near the altar wall; the office and technical areas are located near the main entrance to the church on Lutherinkatu. The altar is visible from the street through the glass doors. It consists of a slab of smooth granite and is approached by three steps. The wall behind the altar is formed by an ice-age rock crevice. During the morning service in the summer this area is illuminated by direct sunlight. Supplementary lighting in the church is provided by spotlights set in the ceiling.

The building is mechanically ventilated. Heated fresh air is admitted into the main area through ducts in the gallery, while return air is drawn into ducts along the wall under the floor through a slit between the rock and the floor. The concrete floor is lightly tinted and polished.

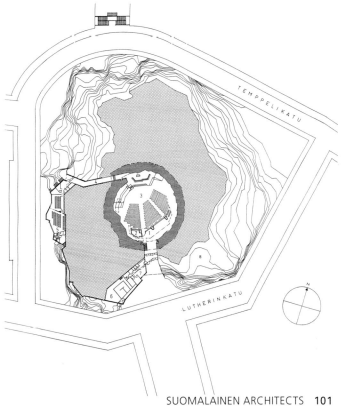

Espoonlahti Church, Espoo, Finland, 1979
OPPOSITE: View towards altar; ABOVE: Entrance courtyard;
CENTRE, L TO R: Ground floor plan; site plan; BELOW: Sections

The essential dialogue with the natural environment that determined the character of Temppeliaukio Church is expressed in subsequent projects by the architects. In Espoonlahti Church, Espoo (1979) granite boulders are used for the front wall of the sanctuary and walls between the congregational hall and the entrance hall. The visible framework of wooden beams corresponds with the free-standing steel column, evoking tree-like associations.

The sanctuary seats 410 people, although if more space is needed an overspill of 270 can be accommodated in the adjoining congregational hall, which is neatly separated by a partition wall. Natural light is admitted indirectly through skylights, animating the lofty space with interesting effects of light and shadow: during worship services the rays of the sun are directed across the altar. Copper panels enrich and add a touch of warmth to the interior.

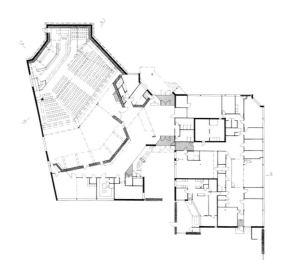

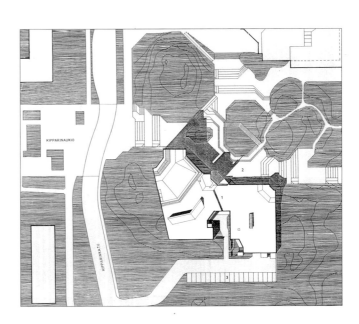

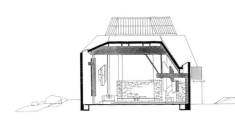

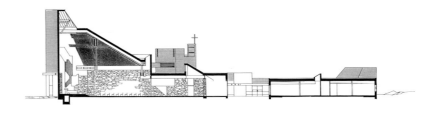

The recent Paijala Chapel, designed for Tuusula Cemetery, Hyryla (1993), aims at a greater degree of lightness and transparency in defining its principal role as a funeral chapel. The chief materials used for the chapel are concrete, glass, stained wood and copper; the latter characteristically applied to doors, window frames and the roof. The shifted geometry of the building envelope opens up to embrace the surrounding environment while providing a sheltered place for contemplation.

The building is laid out in accordance with the processional aspect of the service. Ancillary rooms in addition to the mortuary and main hall include a sacristy, waiting hall, memorial hall and farewell area; a kitchen also offers catering for memorial functions if required. The main hall accommodates around 170 people in pews and movable chairs.

The height of the space is governed by acoustic demands; assisted by wooden surfaces and structural members which draw the eye towards the altar wall and through the glazed partition to

Paijala Chapel, *Tuusula Cemetery, Hyryla, 1993*
OPPOSITE AND ABOVE: Views of exterior; RIGHT: Plan

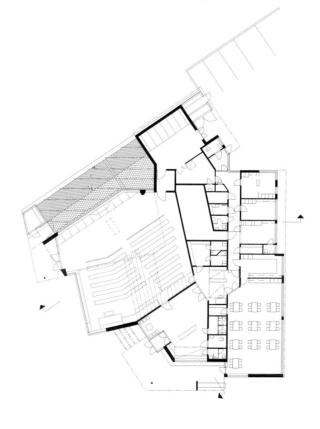

the mottled surface of the cobble-stone wall. The use of this transparent device was introduced by Heikki and Kaija Siren in their Chapel for the Technical University, Otaniemi, executed in the fifties (pages 74-80)

The way in which these structures combine built space with that of nature reflects a typically Finnish approach. With Temppeliaukio Church the architects were fortunate in that they managed to fully exploit the potential of their site when blasting into the rock bed, a process that was less successful for Reima Pietilä's Dipoli Conference Centre in Otaniemi conceived earlier the same year.[2] The underground church is perhaps the most original of the Suomalainens' projects: its atavistic character is steeped with a sense of early Christianity, sensitively restructured for contemporary worship in a built-up environment.

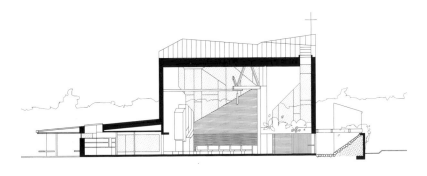

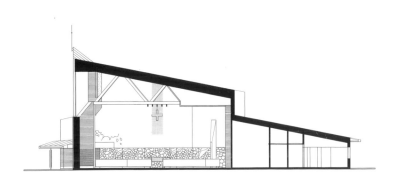

Paijala Chapel
ABOVE: View towards altar and cobble-stone wall; LEFT: Sections; BELOW: Site plan; OPPOSITE: View of interior

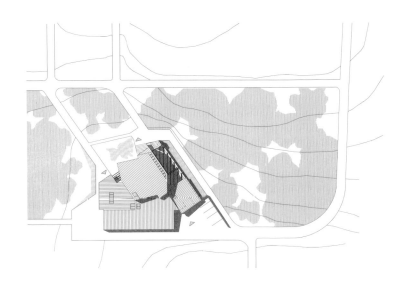

RICHARD ENGLAND

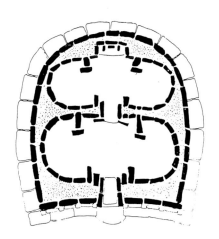

Richard England's first major commission, the Church of St Joseph, Manikata in Malta (1962-74), remains one of his most significant works to date. It was conceived when England was in his twenties, following a brief spell in the Milan office of Gio Ponti before completing his architectural studies. The commission for the church was passed on to England by his father, Edwin, in 1961.

Although England's concept for the church was progressive for its time and unique for the island it was approved by the parish priest and officially sanctioned on the basis that it offered a church that related to the island's indigenous culture rather than the predominant colonial style. While clearly inspired by the spirit of the place, the regionalist qualities of the building owe much to England's collective experience with Ponti in Italy; the trip organised by Ponti to Le Corbusier's pilgrimage church at Ronchamp left a deep impression on the young student, who sought to recapture its primitive quality.[1]

Locally, the church is known as 'girna' in reference to the corbelled, dry-walled structures that are scattered across the island; evoked in the curved exterior of the church. The plan of the building is inspired by the remains of the 5,000-year-old, megalithic temples in Malta. It consists of two interlocking U-shaped forms within which are housed the nave and sanctuary. Adjoining this is a smaller volume (a miniature adaptation of the two forms) which contains the sacristy.

The church is situated on a hilltop on the northern fringe of the village, 250 feet above sea level. The pure geometry of this building contrasts with the rugged landscape that surrounds it. Its curved form is characteristically sculptural, enhanced by the incisions, voids and narrow slits which provide light and ventilation.

The building is raised on a walled podium that follows the gentle contours of the sloping site.

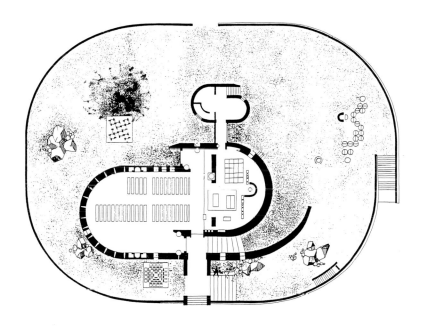

The Church of St Joseph, Manikata, Malta, 1962-74
OPPOSITE: View of exterior; FROM ABOVE: Plan of megalithic temple, Malta; plan of Manikata Church; local 'girna'

The Church of St Joseph
OPPOSITE: View of exterior; FROM ABOVE: Detail of sanctuary; view towards altar

This transitional space provides an open courtyard for the congregation to gather before or after the service, while offering views of the surrounding landscape. The visitor is able to walk around the building, surrounded by various sculptures such as *Labyrinth City* to the left of the entrance canopy, the *City of Towers* on the north-eastern side, and the gargoyle on the south-east of the church. The main entrance on the west side of the building can also be approached from the stairs to the south; passing the belfry, the outside seating and a sundial.

The modest handling of the exterior is repeated in the interior layout of the church where the space is simply ordered and defined with a limited palette of colour. The eye is drawn towards the sanctuary and to the white crucifix that stands out against the rich brown background. The altar is freestanding and carved from a solid block of limestone. It is brought forward and separated from the nave by a shallow podium, effectively forging a link with the congregation which is seated in hardwood benches arranged either side of the nave.

To the left and right of the sanctuary stand the lectern and font; the latter supported by a screen wall which separates the choir. Natural light falls on to the altar through the horizontal fracture created by the different roof heights, while additional lighting is provided by the stalactiform light shafts above. To the rear of the sanctuary the tabernacle is enclosed by a low wall of rough-hewn limestone, recalling the stony landscape of the island.

Manikata Church evolved as an intuitive response to the requirements of the modern church, instilled with the youthful enthusiasm and ideals of one fresh from architectural school who sought to invest the building with an identifiable Maltese spirit. The timeless quality of this early church perhaps makes it hard to reconcile the

building with the architect's uninhibited and colourful post-modern projects of the eighties; however, the interior handling of his churches is more subtle and remains relatively restrained.

Other churches of interest include the little cave chapel at Ir-Razzet Ta' Sanorina, Mgarr, completed in 1989. Here, England provides a meditative space that is devoid of extraneous detail and simply enriched by colour and reflected light. His most recent church, the House of the Good Samaritan (inaugurated in December, 1996) is styled in the manner of its baroque predecessors but diverges with a screen wall that is fractured and partially defined in yellow. The interior makes use of blue-coloured glass blocks to create special light effects but apart from the large crucifix above the altar the space is bare and reduced to its most essential expression.

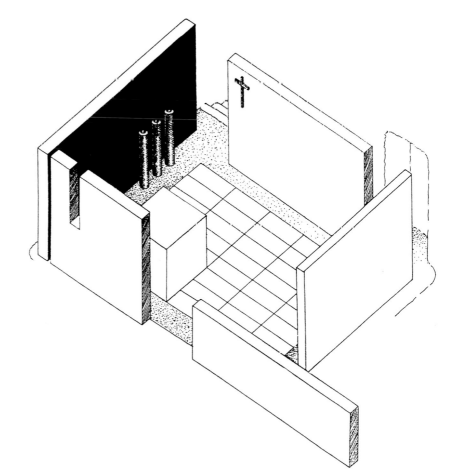

The House of the Good Samaritan, *Malta, 1996*
OPPOSITE: View of interior; ABOVE: Exterior

Cave chapel, Ir-Razzet Ta' Sanorina, *Mgarr, 1989*
TOP AND RIGHT: View of interior; axonometric

PHILIP JOHNSON

In 2004, if all goes according to schedule, Philip Johnson's most recent project, the Cathedral of Hope, will be complete. Described by Johnson as 'the crowning jewel in my lifetime of work', this monumental gesture requires funding in the region of $20 million. The building is 266-feet long and 75-feet high and is designed to accommodate a predominately gay and lesbian congregation of over 2,000 worshippers in Dallas, Texas.

This new church was commissioned by the Dallas branch of the Universal Fellowship of Metropolitan Community Churches to replace the existing church (also called the Cathedral of Hope) which is unable to cater for its fast-growing membership. This will eventually become a fellowship hall when the 13-acre site incorporates

the new building and attendant car park. Inside the present church a model of its successor is currently on display, unveiled by Johnson on his ninetieth birthday, 8th July 1996.

The model shows an esoteric form that has been shaped by an expressionistic treatment of warped planes. These will be made of concrete and finished with coloured acrylic coatings. The building is devoid of ecclesiastic imagery (except for the bell tower) and window-less – daylight will be filtered through discreet skylights. Its stark, imposing form is sculptural, resembling an iceberg.

The plan indicates a fairly traditional layout. Within a long nave two rows of pews are arranged either side of the central aisle and two outer rows distributed laterally, following the contours of the

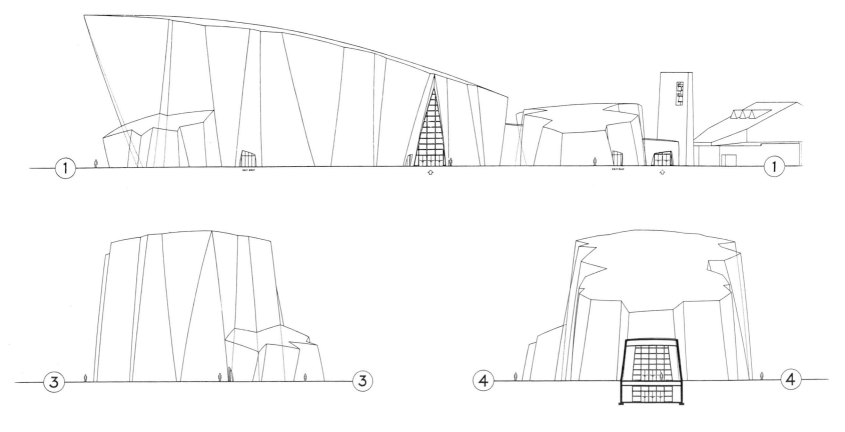

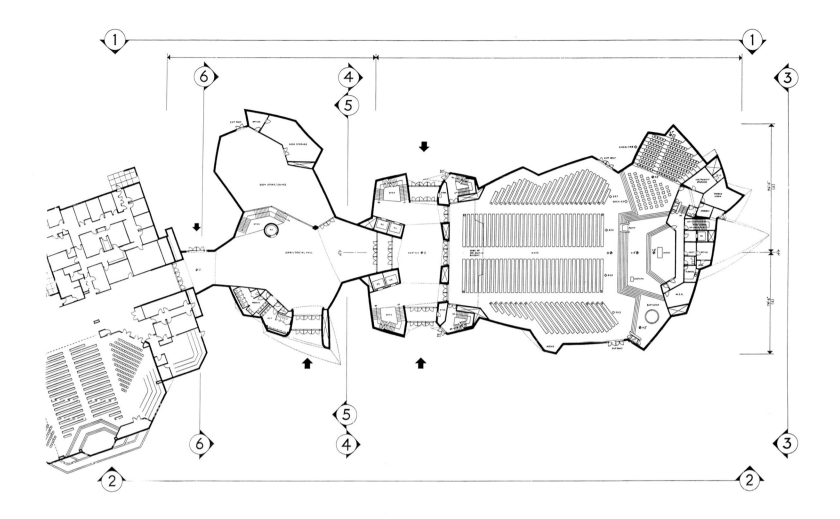

Cathedral of Hope, *Dallas, Texas*
OPPOSITE, FROM ABOVE L TO R: North-east elevation; south-east elevation; north-west elevation; FROM ABOVE, L TO R: Ground floor plan; south-west elevation; south-east elevation; north-west elevation

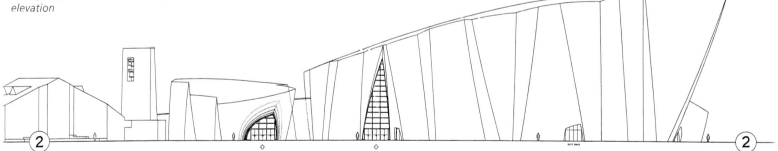

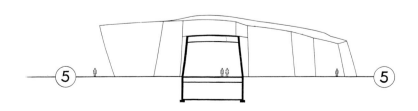

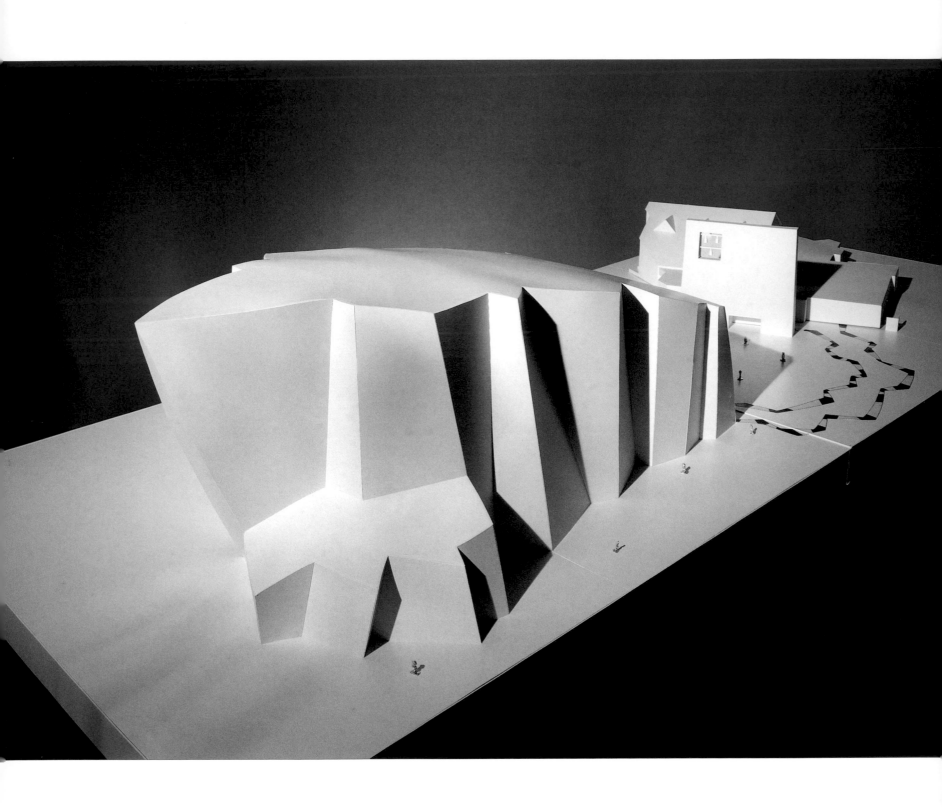

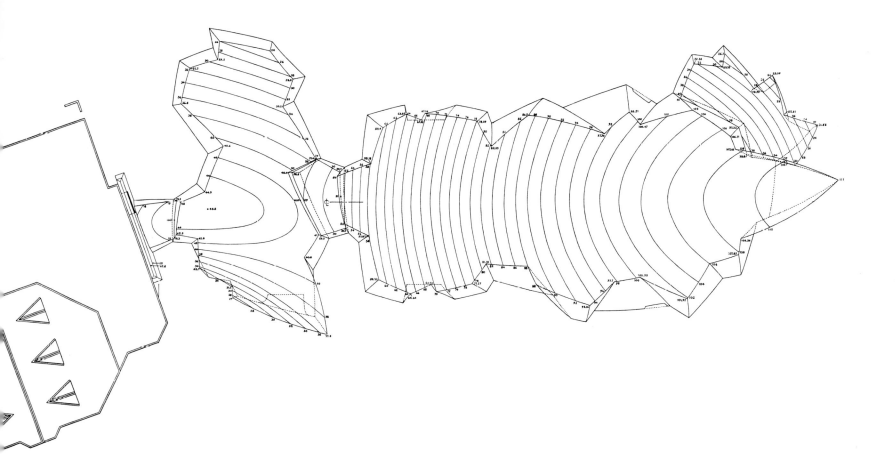

building. At the far end, steps lead up to the pulpit and lectern, positioned to the left and right of the podium respectively. The altar, which is in line with the central aisle, is approached by more steps and therefore placed at a considerable distance from the congregation. The choir and baptistery are located either side of the altar and a balcony sited at the opposite end. The pews in the main area and balcony will be fixed, while those in the choir will be movable. The main floor is designed to seat over 1,800 parishioners with additional seating for 200 in the balcony. In addition to a spacious lobby and bookstore, ancillary areas will be provided for administration, instrument storage, robing rooms,

flowers and WCs. The organ loft will be situated above the baptistery.

The Cathedral of Hope is one of a number of religious projects drawn up by the Johnson office since the 1950s. Those executed include Kneses Tifereth Israel Synagogue, New York (1956); Roofless Church, Indiana (1960); Rothko Chapel, Houston, Texas, consultancy work (1964); Chapel of Thanksgiving, Dallas, Texas (1976); Crystal Cathedral, Garden Grove, California (1977); Crystal Cathedral Chapel and Bell Tower (1990), and the more recent St Basil's Chapel at St Thomas's University, Texas (1997). Unexecuted designs are Vassar College Chapel, New York

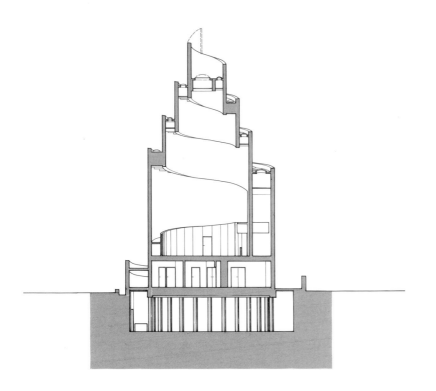

(1955); Greenwich Synagogue, Connecticut (1958); St Stephen's Church, Indiana (1960); St Anselm's Church, Washington DC (1960); Pilgrimage Chapel, Arona, Italy (1992), and Bell Tower, Berlin (1994).

The diverse nature of these religious projects attests to the eclectic streak in Johnson's work, engaging mass culture with a reworking of shapes and historical archetypes; articulating gothic imagery, Byzantine and Renaissance geometry and elements, Islamic architecture (Chapel of Thanksgiving), conical and bulbous forms, egg shapes and, lately, Ando-like planes (St Basil's Chapel) and bold expressionism (Cathedral of Hope).

Chapel of Thanksgiving, *Dallas, Texas, 1976*
ABOVE: Section and exterior of chapel; RIGHT: Site plan;
OPPOSITE: View of stained-glass ceiling which spirals
upward to a height of 90 feet

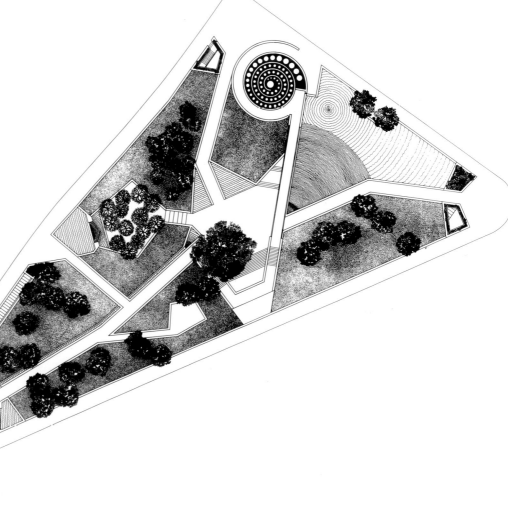

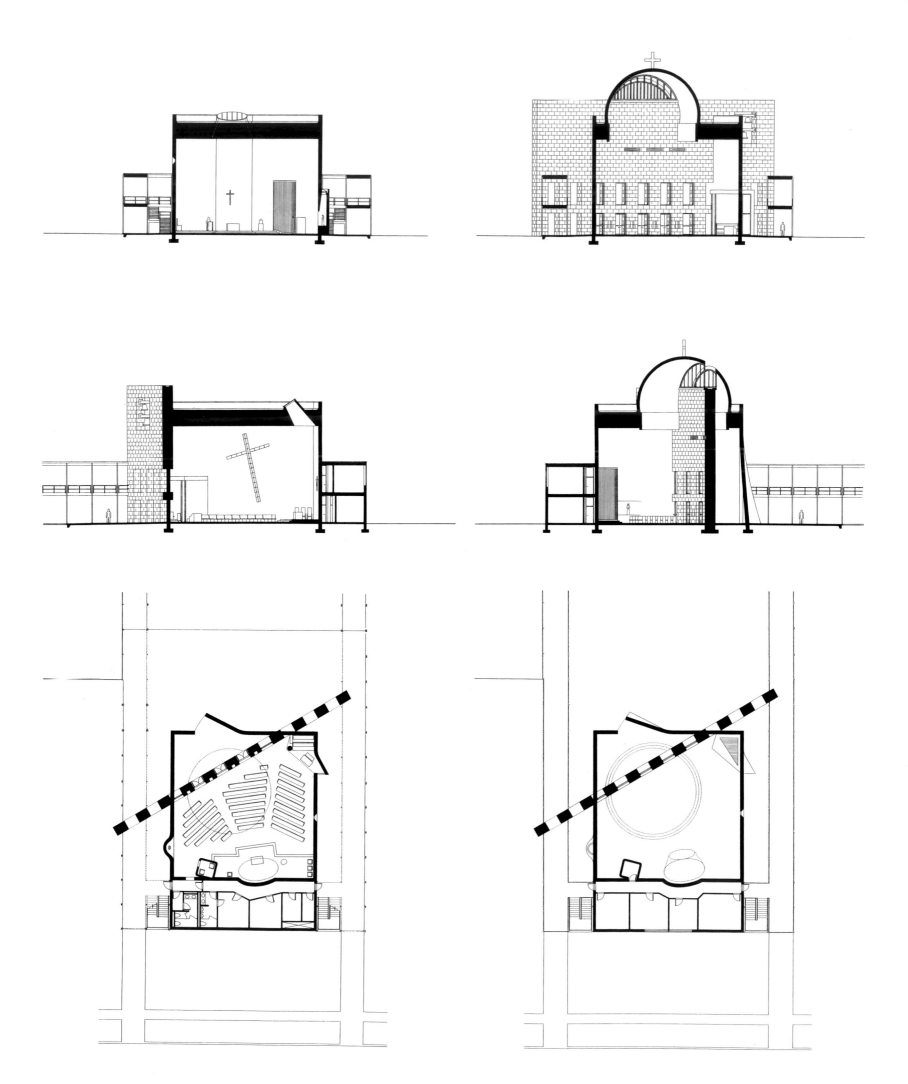

St Basil's Chapel at St Thomas University, Texas (1997) is an interesting intervention which links two university buildings that were designed by Johnson in the 1950s. The structure consists of a 50-foot cube surmounted by a hemispherical dome evocative of a Byzantine church.

The cube and dome are sliced by a vertical plane, a device utilised by Ando in his Church of the Light (see pages 134-7). The intersecting wall of St Basil's Chapel is constructed of black granite and provides a striking contrast to the white-stuccoed cube. The fracture enables light to be filtered atmospherically into the interior, supplemented by smaller apertures in the chapel; externally it acts as a bell tower. The chapel is an intimate space which seats 225 people in three rows of pews, arranged at an angle to correspond with an off-centre altar. The building is still under construction at the time of writing.

St Basil's Chapel, *St Thomas University, Texas, 1997*
OPPOSITE: Sections; ground floor plan; second floor plan;
BELOW: Model

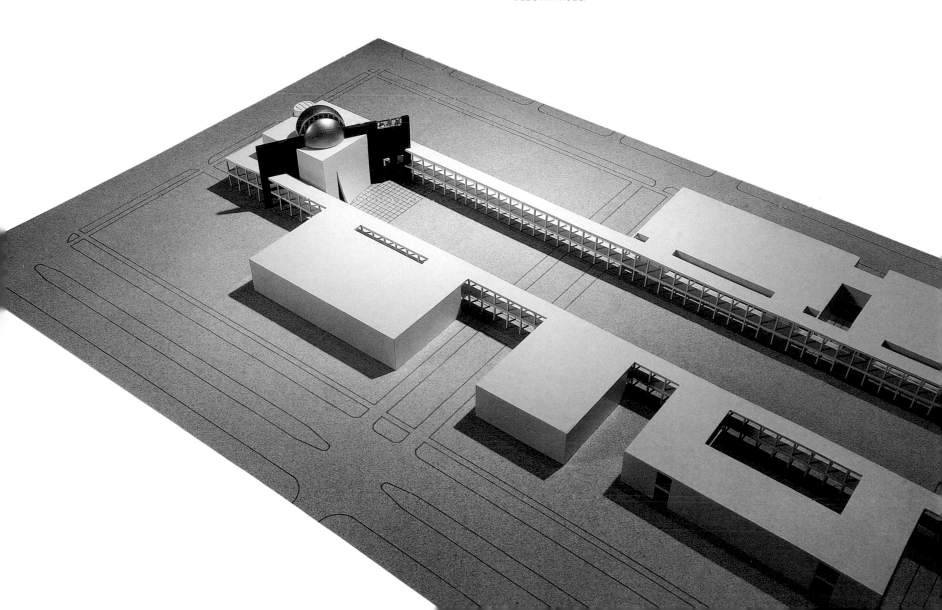

Crystal Cathedral, *Garden Grove, California, 1980*
ABOVE: View of the cathedral and bell tower;
OPPOSITE, FROM ABOVE: Section; ground floor plan;
OVERLEAF: View of interior

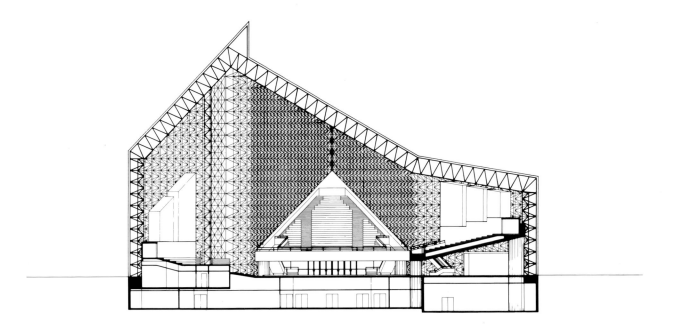

We believe that this is what we're on earth for, to create shapes like this . . . you'll find if you go to Europe, emblazoned over the heads of many a church: 'this building was built for the greater glory of God'.

On this note Philip Johnson ended his dedication speech at the Crystal Cathedral in 1980. This glass church in Garden Grove, California, was commissioned by television evangelist, the Reverend Robert H Schuller, whose 'Hour of Power' attracts millions of viewers. The building evolved from six years of collaboration between Johnson, Burgee and Schuller. Funding for the project, which cost $18 million, was raised by an enormous network of worshippers (Schuller's home congregation alone consists of 10,000).

From the outset Schuller wished to create a wholly inspirational and uplifting building that would embrace the outside world. He urged Johnson to make the church as transparent as possible, elaborating on his original proposal of a glass roof.

The glass casing consists of over 10,000 panes supported by a network of white-painted metal trusses. The reflective silver coating admits only eight per cent of the sun's rays so that the temperature never exceeds that of the outside. The building is naturally cooled. Hot air is drawn up through the roof and ventilation is provided by motorised fin windows.

The plan of the church is an elongated four-pointed star. The transept is 415 feet long and the nave 207 feet wide, adjusting the typical Latin cross plan so that the congregation is more focused on the chancel (no mean feat for a congregation of 3,000).

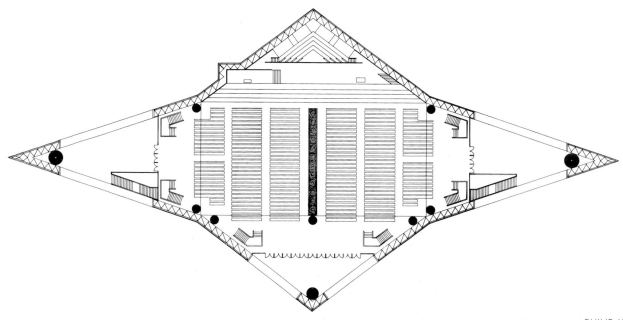

Although the space soars to a height of 128 feet, accentuated by the sweep of the triangular balconies inside, the spatial organisation achieves a surprisingly intimate effect. The congregation is seated in straight rows either side of the central aisle which is lined with twelve fountains representing the apostles. In true theatrical manner, the fountains are activated at the start of the service in concert with the procession, subsiding as the reverend is about to speak (those outside the church are similarly choreographed before the service).

Three points of the star serve as entrances, effectively controlling the flow of the congregation. The balconies above these points act as entrance canopies and draw worshippers into the lofty space. The fourth point of the star contains the chancel which is enhanced by rose-coloured granite, a material that is less in keeping with the spirit of the place. This 185-foot area can accommodate up to 1,000 singers.

Large remote-controlled doors on one side allow worshippers in the parking area to 'receive' Schuller's address while listening to it on their car radios. A useful forecourt is provided by the space between the Crystal Cathedral, the original church designed by Richard Neutra (1959), and the bell tower by Dion Neutra (1967). The reflection of these structures animates the corresponding facade of the Crystal Cathedral.

Johnson's original conception for the cathedral was finally realised in 1990 with the completion of the Crystal Cathedral Bell Tower and the Mary Hood chapel. The tower rises to a height of 286 feet above ground. Its streamlined appearance is achieved by the use of polished stainless steel prisms on a structural steel frame. The little chapel beneath is relatively restrained and surmounted by a hemispherical dome, supported by the coupled arrangement of different coloured marble columns. The gentle curve of the dome is enhanced by the suspended points of the prisms above. These culminate in the nine-foot steel prism that marks the pinnacle of the tower – a dynamic counterpart which evokes the form of a gothic spire.

Crystal Cathedral Chapel and Bell Tower, 1990
OPPOSITE: View of tower; ABOVE AND BELOW: Plans; CENTRE: Close-up of Mary Hood Chapel

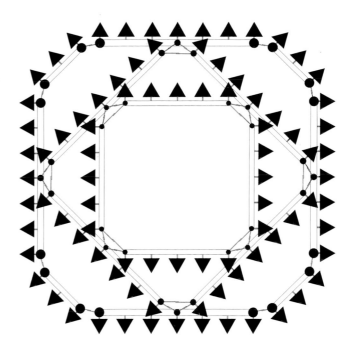

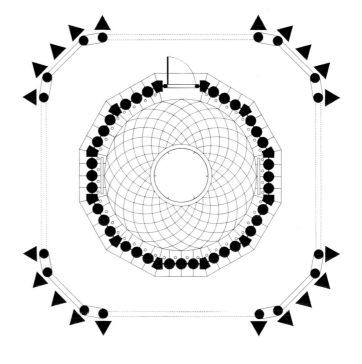

TADAO ANDO

The cultural make-up of the small and over-populated country of Japan reflects a spatial perception that is noticeably different to that of the West. An awareness of this contributes to an understanding of the work of Tadao Ando who is renowned for his skill in manipulating space, intensifying one's relationship with the environment.

In English, the Japanese character *ma* signifies space; or 'place', as has been suggested by Gunter Nitschke, since historically the notion of place precedes our contemporary idea of space as a measurable area.[1] The various uses of *ma* in traditional and modern Japanese include: *ma ga warui* – 'I am uncomfortable, embarrassed' (literally, 'the placing is bad'); *ma dori* – 'design' (literally, 'grasp of place'); *ma-nuke* – 'simpleton', 'fool' (literally, 'someone missing *ma*, space') and *ma chigau* – 'to be mistaken' (literally, 'place differs').[2]

Japanese Buddhists adopted *ma* to convey the notion of emptiness. This is consciously absorbed into Ando's work. Through a reductive process, he draws out the essential nature of a space; simple geometric forms such as cubes and cylinders, uniform materials, and the play of light and shadow, induce and intensify the sense of sacred space within the hallowed enclosure.

The churches featured here – the Chapel on Mount Rokko, Kobe, Hyogo (1985-6), the Church on the Water, Tomamu, Hokkaido (1988) and the Church of the Light, Ibaraki, Osaka (1988-9) – are all set-apart places defined by a concrete bounding wall, an element which takes its cue from early Buddhist temple complexes.

The Chapel on Mount Rokko is approached gradually, by various stages or 'passages'. Its pure white form is ultimately reached by way of a vaulted colonnade of frosted glass. Rather than lead directly into the chapel this signals the other side of the garden. It is only when nearing the end of the colonnade, after descending steps, that the entrance is discernible. A sharply curving passage then leads to the final destination where, uniquely, the eye is directed downward; the pews reached by descending a few steps.

Through the large window to the left, a grass slope rises to meet the concrete wall. Although the

Chapel on Mount Rokko, *Kobe, Japan, 1986*
OPPOSITE: View of chapel and connecting colonnade;
ABOVE: Axonometric; RIGHT: North elevation; section

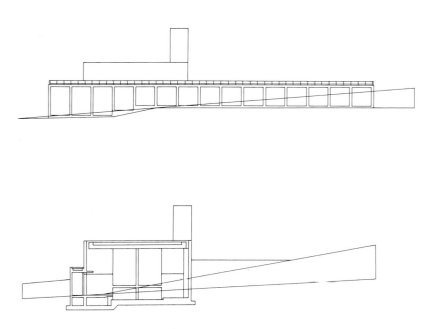

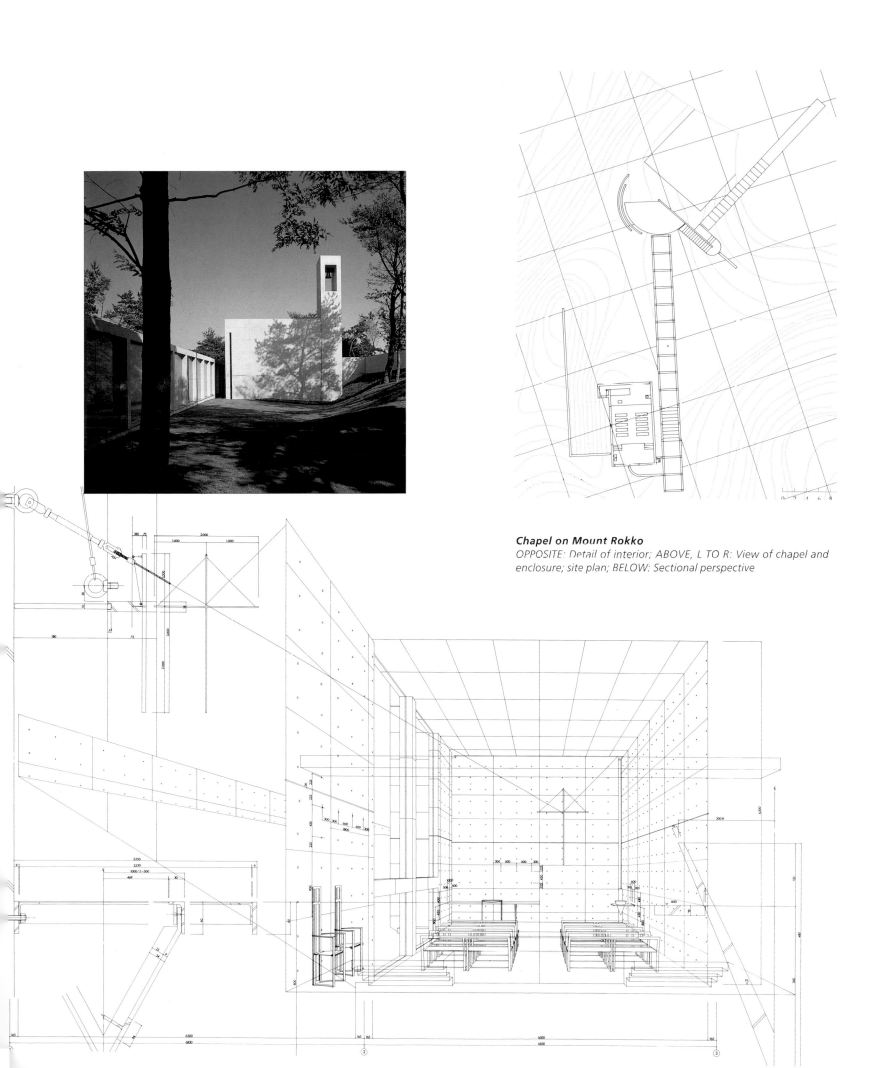

Chapel on Mount Rokko
OPPOSITE: Detail of interior; ABOVE, L TO R: View of chapel and enclosure; site plan; BELOW: Sectional perspective

interior of the Chapel on Mount Rokko is flooded with light there is a strong sense of being submerged. The internal space of the cube is intimate and unadorned; except for the altar in the left hand corner, there is a thin cruciform on the sanctuary wall, a small pulpit, two slender chairs and a flower stand.

The Church on the Water and the Church of the Light were both designed in the years 1985-88 and built respectively in five and eleven months. In the same way as the chapel on Mount Rokko, these structures connect with the surrounding environment while cloistered by a sacred and defined boundary.

The first of these is situated on a plateau in the central mountains of Hokkaido. The site gently slopes down to the river which acts as another boundary, in addition to diverting water to the artificial pond. Approximately three times the size of the Church of the Light, the plan of the Church on the Water consists of two squares (one 15-metres square, the other 10-metres square) which overlap at one corner. The church is reached by way of a circuitous route along the freestanding wall which separates the church from the neighbouring hotel.

A passage leads to the rear of the chapel and up into the enclosure of light: a transparent box which contains four separate but corresponding crosses made of concrete. The translucent base of the crosses acts as a glass roof for the cylindrical chamber situated directly beneath. This light-filled vestibule is succeeded by a darker passage as the visitor descends into the main chapel by way of a curved stairway. Here one is confronted with a spectacular view across the water, directly centred on the large cross which is framed by the encircling beech trees and the binding wall on the left.

A movable glass wall extends the length of the chapel allowing the space to be opened up completely. The interior is unadorned, with wooden pews arranged to create a central aisle. Ando's use of the glass wall and free-standing cross seems directly influenced by Kaija and Heikki

Church on the Water, *Tomamu, Hokkaido, Japan, 1988 OPPOSITE, FROM ABOVE: View from interior; view of enclosure and transparent vestibule containing four crosses; FROM ABOVE: Axonometric; elevation; section*

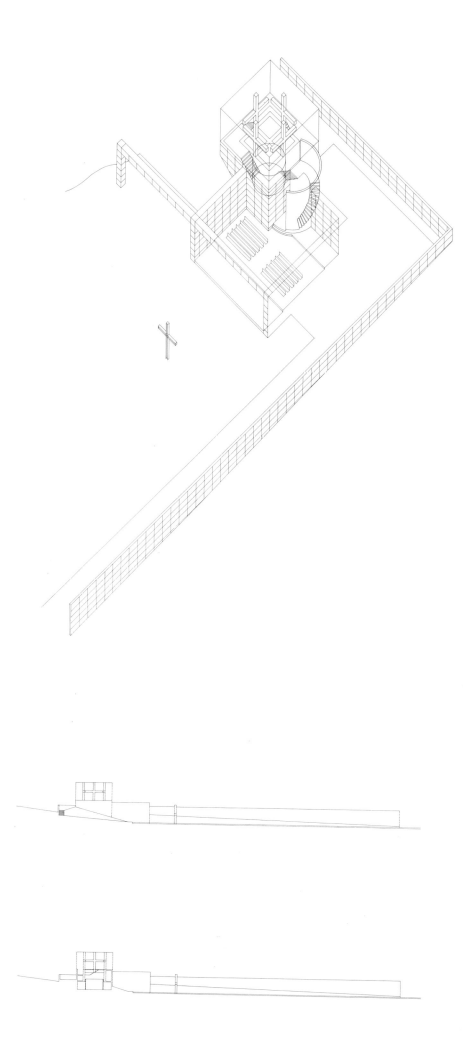

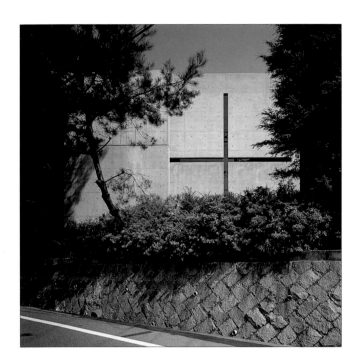

Siren's chapel in Finland for the Technical University, Otaniemi. The Sirens used these devices to extend one's perception of space, while introducing a strong link with nature (see pages 74-81). In the Church on the Water, Ando intensifies the union by incorporating a sliding glass wall which ingeniously dissolves the boundaries.

In the Church of the Light the large cruciform aperture is the most effective medium in enforcing such a relationship within a limited space. It is as much an economic gesture as a symbolic device. The building is rectangular in form and extremely compact (113 square metres). It is situated on the corner of two streets in a quiet residential area where it fits snugly into its urban context. The sacred boundary is signified by a wall that slices

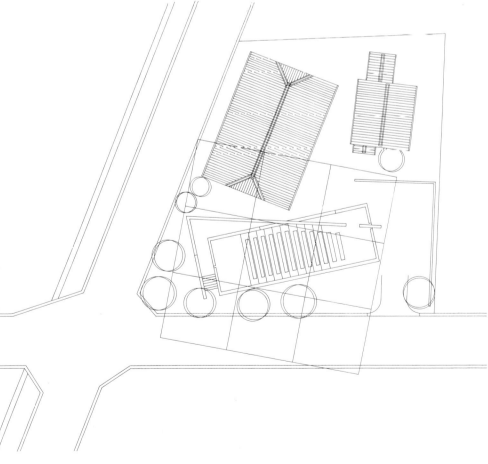

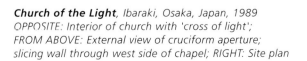

Church of the Light, *Ibaraki, Osaka, Japan, 1989*
OPPOSITE: Interior of church with 'cross of light';
FROM ABOVE: External view of cruciform aperture;
slicing wall through west side of chapel; RIGHT: Site plan

the west side of the building at a 15-degree angle, piercing the back of the building. This dramatic device postpones entry into the church and heightens the worshipper's expectations. Additionally, it acts as the entrance to the church itself once the outer enclosure has been penetrated.

The interior is austere and offers a highly focused and meditative space in which to worship. The altar and lectern are situated in front of the cruciform aperture and the pews placed uniformly either side of the aisle in line with the cross. Light filters into the interior through the cruciform aperture and through a glass opening that emphasises the angled wall. Supplementary lighting is also provided by small light fittings.

The churches discussed here are distinguished by a sophisticated treatment of space and light, and a distinct lack of the customary paraphernalia associated with the church; benefiting from a cross-cultural infusion. The artist James Turrell referred aptly to the spiritual rift between East and West: 'When we want to go into the universe we can't look at a rock, like the Japanese. We have to actually go to the moon. We're so literal.'[3]

Church of the Light
OPPOSITE: View of slicing wall through glazed opening of chapel; FROM ABOVE, L TO R: Detail of pews with cross motif; plan; axonometric; section

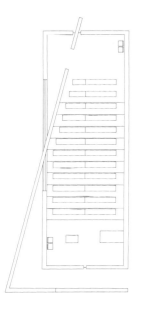

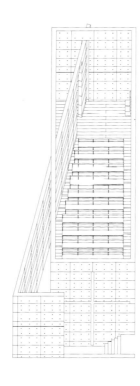

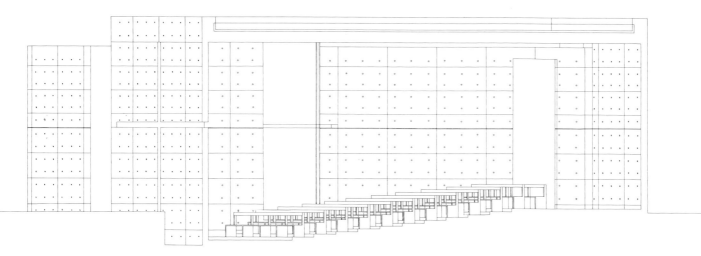

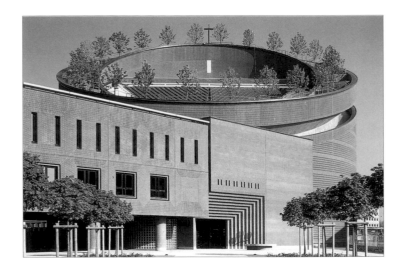

Cathedral of the Resurrection, Evry, France, 1988-95
Church in Pordenone, Italy, 1987-92
Church in Sartirana di Merate, Italy, 1987-96

MARIO BOTTA

Mario Botta's buildings evolve from a rational approach to architecture, characterised by a distinctive vocabulary of strong geometric forms. Of his religious buildings the cathedral for the new town of Evry in France is especially well known. This twelve-storey building, completed in 1995, was designed to house a congregation of over a thousand (incorporating a large projection screen and stereo sound in the scheme). The reinforced-concrete cylinder and red brick cladding is a combination favoured by Botta and appears in other projects such as the Church in Pordenone (1987-92) and the Church of San Pietro Apostolo in Sartirana di Merate (1987-96) in Italy.

Although the exterior of Evry Cathedral is a little puzzling – somewhat confused by the configuration of elements such as the array of 'shot-hole' windows and the 'crown' of lime trees – the interior space is atmospheric and well lit. The sloping glass roof allows a good degree of natural light to be filtered into the circular nave where the synthesis of red brick, wooden pews and black stone floors

works well. The altar, font and crucifix are clearly emphasised in white; the former raised on a podium of six steps to ensure maximum visibility for the congregation. Behind the altar a large semi-circular window depicts the Tree of Life. The upper floors encircling the nave house a museum of religious art, while the vestry, choral chamber, organ and offices are located below. Provision is made for an additional chapel and parish facilities in the rectangular wing on the south-east side of the cylinder.

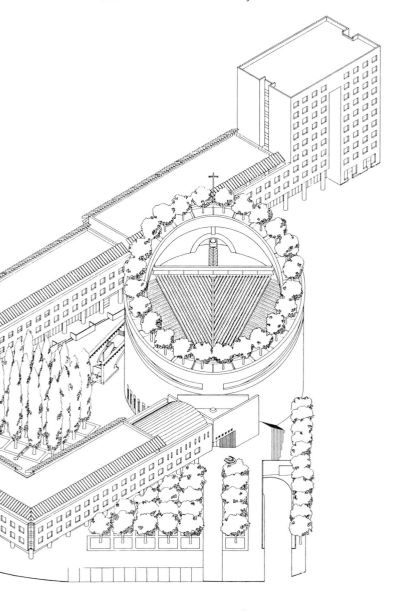

Axonometric of Evry Cathedral

Cathedral of Evry
OPPOSITE: View of exterior; CLOCKWISE, FROM RIGHT:
Plans; sections; view towards altar

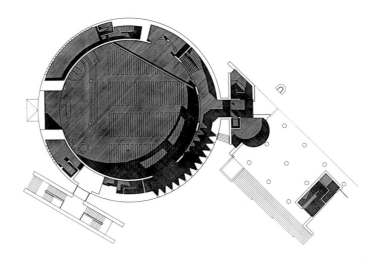

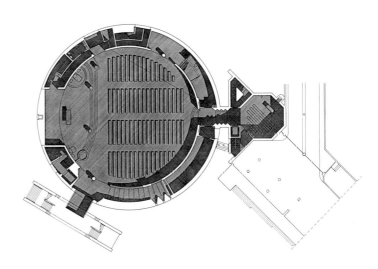

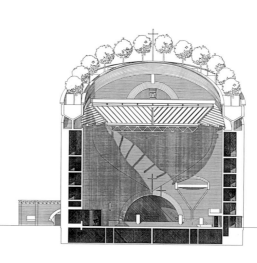

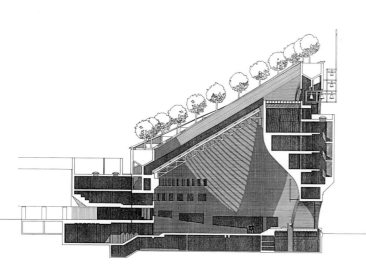

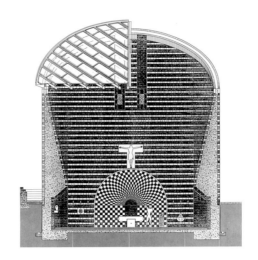

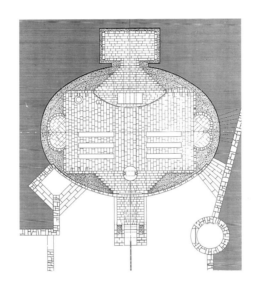

San Giovanni Battisti, *Mogno, Switzerland, 1996;*
OPPOSITE: The chapel and surrounding landscape; ABOVE:
Exterior and interior views; RIGHT, FROM ABOVE: Section; plan

The centralised form crops up consistently in Botta's architecture where it is exploited for both ecclesiastical and secular works. The sliced cylinder used for Evry Cathedral also defines the small valley church of San Giovanni Battisti, Mogno in Switzerland (1986-96) which is beautifully detailed in different types of stone, and the Chapel of Santa Maria degli Angeli, Monte Tamaro, Ticino, Switzerland (1990-6). Alternatively, the Church of Beato Odorico, Pordenone, Italy (1987-92) is structured as a cone within a rectilinear envelope (reminiscent of Le Corbusier's unfinished project in Firminy), while the cylindrical core of the Church of San Pietro Apostolo, Sartirana di Merate, Italy (1987-96) is shrouded in a cube. Although more intimately scaled, the latter shares features with Evry, notably the altar window in the sanctuary.

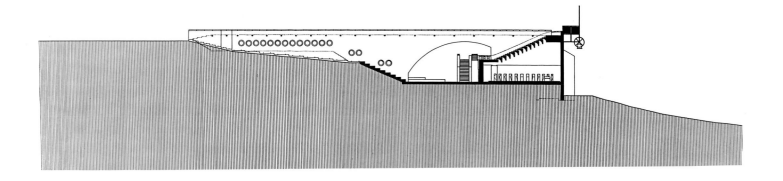

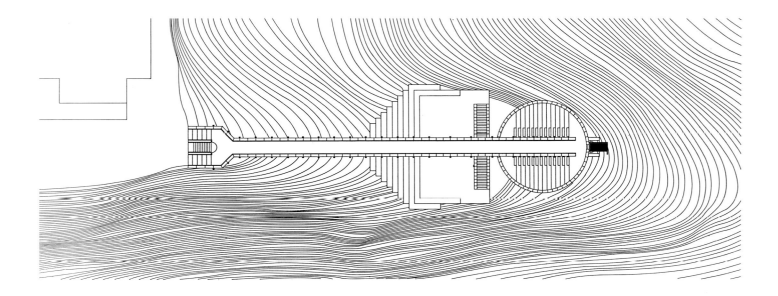

Chapel of Santa Maria degli Angeli, Monte Tamaro, Ticino, Switzerland, 1996; OPPOSITE: Views of exterior, FROM ABOVE. Section; plan

The Chapel of Santa Maria degli Angeli on Monte Tamaro, Ticino, is an interesting departure from Botta's formal grammar, though a clear descendant. The chapel stands at an altitude of 1,500 metres in the Foppa Alps, reached by cableway from Rivera, near Lugano. It was commissioned by the proprietor of the cableway, Egidio Cattaneo, and completed in 1996. The concrete structure is clad in porphyric stone and strung out along the edge of a natural terrace, exploiting its spectacular location.

The appearance of the building suggests a fortress or an arched bridge rather than a religious building. A slender crucifix identifies the little chapel: a cylindrical structure of 15 metres in diameter. This is approached by a 65-metre long, open walkway which terminates in a belvedere – an extension of the metal structure supporting the bell. From this point panoramic views are opened up over the alpine scenery and valley beneath. The passage is then one of descent by way of the stepped roof of the chapel and an arched staircase which is set at right angles to the chapel. In front of the entrance there is a rectangular platform with steps cut into the slopes of the mountain on one side. The chapel can also be reached by a corridor beneath the walkway.

Botta's approach to the chapel exploits similar devices to Tadao Ando. The processional route recalls that at Mount Rokko, Kobe (see pages 128-131), where the church is reached by way of a long passage that opens on to a scenic view. Similarly, one must then turn back on oneself to enter the church, followed by a movement of descent. The intersection of Santa Maria degli Angeli also encourages comparison with the slicing wall of Ando's Church of the Light, Ibaraki (pages 134-7).

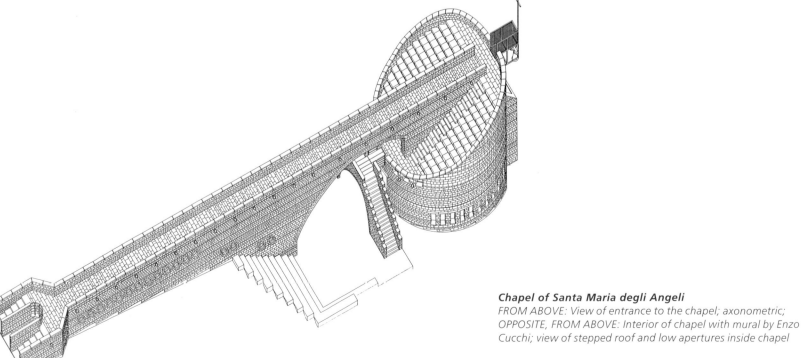

Chapel of Santa Maria degli Angeli
FROM ABOVE: View of entrance to the chapel; axonometric;
OPPOSITE, FROM ABOVE: Interior of chapel with mural by Enzo
Cucchi; view of stepped roof and low apertures inside chapel

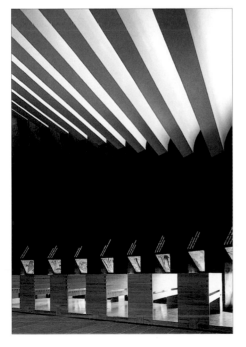

However, rather than penetrate the interior entirely, this feature is defined as a vaulted central nave, leading to a small apse that protrudes externally from the principal volume. Here, natural light illuminates the image of offering hands painted by the artist Enzo Cucchi.

Either side of the nave, light is filtered through the horizontal slits in the risers of the stepped roof. Small apertures also punctuate the walls of the chapel at floor level, offering partial views of the landscape below. Decorative tiles relating to the Virgin Mary are set into each opening, of which there are twenty-two in total.

JUHA LEIVISKÄ

Juha Leiviskä has practised architecture in his native Finland since the early sixties. He set up on his own in 1967 and entered into partnership with Vilhelm Helander in the late seventies. By this time he had developed a coherent approach to architecture that was rooted in the tradition of Finnish modernism, consolidated by architects such as Alvar Aalto. With Nakkila Parish Centre (1968-70) Leiviska was brought into close contact with the work of Erkki Huttunen, architect of Nakkila Church (1935-7), and his intervention reflected a sensitive approach to the existing structure and topography, fused with the atmospheric quality of the late eighteenth-century wooden church he was also restoring.

In addition to religious buildings, Leiviskä has designed and built schools, libraries, embassies, offices and public and private housing. His design for the Church of St John and Parish Centre, Männistö (1986-92), in Kuopio, won first prize in an invited competition. It builds on the accumulative experience of Myyrmäki Church and Parish Centre, Vantaa (pages 153-5) and the Church of St Thomas, Puolivälinkangas, Oulu (pages 156-7).

The Männistö church is striking in appearance, articulating a dramatic interplay of vertical and horizontal planes composed of concrete wrapped in brick. The complex is raised up and stretched across an east-facing site that slopes down from uninspiring 1960s high-rise apartment blocks towards wooded parkland and a busy road. Provision will also be made for a leisure centre along the western edge.

The overall effect of the composition is intended to evoke the feel of an ancient hill town. It evolves from the spatial planning of public and private areas pursued in the Church of St Thomas and the town plan for the Centre of Puolivälinkangas. Horizontal orientation of the complex enables the park area in the foreground and a clump of pine trees to the north to be preserved as part of the park, while that behind – between the church and parish centre and the apartment blocks – is made into a pedestrian route, softened by the fences and planting of the upper level courtyards.

As established in Leiviskä's previous churches, the almost square plan of Männistö is foreshortened in order to create a stronger link between the

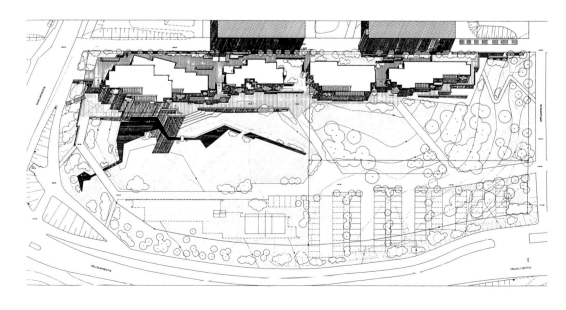

Church of St John and Parish Centre, *Männistö, Kuopio, 1992*
OPPOSITE: Detail of exterior; LEFT: Site plan

congregation and the altar. The main area and gallery provide seating for over 450 worshippers, while three-part sliding doors allow another 140 to be accommodated in the parish hall: a feature utilised by Aalto in Vuoksenniska Church.

Externally, the geometry of Männistö's overlapping planes is enhanced by the limited set of materials; alternating white-washed concrete and red brick. The 114-foot-high bell tower is a separate component composed of two vertically cantilevered concrete slabs. When seen from the park it appears to be united structurally. From every perspective the structure is rendered with a staccato quality that is difficult to attain in

architecture but perhaps comes naturally to one who is deeply musical, as Leiviskä is.

The church, the fellowship hall and the parish centre are entered from the terrace facing the park, a situation which maximises use of natural light. The first stage of progression is marked by the aula, a transitional space which conducts movement through the complex while creating a series of foyers, distributing areas according to their use and importance. This softly lit artery suspends entry into the worship hall which, in contrast, is flooded with natural light. This suffuses the interior indirectly from above and from the sides.

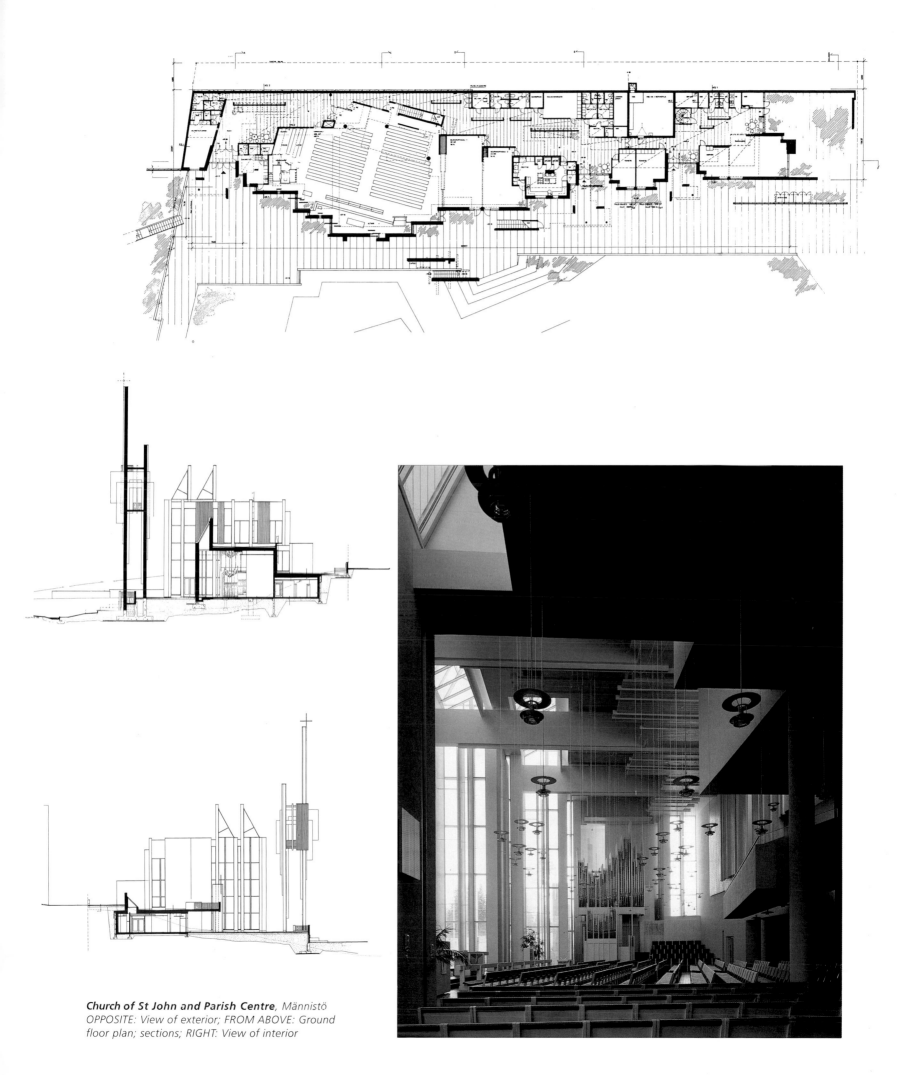

Church of St John and Parish Centre, *Männistö*
OPPOSITE: View of exterior; FROM ABOVE: Ground
floor plan; sections; RIGHT: View of interior

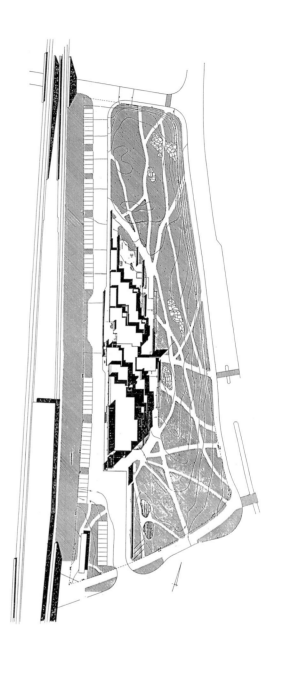

Myyrmäki Church and Parish Centre, *Vantaa, Finland, 1984*
Contextual considerations are consistently woven into Leiviskä's projects in line with his belief that the existing make-up of a place can always be improved by new building. With his design for this church and parish centre, Leiviskä resolved the problem of a narrow site by tightly clustering the building mass and service areas alongside the railway embankment. This not only creates a protective wall but enables the rest of the site to become a continuous park.

OPPOSITE AND ABOVE: Views of exterior; ABOVE RIGHT: Site plan

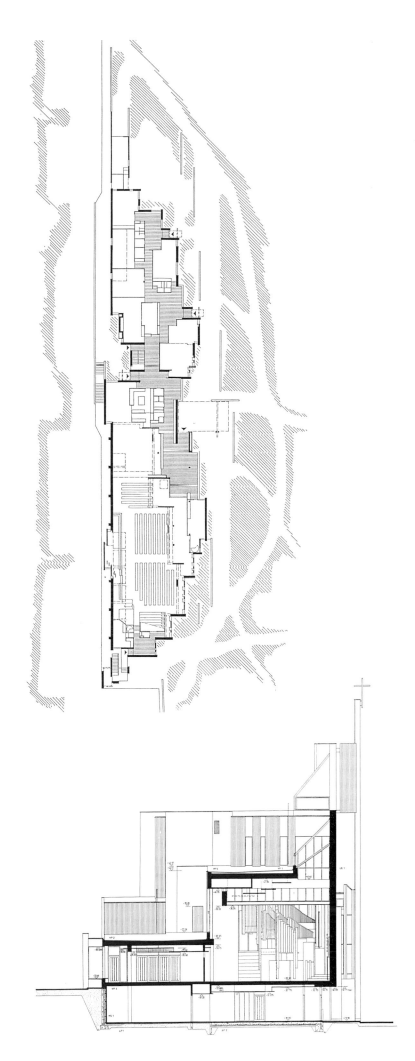

Myyrmäki Church and Parish Centre
OPPOSITE AND ABOVE: Interior of church hall;
RIGHT, FROM ABOVE: Site plan; section

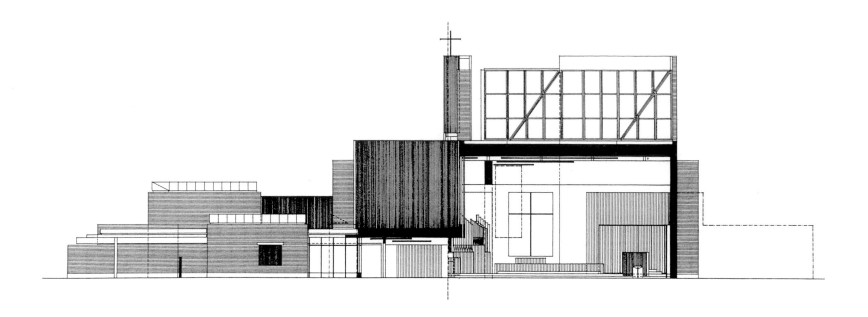

In handling the interior space of his churches, Leiviskä carefully orchestrates light and shade, and vertical and horizontal elements. He builds on the experience of an early work, the Church of St Thomas, Puolivälinkangas, Oulu – where he aimed 'to create a continuously changing, shimmering veil of light' – and Myyrmäki Church, Vantaa, which was inspired by the spatial layering of Balthasar Neumann's great abbey church at Neresheim in southern Germany.

The dynamic treatment of light and form in his interiors is reminiscent of the work of Alvar Aalto, particularly his church at Vuoksenniska, Imatra. While Leiviskä's buildings nurture a variety of influences they are distinct, personal symphonies offering a unique spatial experience, and finely tuned expressions of his approach. He states:

Architecture is closer to music than the visual arts. To qualify as architecture, buildings, together with their internal spaces and their details, must be an organic part of the environment, of its grand drama, of its movement and of its spatial sequences. To me, a building as it stands, 'as a piece of architecture', is nothing. Its meaning comes only in counterpoint with its surroundings, with life and with light.[1]

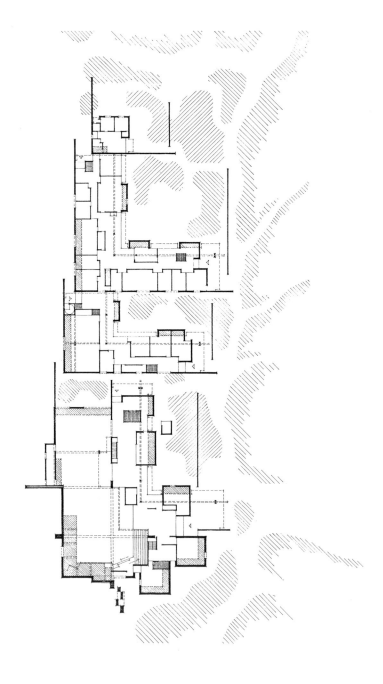

Church of St Thomas, Puolivälinkangas, Oulu, 1975
FROM ABOVE: Section; ground floor plan; OPPOSITE: Views of exterior and interior

In the Männistö church, the gallery is detached from the side walls and accentuates the staggered form of the interior and the play of horizontal and vertical elements; complemented by the slatted wood panels attached to the walls, which conceal mechanical and electrical services, and by the light fixtures suspended at different heights.

Leiviskä is the architect of the building, but light is the conductor, unifying and animating interior components like the chords of a musical instrument. The morning sun is brilliantly reflected into the space through glazed windows that separate the vertical planes; double or triple glazing helps retain the warmth during Finland's harsh winters. The reflections in Männistö are at their most intense in the late morning (during the morning service), maximised by the orientation of the worship space which is set at an angle of 15 degrees. The effect recalls the side lighting in Erik Bryggman's cemetery chapel near Turku (1941). The magical quality is further enriched by the play of artificial light from Leiviskä's delicate light fixtures. Leiviskä outlines his approach:

> I have tried especially to ensure that all the components of the space, such as the slanting gallery, the organ etc, belong together and form an entity. A living interaction of large and small, open and shut, high and low, light and shade, spaces 'as instruments for light to play on'.[2]

The white stucco interior of the church is enhanced by delicate strips of colour, synthesising tones of yellow, green, turquoise, blue and purple. These are painted by the artist Markku Pääkkonen and applied to the walls around the altar to correspond with the reflections.

The quality of Leiviskä's work was recognised in 1993 when he was chosen from over fifty candidates to receive the Carlsberg architecture prize. This, the second of its kind, is awarded to architects for the creation of works 'of lasting architectural and social value'.

Church of St John and Parish Centre, *Männistö*
OPPOSITE: Interior of church hall; FROM ABOVE: View of gallery; aula

IMRE MAKOVECZ

Imre Makovecz has designed numerous religious projects in his native Hungary over the last few decades: Roman Catholic, Lutheran and Baptist churches, mortuary chapels, memorial structures, and forest and rock chapels. Not all of these have been built although at least a dozen have been designed in the last decade. Makovecz's initial drawings are sketched idiosyncratically in pencil and often involve a variety of individuals interacting with the building in groups or alone. They, like his buildings, exhibit personal attributes and are conceived as participants, a fundamental element of Makovecz's architecture and an important directive of the Church today.

The power of his buildings is such that if the iconography is not understood in its entirety it acts as a stimulus. The unusual form of Makovecz's buildings is bred from animal and bird metaphors, trees, plants, decorative motifs and mythical themes. It is invested with the rich cultural heritage of Hungary and draws on sources of Magyar folk art and ancient forms from Scythian and Celtic culture, explained in detail by Edwin Heathcote in his recent monograph.[1] Makovecz's approach, we learn, is not predisposed to nostalgic or aesthetic concerns but has deep foundations. The architect uses archetypal symbolism to tap into the underlying spirit of European culture; the 'collective unconscious' described by Jung.

While the organic nature of Makovecz's buildings is often perceived in terms of its intrinsic unity or symbiotic relationship with the environment, it should also be recognised for its potential to encourage an identifiable and participatory relationship with us.

RIGHT: **Budapest-Gazdagrét Church and Community Centre**, *sketch of main elevation; OPPOSITE, FROM ABOVE: Sketches of* **Budapest-Rákoskeresztúr Memorial Church of the Hungarian Martyrs** *and* **Mátraháza Church of the Forest**

Halottak Templома.

The Lutheran church built in Siófok, Hungary (1985-90), is an arresting structure which seems to have risen up from the surrounding soil. The front elevation is almost entirely camouflaged by grass-covered earth berms which reach towards the extended canopy of the roof. This is a protective skin which Makovecz has emphasised and made a key feature of the design; its curved and undulating form is reminiscent of a boat, evoking the symbolism of the Ark.

An early sketch of the main elevation of Siófok Church shows a group of eight angels arranged vertically either side of the doorway with their arms raised up and wings outstretched towards Heaven. Although Makovecz maintains this theme, in the executed design, it is a more refined and abstract version. The squat, central tower with feathered wings is evocative of a ceremonial mask. Beneath the 'eyes' of the mask the extended wing-span intimates a motion of flight towards heaven; likewise, the slender black cross emerges from a cluster of plant-like forms, reminiscent of Steiner's boiler house for the first Goetheanum. This relationship is more pronounced in the first sketch for Siófok, in which similar forms are unfurled from

Siófok Lutheran Church, Hungary, 1990
OPPOSITE: Exterior; ABOVE: First sketch;
BELOW L TO R: Sketch of church and vicarage; early sketch

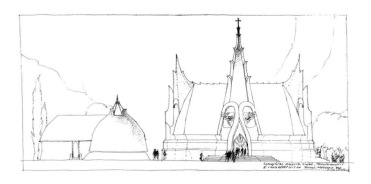

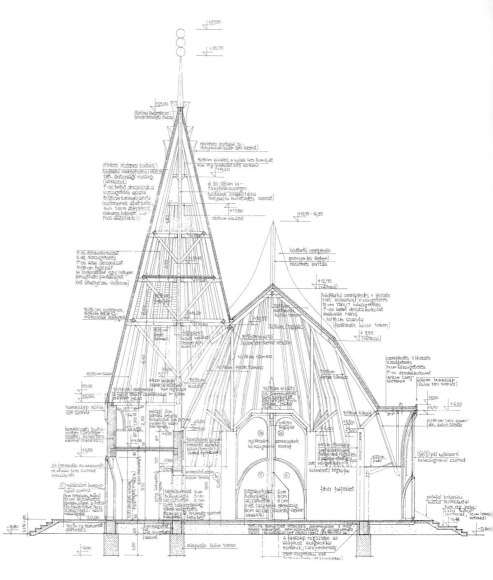

the base of the tower, delineating the upper body of the structure with a jagged edge.

Locally, the church is referred to as 'Christ's boat', an association which is reinforced internally by the wooden ribcage and configuration of exposed structural members, recalling the interior of Farkasrét Mortuary Chapel (1975). The space inside the church is intimate and focused on the funeral bier. The theme of transcendence is conveyed by the wooden bridges which support the sculpture of the risen Christ, and by the winged tree-columns. Makovecz uses natural materials such as wood in a reverential way, recognising its enduring qualities and its symbolic strength. The material lives on in his buildings in structure and form; often alluding to the Tree of Life, the link between heaven and earth.

Siófok Lutheran Church
FROM ABOVE, L TO R: Sculpture of Christ inside the church; section; view towards altar; OPPOSITE, FROM ABOVE: Section; plan

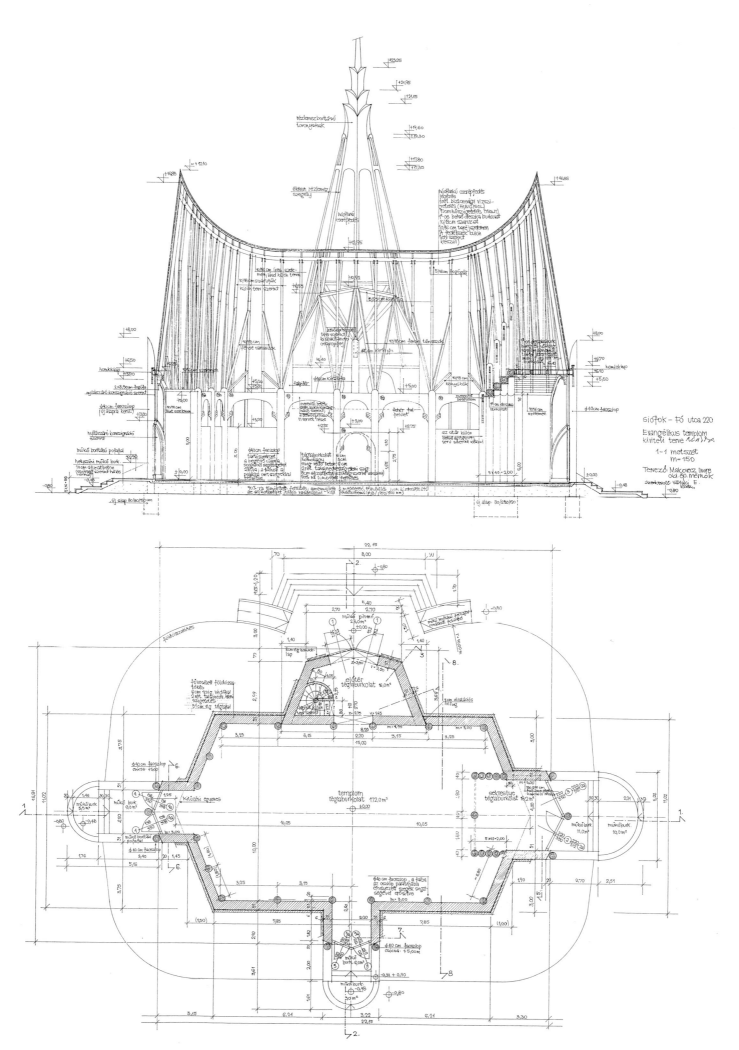

The plan of the Roman Catholic Church in Paks (1987-91) is formed by the juxtaposition of two S-shaped runic symbols, a motif repeated in the landscaping of the site which is based on a Celtic warrior's sword.[2] The building is distinguished by the smooth texture and gentle contours of its scaly form and encourages comparison with the shingled roof of the Price Residence by Bart Prince. At Paks, the rippled surface was created by using hand-cut grey slates and is beautifully expressed in the gateway to the church: a freestanding bell tower which splinters to provide a trinity of antennae-like spires. The soaring verticality of this structure and the arched openings reinterpret the spirit of gothic cathedrals. The highest spire terminates in a cross, complemented by the sun and moon which cap the spires beneath.

Sculptures of the archangels Michael and Gabriel signal the entrance to the church, poised either side of the arched doorway with wings outstretched to heaven. These rest on the outward curving scrolls of the plan, while the inward curves provide a pair of circular, domed chapels either side of the altar (see overleaf), one of which functions as a baptistery. In between the chapels a sculpture of the risen Christ is flanked by two angels.

The altar rests on a shallow podium positioned directly beneath the heart-shaped skylight above. This skylight echoes the plan of the building in stained-glass, though here the scrolls intersect. The benches are oriented towards the altar, in line with the liturgical reforms of Vatican II encouraging greater participation of the congregation.

In many ways unique, Makovecz's architecture has evolved as a conscious reaction to the inert and poor quality modernist architecture in Hungary (such early, spirited interpretations as the Sárospatak Cultural Centre in the seventies were to lose Makovecz his job with the state offices, restricting his work to the National Park at Pilis). While some may feel that his buildings would look out of place elsewhere – perhaps lacking the 'rational', streamlined refinement of 'modern' counterparts – they are instilled with a timeless iconography that is of universal appeal. Such skilfully crafted works are conceived on an interactive and human scale, responding to the language of the body (and that of the mind through powerful symbolism). They will no doubt continue to stimulate and fascinate those who are brought into contact with them. Such is the strength of architecture.

Roman Catholic Church, *Paks, Hungary, 1991*
OPPOSITE: Exterior; BELOW L TO R: Sketch of main elevation; sketch of interior

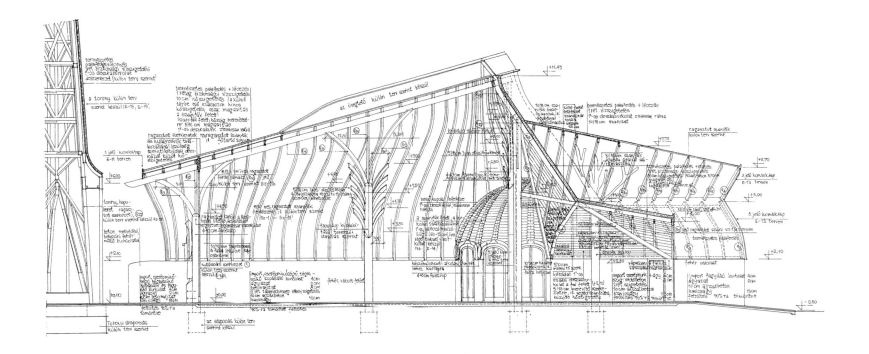

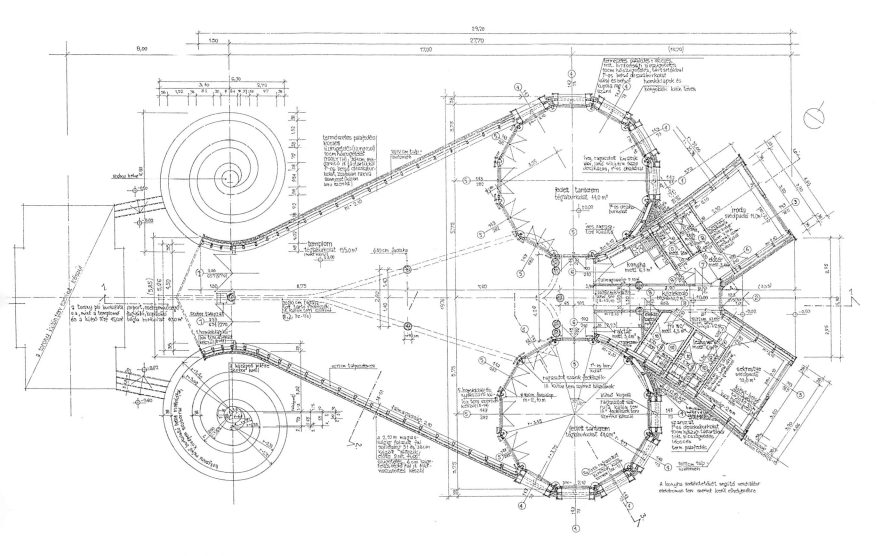

Roman Catholic Church, Paks
OPPOSITE: View of altar; FROM ABOVE: Section; ground floor plan

LEGORRETA ARQUITECTOS

The Metropolitan Cathedral of Managua, Nicaragua, completed in 1993, is Legorreta's first venture in ecclesiastical architecture and has had a profound impact on the Mexican architect. He refers to the building of the cathedral as one of the deepest experiences of his life, in which he was 'able to deal with poverty and faith, humanism and politics, but above everything had the opportunity to offer a country a truly spiritual space to pray'.

Legorreta Arquitectos is well known for producing works which evoke the spirit of the Mexican vernacular, such as the Hotel Camino Real in Mexico City (1968). Often monumental in form, such buildings bring into play Ricardo Legorreta's love of bold colour and simple form, combined with effects of light and texture and an articulation of open and cloistered spaces. Since the 1980s the practice has taken on board a variety of projects in other countries.

The commission for Managua Cathedral arose as a result of the devastating effect of the 1972 earthquake on Managua. The Catholic cathedral was considered to be beyond restoration and it was decided to replace the old colonial building with a new cathedral. Fortunately, the necessary support and sponsorship for such a large-scale commission was provided by the Christian Chapels Foundation, an organisation set up by an American businessman, Tom Monaghan, to finance the building of chapels in underdeveloped countries.

An alternative site was sought for the new cathedral, which it was decided should be relocated in the upper part of the city, and in 1990 Legorreta was elected to draw up designs. Working very much with the concerns of the Second Vatican Council in mind, his scheme for Managua Cathedral attempts to engage the congregation in a more participatory role with ecclesiastical authority, and ensure that a more appropriate sense of space is created within the new cathedral.

The Metropolitan Cathedral of Managua, Nicaragua, 1993
OPPOSITE: View of south facade; BELOW: Site plan

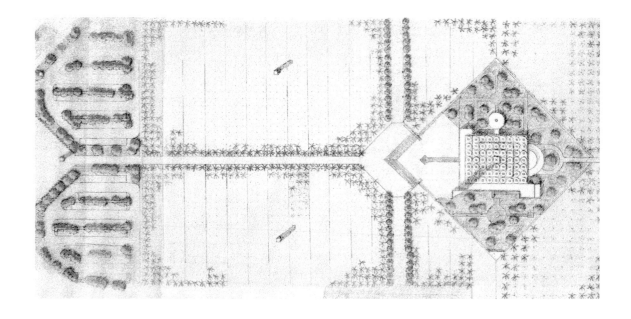

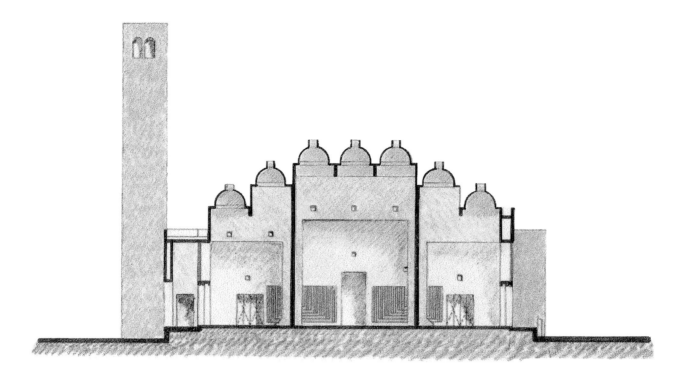

The altar is placed on a circular podium of six steps, bisecting the semicircular sacristy. This encourages a more direct relationship with the congregation. In order to avoid the feeling of detachment that occurs within buildings of such magnitude (induced by the traditional layout of many cathedrals), Legorreta places the highest of the 63 domes above the the main congregational space; this is extended to a height of around 20 metres. The church frequently holds a thousand people for Sunday mass and the shift in emphasis provides a more adequate sense of scale and unity for the worshipper when there is a large concentration of numbers or when the congregation is at a low ebb; it also centres the composition.

The central area is animated by a rich, yellow colour that is applied to the underside of the roof structure and skirts down the inside of the cruciform columns. This artistic stroke defines the area with great simplicity while conveying a sense of enclosure.

Three ancillary chapels adjoin the central worshipping area: the Santismo Chapel, the baptistery, and the veneration chapel. The first is rectangular in form and used for daily mass, therefore a more intimate space. At one end, the wall is pierced with a cruciform aperture through which light is effectively filtered and distilled, providing an atmospheric area for regular celebration of the Eucharist. This device occurs in Tadao

OPPOSITE, FROM ABOVE: View of east facade; view towards altar;
FROM ABOVE: North-south section; west-east section

Ando's little Church of the Light (see pages 134-7). The same effect is achieved in the baptistery by way of conducting light through slits in the walls and the oculus above.

The third chapel is dedicated to the image of the *Sangre de Christo*, an ancient crucifix rescued from the original cathedral in Managua which is placed in a glass dome in the centre of the circular space. The orange painted interior of the domed chapel is resplendent with an array of points that pierce the surface to admit natural light, like stars within the vault of the sky. The colour is enriched by the glow of candles placed on the steps of the podium beneath the *Sangre de Christo*. As evening falls, the exterior of the chapel invokes the constellation, with glints of light punctuating the dome.

The formidable austerity of Managua Cathedral, which arises from the use of *in-situ*, reinforced concrete (and the sheer scale of the project), is relieved by defined areas of bold colour and by the skilful juxtaposition internally and externally of rough and smooth surfaces, concave and convex forms, solid and void, and light and shadow. This is facilitated by the lack of decoration and the paring down of extraneous detail, consigned internally to the geometrical arrangements of coloured tiles on the floor.

In recognition of their design for Managua Cathedral, Legorreta Arquitectos received the 1994 Award for Religious Architecture from the American Institute of Architects.

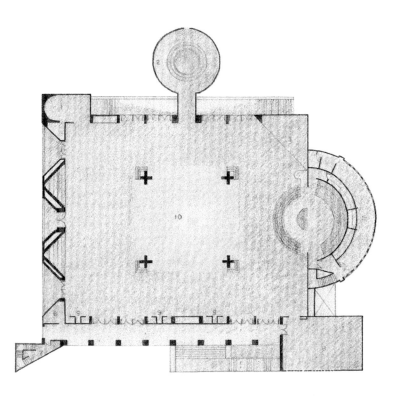

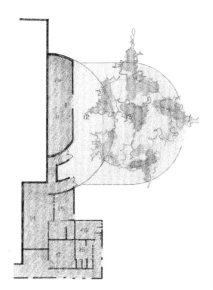

OPPOSITE: View of nave; FROM ABOVE: Veneration Chapel; plan of Managua Cathedral

FAY JONES

The integral relationship between Fay Jones' buildings and their surroundings evolves from a deep respect for nature. This is reflected in the use of natural materials such as indigenous stone and different types of wood which are employed with great sensitivity. Equally, with materials such as steel, brick or glass, Jones draws out the essential nature of the medium, endowing the structure with an organic wholeness that is characteristic of his approach, one which embraces the principles of Frank Lloyd Wright and the Arts and Crafts movement.

Following his apprenticeship with Wright and a period of teaching with Bruce Goff at the University of Oklahoma, Jones returned to work and teach in Fayetteville, Arkansas, in 1953. He set up his own practice in 1956 and was later joined by Maurice Jennings, a former pupil. The reputation of the practice was established early on with the success of residential commissions, which make up about seventy-five per cent of their workload. The religious projects evolved from the vocabulary of the woodland houses.

The Thorncrown Chapel, Eureka Springs, Arkansas (1981) and the Mildred B Cooper Memorial Chapel, Bella Vista, Arkansas (1988) are located in wooded settings in Arkansas. In response to the nature of the site they interact with their surroundings as 'open' structures, sheathed in a transparent skin which forges an immediate relationship between the inside and the outside. Both chapels are slender in form and rectangular in plan; grounded with a base of native stone, around which runs a low supporting wall. Inside, wooden pews are arranged uniformly to create a central aisle with steps leading up to the sanctuary.

Mildred B Cooper Memorial Chapel, *Bella Vista, Arkansas, 1988*

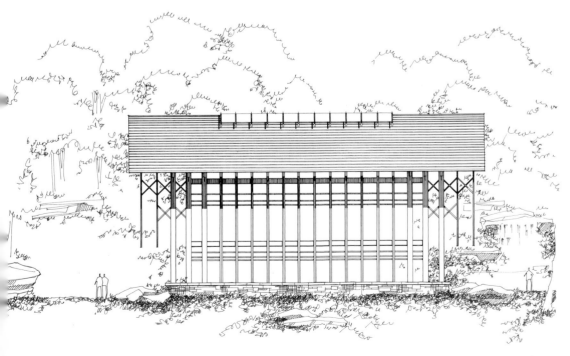

The chapels were constructed from components and materials that were easily transportable without the aid of earth-moving equipment, so that the natural setting of trees amongst stone outcroppings and boulders would not be damaged; the 'kit of parts' aspect of the construction proved to be inspirational to the design process.

In the Thorncrown Chapel, the interior space is enlivened and effectively extended by a stabilising web of cross-bracing, reminiscent of Rudolf Schwarz's glazed wall of St Maria Regina, Frechen, 1954. The dynamic interplay of wooden structural elements, seemingly infinite, charges the interior with the atmosphere of a gothic church, lifting the eye upwards and beyond the 48-foot high enclosure. Light filters through the ridge skylight and the glazed skin of the chapel, animating the pattern of the cross-bracing and providing natural ornamentation for the interior. In order to blend with the bark of the surrounding trees the wood used for the chapel was hand-rubbed with a greyish stain.

With simple means, and by sensitively reworking and translating gothic imagery into a contemporary

Thorncrown Chapel, *Eureka Springs, Arkansas, 1981*
ABOVE: Views of exterior and interior;
BELOW, L TO R: Elevations; section; floor plan

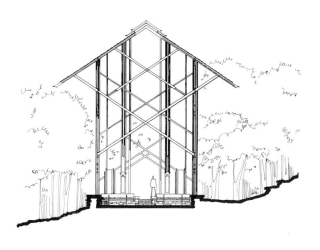

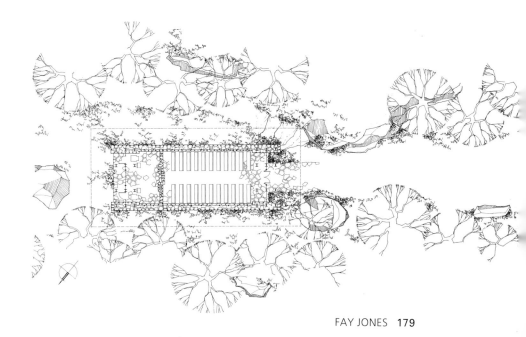

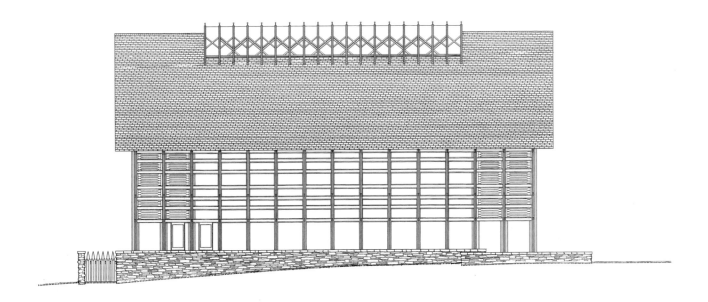

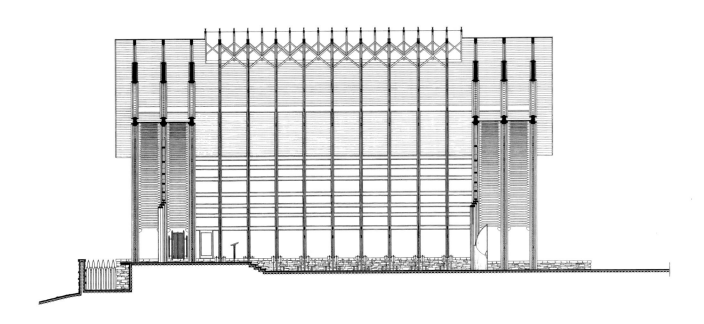

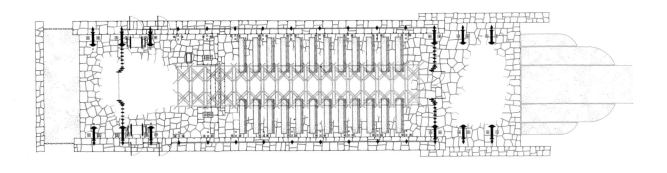

Mildred B Cooper Memorial Chapel
*FROM ABOVE: Elevation; section; plan; OPPOSITE, LEFT: Detail of
exposed steel structure and interior; OPPOSITE, RIGHT: Elevation; section*

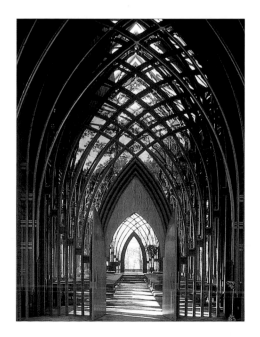

idiom, Jones creates a wholly inspirational setting in which to worship. The Thorncrown Chapel represents a fertile breeding ground for the development of an appropriate style and vocabulary for church design, achieved through the repetition of structural elements which are knitted together to create an organic entity.

While Thorncrown Chapel rekindles the essence of the gothic style, the Mildred B Cooper Chapel evokes its imagery more specifically; exploiting a distinctive feature of the style, the pointed arch. This becomes the keynote of the whole design. Externally, it defines and accentuates the front and rear elevations; internally it reverberates in the characteristic geometry of the exposed steel

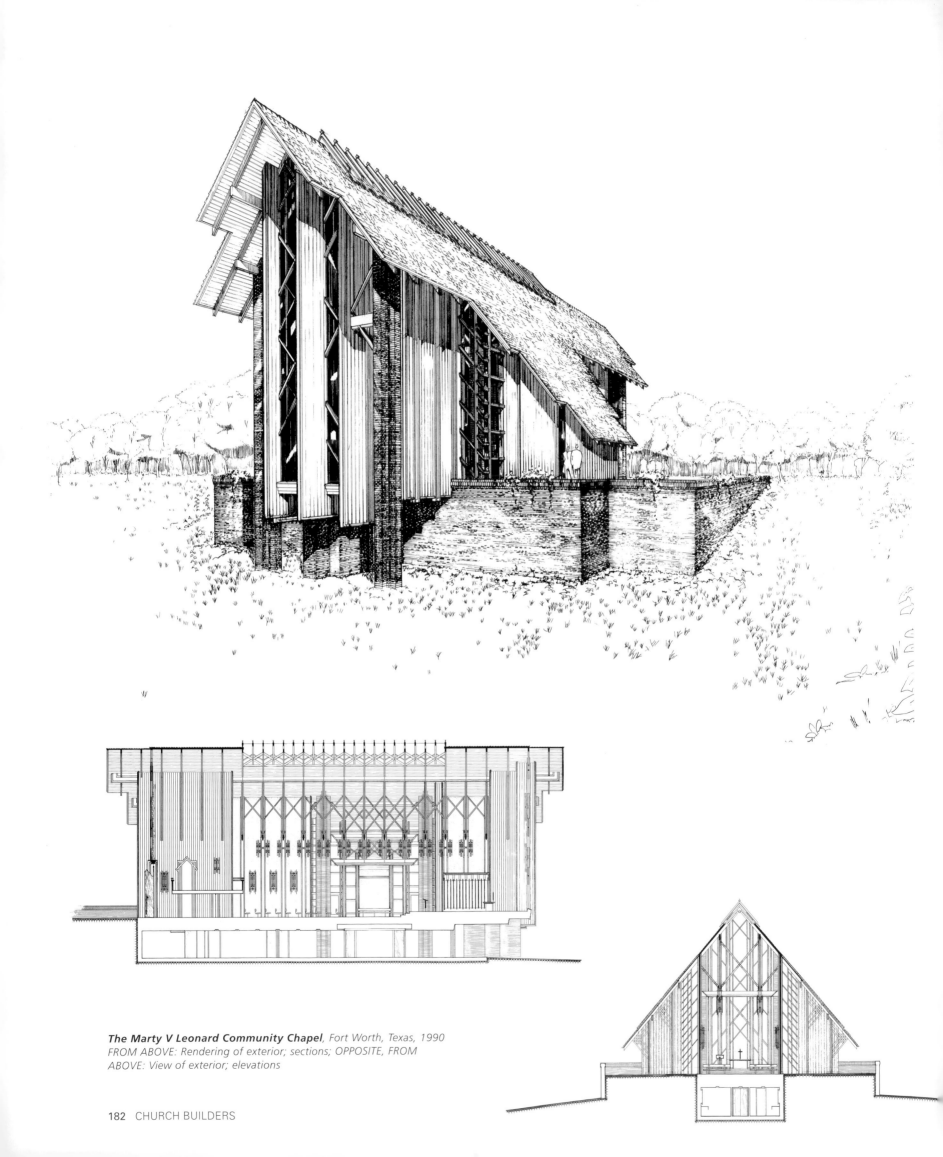

The Marty V Leonard Community Chapel, *Fort Worth, Texas, 1990*
FROM ABOVE: Rendering of exterior; sections; OPPOSITE, FROM
ABOVE: View of exterior; elevations

ribcage. With modern materials Jones reinterprets the style with great delicacy. The orchestration of elements and the synthesis of steel, wood and glass is dynamically expressed. Like the Thorncrown Chapel, this chapel is devoid of ornamentation, made unnecessary by the rhythmic arrangement of elements and by the transparent nature of the building.

The Thorncrown Chapel and the Mildred B Cooper Chapel are fortunate in their natural settings and thus correspond with their surroundings as open structures, an aspect fully exploited by Jones in the Pinecote Pavilion in Picayune, Mississippi (1986). The Marty V Leonard Community Chapel in Fort Worth, Texas (1990) prompted an alternative response.

This chapel was designed for the Lena Pope Home, a treatment centre for neglected and abused children, while additionally catering for community services. Although the chapel uses much of the same vocabulary as its predecessors, similarly inspired by the spirit of gothic cathedrals, it is a distinctly protective enclosure. Sheltered by a broad pitched roof, it sits on a relatively barren, sloping site close to the highway and is a domi-

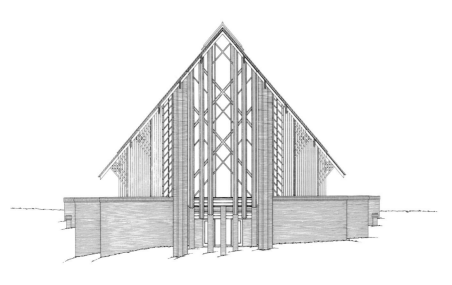

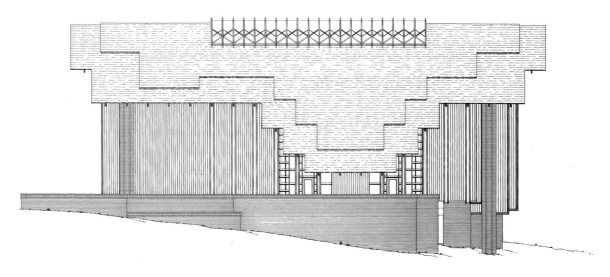

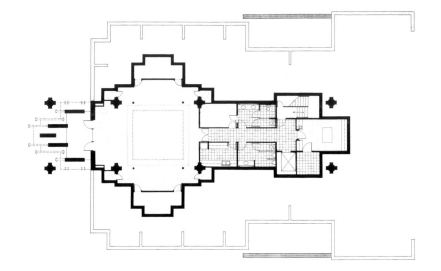

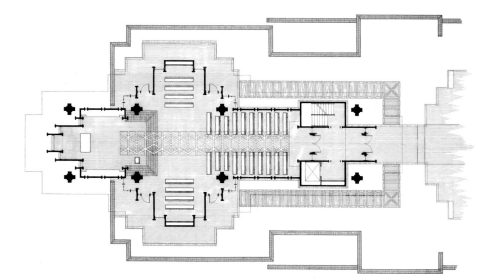

nant feature of the landscape, raised up on a brick podium which contains administration space. This feature acts as a forecourt, sealed by a water wall at one end.

In contrast to Jones' previous designs, the Leonard Chapel is cruciform in plan. It is also more introverted as a result of its setting. To avoid views of the nearby freeway the lofty interior is devoid of side widows and has low pews (which seat up to 150), thus creating an enclosed space for contemplation. An ante-room, with low ceiling, precludes entry into the soaring, 52-foot high space which is animated by effects of light and shadow.

Light is filtered through the ridge-skylight that spans the length of the nave, interacting with the dynamic web of cross-bracing to create a dappled effect reminiscent of Jones' forest structures. Hand-crafted features and the predominant use of wood throughout the Leonard Chapel contribute to providing an atmospheric setting for worship while offering a warm retreat for the young residents of the Lena Pope Home.

When set alongside its predecessors, the Leonard

The Marty V Leonard Community Chapel
FROM ABOVE: Basement plan; ground floor plan; site plan

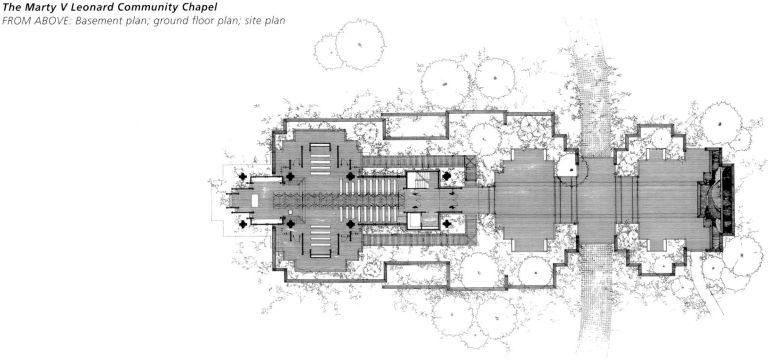

Chapel has more affinity with the Thorncrown Worship Center (1989), a similarly focused space which is hemmed in by solid walls and enlivened by sconces, light fixtures and other features, which are usually designed by the practice. The form of the Leonard Chapel is also recalled in a large chapel which is currently under construction in Rose Hills Memorial Park, California.

Fay Jones and Maurice Jennings have also recently designed chapels for Chapman University in Orange, California, Powell Gardens near Kansas City and the Lindsey Wilson College Chapel in Columbia, Kentucky. The latter, which is shortly to begin construction, departs from the formal language of its predecessors. In response to its urban location the chapel is an introverted structure but this time it is almost entirely constructed of brick; consisting of two cylinders which are connected by a barrel vault. Natural light is drawn into the window-less form through the large, circular skylights in each cylinder. An open 'crown of steel' marks the transition from the heavy brick base to the sky above.

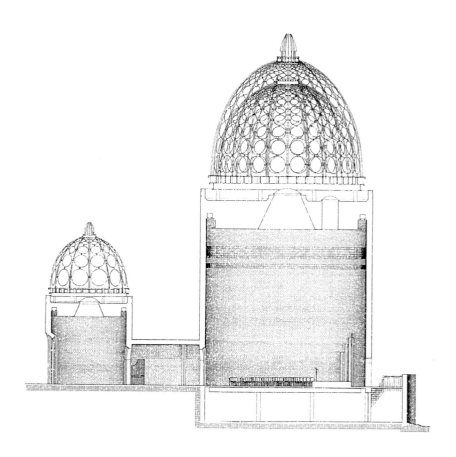

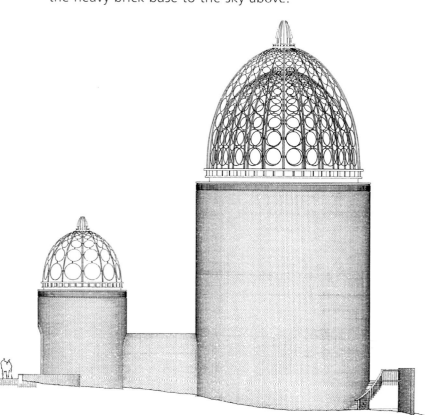

Lindsey Wilson College Chapel, *Columbia, Kentucky*
FROM ABOVE: Section; elevations

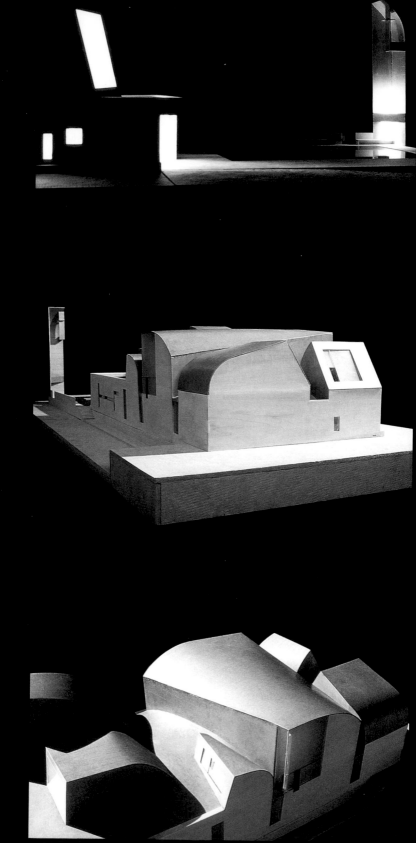

STEVEN HOLL ARCHITECTS

The new Jesuit Chapel of St Ignatius at Seattle University, Washington (1994-7) is still under construction at the time of writing. The building is designed by Steven Holl Architects in association with Olson/Sundberg Architects. It builds upon the experience of projects such as Stretto House and a small chapel in Port Ludlow, Washington (completed in 1992). Curved and square forms are brought into play with maximum exploitation of natural light which is filtered through clear and coloured glass, beautifully capturing the morning light from the east. In *Anchoring*, Holl writes:

> Light subjects space to uncertainty, forming a kind of tentative bridge through fields of experience. What a pool of yellow light does to a simple bare volume or what a paraboloid of shadow does to a bone white wall presents us with a psychological and transcendent realm of the phenomena of architecture.[1]

Holl believes that architecture and site should have an experiential connection, a metaphysical link and a poetic link. His writings are peppered with references to Benedictine monasteries, Romanesque churches, cathedrals, nunneries and the ancient temple architecture of Japan and Egypt.

The Chapel of St Ignatius corresponds to the grid system which connects campus buildings to each other across grass zones and is sited to form a new campus quadrangle green space to the north, the west and, in the future, to the east. A concrete bell tower placed discretely at the south-east corner defines the inner boundary of the site, while a reflecting pool to the south provides a framework that the architects refer to as a 'thinking field'.

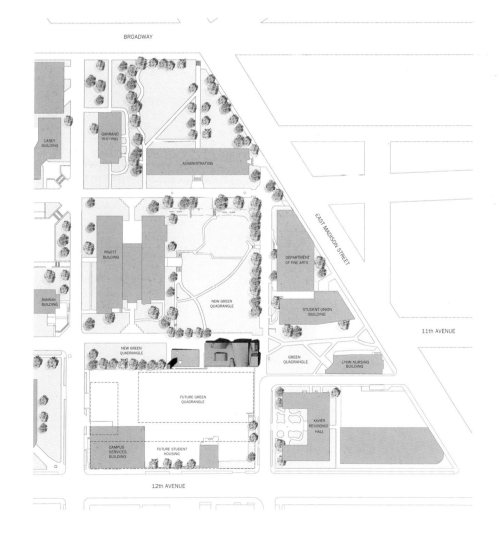

Chapel of St Ignatius, *Seattle University, Washington, 1997*
OPPOSITE: Model views; RIGHT: Site plan

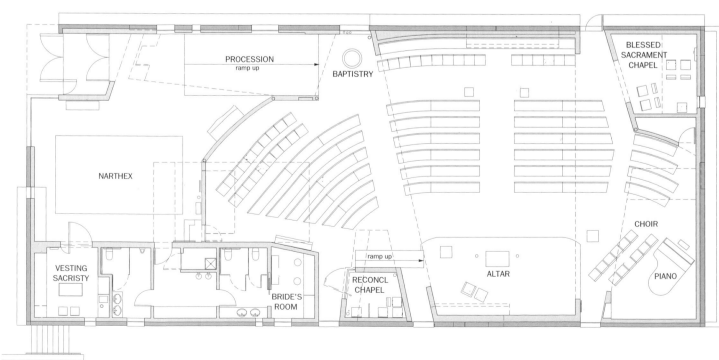

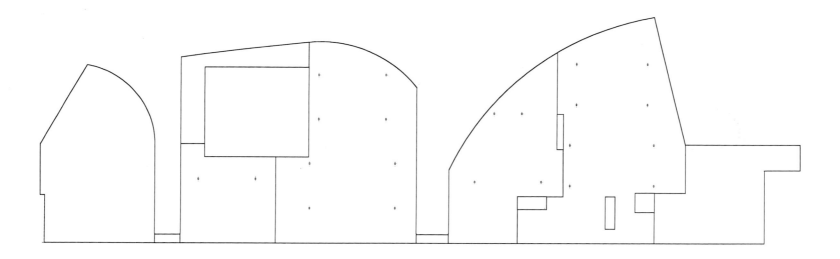

The plan of the building is an elongated rectangle, taking into account the processional aspect of the Catholic liturgy. Within the irregularly shaped nave, pews are grouped around the altar, which is situated between the choir and Reconciliation Chapel and approached by way of a ramp.

Conceived of as a 'stone box', the building locks together lift-slab, concrete perimeter walls, bearing tubular-steel, lightweight metal vaults, covered with insulation and zinc roofing. For the roof, steel tubes were bent by magnetic induction through a computer-driven process (also used for Stretto House). To hoist the slabs into place (the heaviest was 77 tons) the crane required hooks which will be retained when the wall is in place; the covers will be cast in bronze and applied over the holes, reinforcing the materiality of the construction. The architects also intend to design furniture, pews and carpeting for the chapel.

Chapel of St Ignatius
OPPOSITE, FROM ABOVE: Construction of the chapel using lift-slab concrete walls; ground floor plan; FROM ABOVE: West elevation showing pick-pocket points of lift-slab concrete walls; crane hoisting slabs into place; detail of pick-pocket point plug

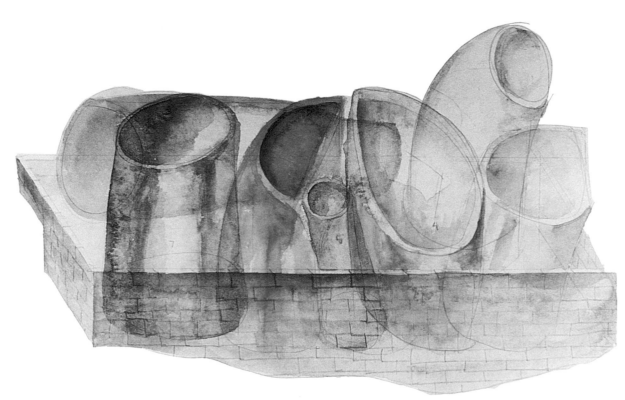

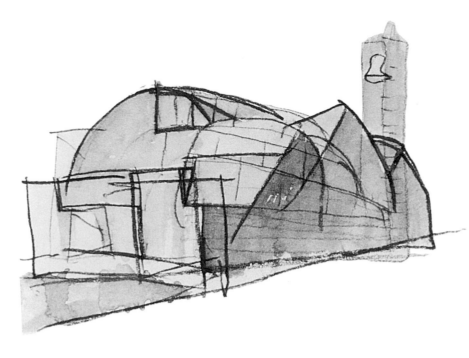

The warped geometry of the building gives it a kinetic quality that is experienced internally. The 'box' is volumetrically structured as a continuum of seven vaults, which Holl visualises as 'bottles of light'. The concept of a gathering of different lights relates to the diverse cultural make-up of the university, while each light volume corresponds to a part of the Jesuit Catholic ceremony: the south-facing light, to the processional way and adjacent narthex; the city-facing north light, to the Chapel of the Blessed Sacrament and to the mission of outreach to the community; the east and west light, to the main worship space.

Holl also introduces various fields of colour. As one moves deeper into the chapel, the spatial experience is enriched by the glow of reflected colour fields as light bounces off coloured panels and is filtered through stained glass lenses. Each lens contains the complementary colour of each field (tested by the Pilchuck Glass School in Seattle):

1	Procession	Natural sunlight
2	Narthex	Natural sunlight
3	Nave	Yellow field with blue lens (East)
		Blue field with yellow lens (West)
4	Blessed Sacrament	Orange field with purple lens
5	Choir	Green field with red lens
6	Reconciliation Chapel	Purple field with orange lens
7	Bell Tower and pond	Projecting, reflecting night light

Chapel of St Ignatius
OPPOSITE, FROM ABOVE: Night view of 'bottles of light' (model exterior); conceptual watercolour rendering of 'bottles of light'; FROM ABOVE: Renderings of exterior and interior

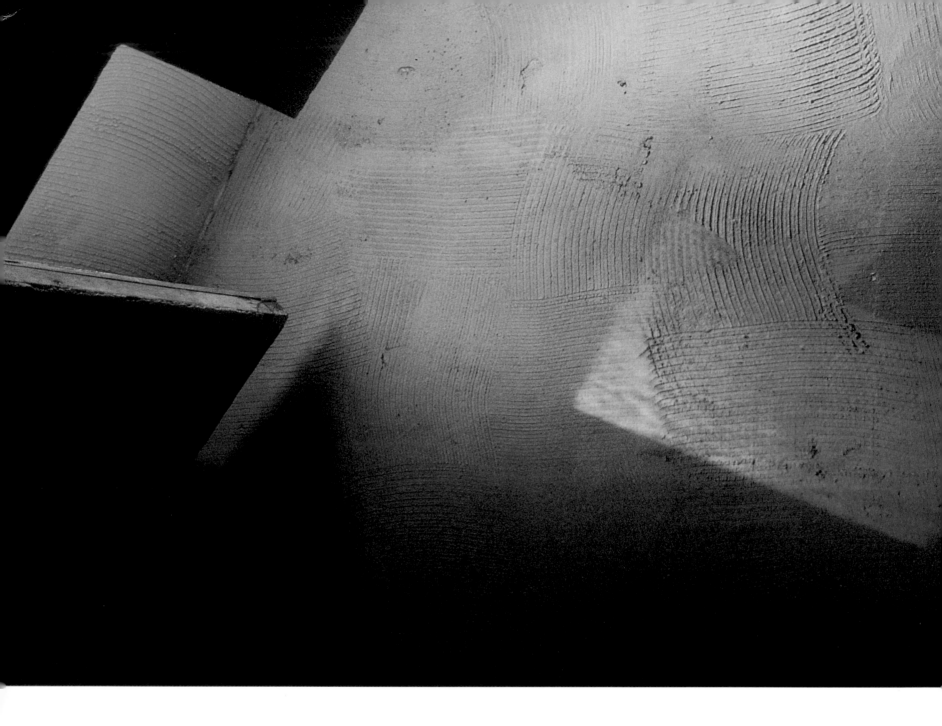

Holl's concept for the chapel very much attempts to provide a sensory experience, embracing site and tectonics. With economic use of materials and by substituting the traditional patchwork of colour (ie. stained-glass) with an aura of colour that dissolves boundaries, Holl seeks to produce a timeless and more unified space. In such a context one's perception will no doubt be ably extended. Holl writes of his work:

> Whether reflecting on the unity of concept and sensation or the intertwining of idea and phenomena, the hope is to unite intellect and feeling, precision with soul.[2]

FROM ABOVE: Study of reflected and projected light; study of interior light

FROM ABOVE, L TO R: Mock-up of baffle and cast-glass lens; view
towards choir ceiling, model interior; altar ceiling reflected and
projected light, model interior

Tokyo Church of Christ, Tomigaya, Tokyo, Japan, 1995
ABOVE: View of exterior; OPPOSITE: Sketch of main hall interior

MAKI AND ASSOCIATES

The Tokyo Church of Christ in the Tomigaya neighbourhood of west-central Tokyo was completed by Maki and Associates in 1995. It replaces a modest, wooden church built in 1949 which was no longer able to accommodate a growing congregation.

The brief for the church requested a worship hall for an assembly of 700 people. There were various site restrictions that needed to be taken into consideration: firstly, the building was not to cast shadow on the small-scale residential neighbourhood to the rear; secondly, the government planned to widen the road bordering the site to make room for an entrance tunnel to an underground highway.

With this in mind, Fumihiko Maki placed the ancillary functions of the church on the ground floor and raised the worship hall to the second level. The church was set back 15 metres from the front boulevard to make way for future street-width expansion.

From the outset, the building was sketched with a gently curving roof to symbolise the celestial vault. Externally, this is complemented by the angular projection supporting the slender stainless-steel cross. The exterior of the church is predominately of glass and exposed concrete, imprinted with the texture of the cedar boards used as formwork. Parapet caps and drip were incorporated to avoid waterstaining.

While the architects wished to create a light-filled space for the worship hall that was both uplifting and suitable for spiritual reflection, the visual distraction and noise of the surrounding urban environment needed to be concealed. This was resolved by devising a translucent 'wall of light' for the sanctuary, which is revealed externally as a double-layered curtain wall system. The outer

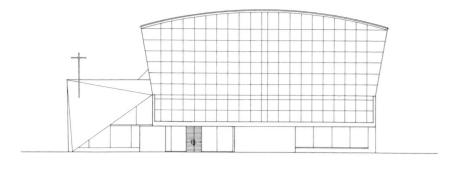

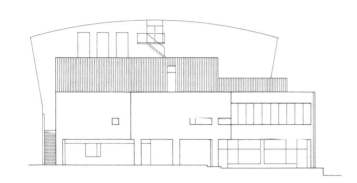

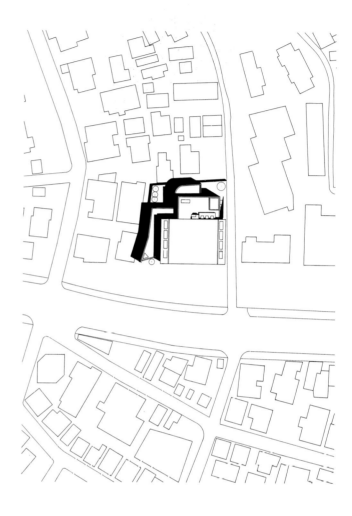

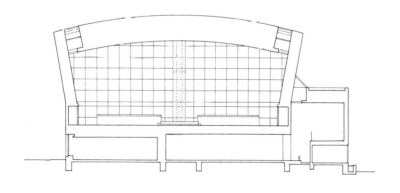

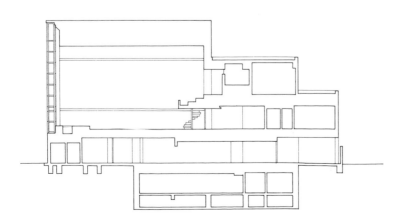

Tokyo Church of Christ
OPPOSITE: Night view of exterior; LEFT, FROM ABOVE: West elevation; east elevation; sections; ABOVE: Site plan

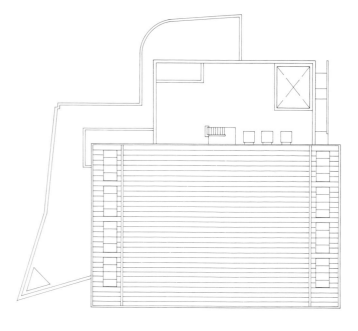

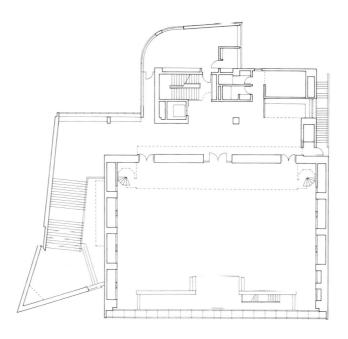

layer of the exterior membrane is treated with a ceramic dot pattern which veils the truss structure and the second layer of glass behind. Maki consistently makes use of dotted lines in his sketches to express unfixed notions and spatial boundaries. Here the dotted screen is a fixed device which acts as a responsive filter. The double-layered curtain wall effectively screens out a portion of the expected heat gain and offers acoustic insulation from the noise of traffic on the Yamate boulevard. The screen appears in other projects by Maki such as the Congress Center in Salzburg, where it consisted of perforated metal and extended from the elevation to the roof.

The interior layer of glass for the sanctuary is composed of thin layers of translucent glass fibre tissue sandwiched between two panes of glass. The wall of light changes in accordance with the time of day and the weather. In order to avoid reflection at night it is sandblasted, giving the impression of a large *shoji* screen. Skylights on the left and right sides of the ceiling counterbalance the light admitted through the glass wall, while the side walls are tilted outward to receive light from above which is softened by aluminium louvers. The space is atmospheric and unadorned, exploiting effects of texture and filtered and reflected light. White birch wood (imported from Finland) is used throughout the building, harmonising the simple vocabulary of elements.

Tokyo Church of Christ
OPPOSITE: Interior of worship hall showing the 'wall of light' during the day; FROM ABOVE: Roof plan; second floor plan; first floor plan

In front of the wall of light the altar is raised on a podium of three steps. Its prominence is reinforced with great simplicity by the diaphanous cruciform suspended directly behind. The restrained interior of the rectangular worship hall is enriched by tubular wall sconces and the constellation of chandeliers. These provide reading light for the congregation and are arranged in clusters of five, suspended at different levels. Stacking chairs offer flexible seating arrangements for the main floor while built-in benches correspond with the stepped form of the balcony which is reached by

way of two spiral staircases at the back of the hall.

Amidst the bustle of the neighbourhood, the church offers a place of welcome and repose. The building involves a sophisticated level of craftsmanship and sensitively fuses traditional and contemporary features to create a harmonious environment.

The architects originally conceived the church in the image of a house and provide a series of interrelated spaces with seating areas: built-in benches are positioned in various circulation points where people are most likely to pause or to gather.

Tokyo Church of Christ
ABOVE: The main worship hall in the evening; OPPOSITE: View of the balcony and skylight

FROM ABOVE: Interior of worship hall, looking towards altar; plan
of site showing areas affected by urban reform initiative

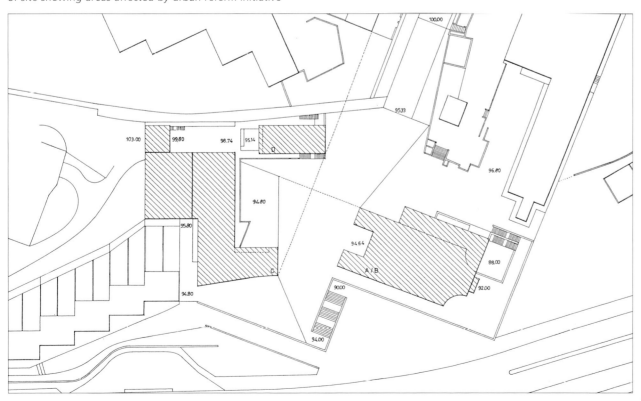

The church provides the neighbourhood with a landmark that is distinctly sculptural in form. Its presence is both neutral and monumental, amplified by the use of simple materials such as white stucco and grey granite facings, and by a process of refinement which emphasises the essential nature of the worship space, evoked symbolically by the height of the nave which is anticipated by the huge entrance doors.

The furnishings reflect this approach and are carefully rendered in materials such as wood or marble in keeping with the reduced palette. Less successful in the planning of the interior is the organ, which at the time of writing is raised on a platform above the entrance to the bell tower at the rear of the church. This appears awkward and unrelated to the overall design; at the same time it draws attention to the homogeneous unity of the space.

What is particularly remarkable about the church is Siza's handling of natural light. This is skilfully directed through seen and unseen sources and defined by slender incisions. The effect of this is atmospheric, constantly intensifying the essential relationship of solid and void within the luminous interior.

Church at Marco de Canavezes
OPPOSITE: View of interior with baptismal font in the distance; ABOVE AND CENTRE: Detail of apertures; LEFT: View towards entrance to the bell tower with organ above

Church of the Year 2000, *schematic renderings of church interior and sunken colonnade, Tadao Ando*

CHURCH OF THE YEAR 2000, ROME

For the Holy Year of 2000, as for all the preceding since the year 1300 (under Pope Boniface VII) the churches will pilgrimage to the See of Peter. They will come to Rome. It will be almost a pilgrimage of response [. . .] to the many apostolic pilgrimages made by Pope John Paul II. The Church of Rome will welcome the Church disseminated over the earth.

In order that, beside the other signs, there remain a sign of the pilgrimage for the Holy Year 2000, and of welcome by the Church in Rome, a church will be built, together with its services and with such elements as will permit it to play a role of expressed welcome for the communities in its neighbourhood. The site chosen is on the city's extreme outskirts where everything, whether from the standpoint of the territory or from the sociological and pastoral standpoints, states its need of welcome. It is not a 'noble' place from the town-planning standpoint [. . .] In fringes of territory that are in no way 'strong', the new church will play a role of upgrading. Thus, the modern problem of going to a difficult place is proposed, together with the problem of the church of today, the 'new evangelization'.

What is being asked of the architect is to design a 'place of welcome, place of convocation, a churchly place'. This is the only significance requested [. . .] Moreover, it is asked of the architect, while aware that daring words are being pronounced, that he make the effort to express the up-to-dateness of the beautiful, to use an expression dear to H Gadamer.[1]

Thus the Vicariate of Rome outlined its brief for a new Catholic church in the Tor Tre Teste district in Rome, designed to celebrate the 2,000th anniversary of the birth of Christ. Six architects were invited to participate in the competition: Richard Meier, who provided the winning entry, Günter Behnisch, Tadao Ando, Santiago Calatrava, Frank Gehry and Peter Eisenman. No experience of ecclesiastical design was requested, nor was the architects' faith considered relevant (indeed, three

of those selected were of Jewish background). In many respects it was surprising that no Italian was invited to compete; hundreds of Italian architects had submitted entries for a church competition in Rome not long before, which must have stimulated original thought.

Although this Catholic church for a poor district in Rome is to be relatively small-scale and just one of fifty new churches planned for the city, the project is highly symbolic. Significantly, the involvement of six internationally renowned architects guaranteed the scheme considerable exposure. Four of the competition entries are illustrated in the following pages, with the exception of Gehry and Eisenman who were unable to provide material for publication.

Tadao Ando

Ando's approach to the project continues the thread of previous designs (see pages 128-137), interweaving anticipatory devices with a sophisticated treatment of space and carefully modulated light. The church is approached from the gently sloping south side of the site, via an eight-metre wall on the left hand side. Its unadorned, bare surface set against the sky is designed to clear the mind of the worshipper so that he arrives at the church in a more contemplative state.

The church is integrated with an underground community centre and colonnade. The cleric's residence is located to the west and the parking area and sports field to the north. The water garden enclosed by the sunken colonnade offers a place to calm and restore the spirit, and somewhere to gather.

The structure is conceived as an isosceles triangle with the apex pointing east. Internally, the chapel is laid out in a centripetal manner with a stepped floor leading down to the area of the sanctuary. This ensures maximum visibility of the altar for the

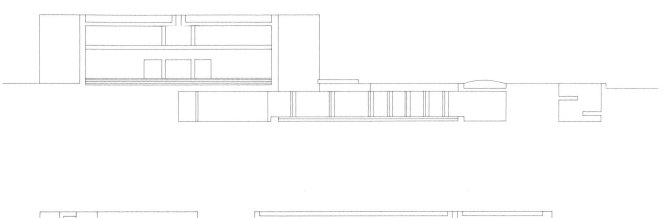

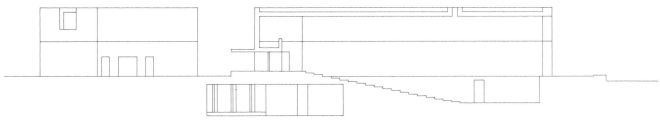

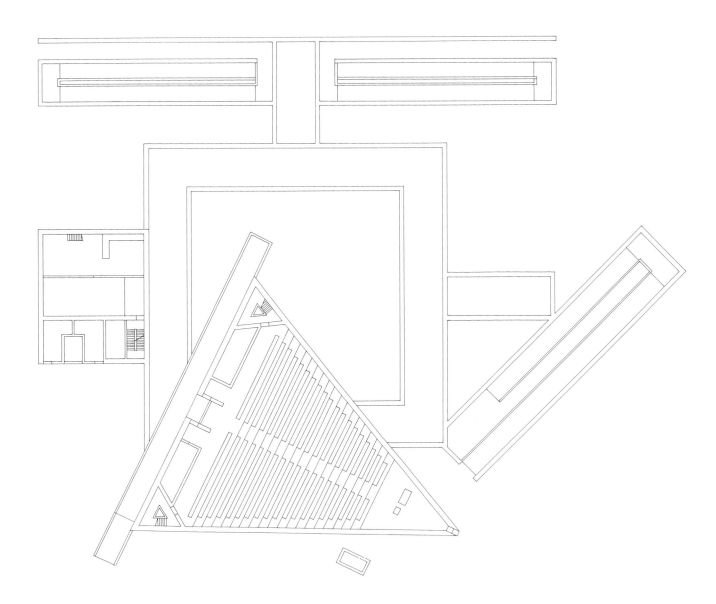

congregation, with the area surrounding the altar placed at the lowest level (an arrangement exploited by Fay Jones in the Thorncrown Worship Centre, Arkansas, 1989).

The choir and a pipe organ are placed at the rear of the aula in the balcony. Light is filtered through a slit at the apex of the chapel, behind the altar, and diffused through the slit in the ceiling, which is a development of the cruciform aperture used for the Church of the Light (pages 134-7). This symbolic device creates an atmospheric space for worship. Individual rooms for Holy Communion, the celebration of the Sacrament of Penance, and the sacristy are placed on either side of the altar. The sacristy can be accessed directly by parishioners from the Community Centre area which is situated around the periphery of the colonnade.

To the right of the entrance wall on the south side of the church a sloping path leads down to the underground colonnade, water garden and community centre. The colonnade is also accessible from the sports field and parking area on the north side and opens on to meeting rooms, an auditorium, clerical offices, the entrance to the cleric's residence, the Weekday Chapel, class rooms and various ancillary spaces. The cleric's residence, on the west side of the site, is enclosed by walls to maintain privacy and connected to the colonnade by an underground level, thereby offering the priest access to all the facilities.

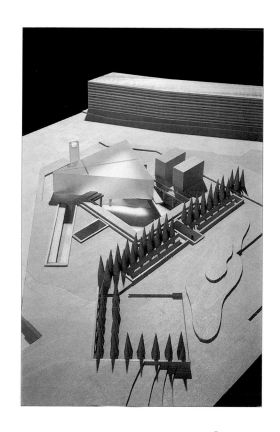

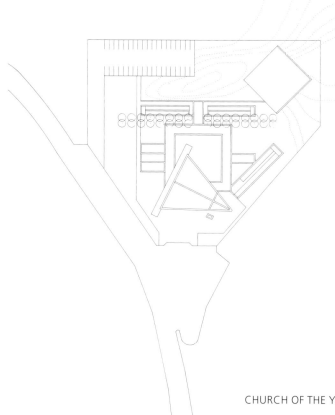

OPPOSITE, FROM ABOVE: Sections; plan; ABOVE: Model; RIGHT: Site plan

Günter Behnisch

In his proposal, Behnisch expressed some concern for the potential of the site to fulfil the aims and intentions of the brief. With reference to the tracts of waste land he stated:

> Even the rather pretentiously laid out central square seems to be half waste land, half parking lot. An appropriate community life cannot develop in such a situation. . . the Church should begin here, and try to eliminate at least some of the existing deficiencies with a project of its own.

Behnisch envisioned a garden of paradise laid out with areas of 'freedom'. Gradually, the church buildings would grow out of a green oasis oriented towards Jerusalem, the corresponding venue for the anniversary celebrations. The traditional bell tower was possibly to be substituted by a freestanding sculpture, perhaps of hewn wood stacked vertically.

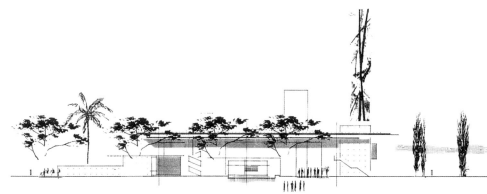

Inside the church, Behnisch intended the atmosphere to reflect that of its immediate environment, proposing an open and flexible composition. The outer walls are planned as movable elements of wood to create more space around the altar area if necessary. The altar, like an organism, acts as the focal point from which everything stems. In hot weather, natural thermal currents carry air from the vegetation and water under the roof to provide ventilation. The opened sections admit natural light into the interior which changes during the course of the day. In contrast, the Weekday Chapel is more introverted and closed off (designed as a more meditative space).

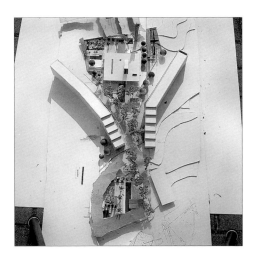

In this ideal context the objective of the church was to provide an interactive public space in a magnificent natural setting. Although the landscape was a challenging venture, this aspect was wholly embraced by Behnisch: 'It would be in the tradition of the Church, eg the Cistercians, and would support the Church's efforts in the cause of mankind and Creation.'

TOP, L TO R: Model; site plan; CENTRE, L TO R: East elevation; west elevation; model; ABOVE, L TO R: Model; north elevation; RIGHT: South elevation

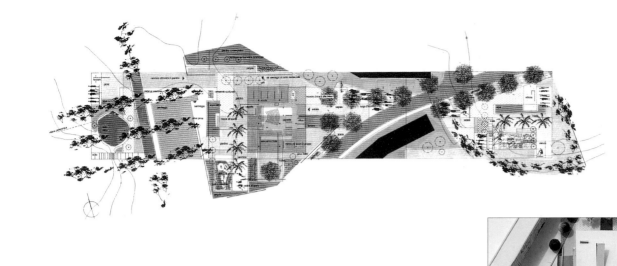

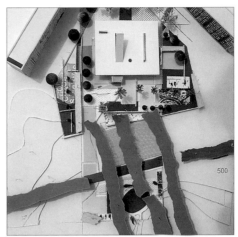

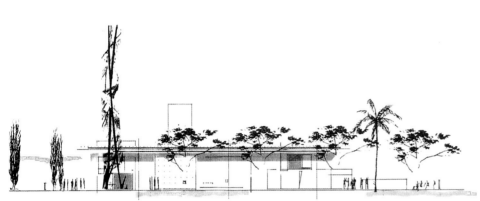

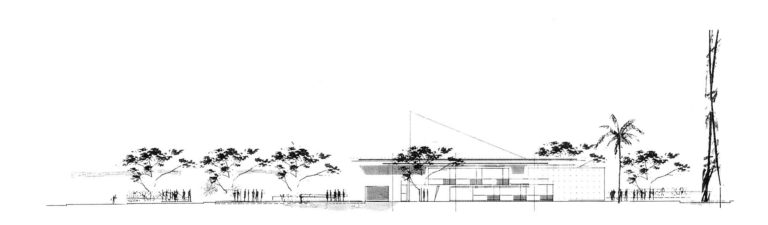

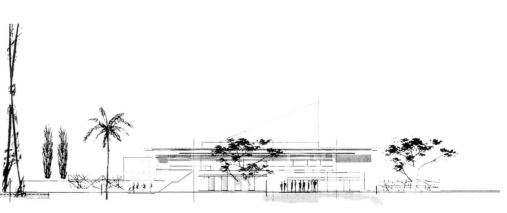

Santiago Calatrava

Calatrava's project for the Tor Tre Teste is distinguished by the dual nature of the complex. An interactive relationship is formed between two distinct buildings as the 'wings' of the church and community centre open to reveal a second building comprising the priest's residence and offices. Their opening transforms the building into a symbolic emblem that visibly engages with the landscape.

The church is located on the upper piazza, offering generous views of the park, and is approached by axially crossing the lower piazza or

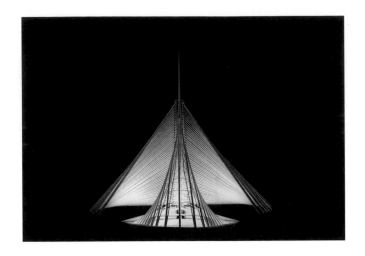

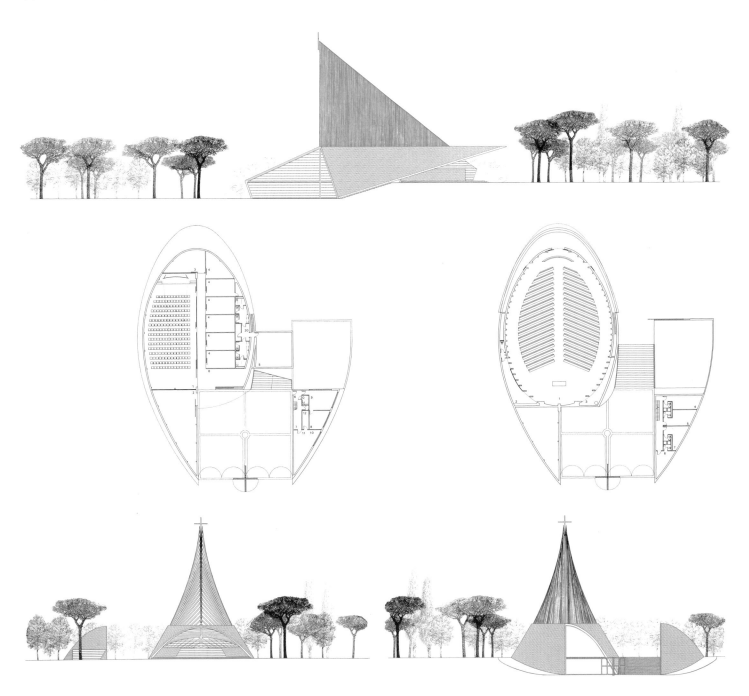

FROM ABOVE, L TO R: Rotating 'wings' of the model, elevation; plan of community centre and church; garden and entrance elevations

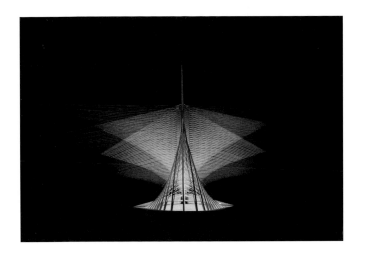
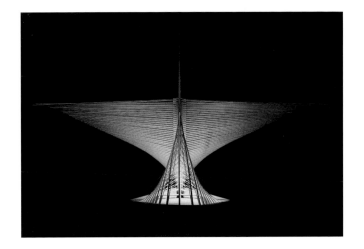

FROM ABOVE, L TO R: Section; closed structure; open structure; garden and entrance elevations

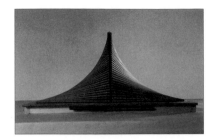

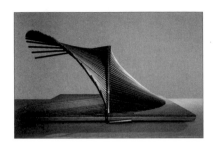

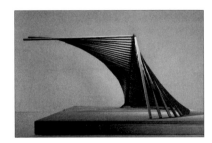

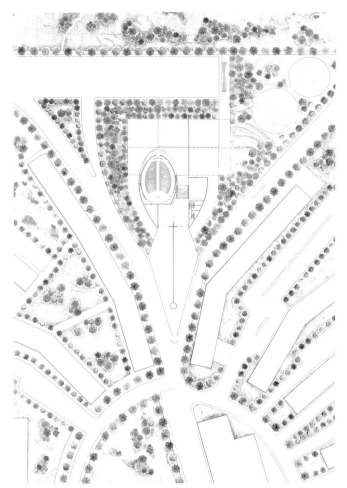

Site plan

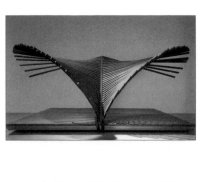

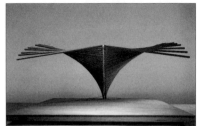

by way of ramps adjacent to the side wings. The lower piazza provides access to the priest's residence, the auditorium and the catechism classrooms.

The church derives its geometric form in plan and volume from the intersection of a cone with an inclined plane. The ribs constituting the structure are generated by the intersection of two parabolas. The wings of the brise-soleil cover up the roof, which is composed of exposed prefabricated reinforced-concrete ribs. Inside, guided by the movement of the wings, light illuminates the spatial play created by the arches, accentuating the sacred and symbolic character of the interior.

The altar is placed at the highest point of the church, and the baptismal font and sacristy to the rear of the building. The enveloping character of the vault is designed to create an atmosphere that is welcoming and intimate. Natural light is exploited and regulated by the brise-soleil wings, composed of steel blades that move independently. A large, central hinge with one single electric motor enables all the necessary rotations and

oscillations of the filtering of light, depending on the inclination and greatest intensity.

Calatrava's previous venture in the field of religious architecture was in 1991 when he won first prize in a competition to complete Heins and La Farge's unfinished neo-gothic cathedral in New York: the Cathedral of St John the Divine.

A bio-shelter had been planned for this cathedral in the late seventies but was shelved due to lack of funds. In Calatrava's scheme this is placed directly beneath the glass and steel roof construction, representing the 'foliage' of the symbolic Tree of Life which was the basis of his design (roots–crypt, earth–nave, trunk–transepts, branches–vaulting, foliage–bio-shelter). The result was an organic and wholly contemporary expression of the gothic, uniting the art of architecture with that of engineering. A close relative is a soaring, skeletal construction by Calatrava for a gallery and heritage square, BCE Place in Toronto, 1992, which relates the dynamic force of modern materials. Motivated by the same concerns, this project for the Rome competition progresses one step further.

Frank Gehry

Gehry's design (not illustrated) focused on integrating the community while seeking to create a sacred atmosphere, referred to as a 'special sense of place and light within the sanctuary'. The model was characteristically sculptural, articulating four discrete volumes as a cluster of mutating forms within a cloister-like configuration.

The church and little Weekday Chapel are sited in the northern half of the site to avoid the shadow cast by the housing development to the south. A linear building, strung out along the north-eastern edge of the site, contains the community centre, cleric's residence and offices, with the main living spaces open to the large reflecting pool to the west of the site. The auditorium/multi-purpose hall and bell tower are located respectively at the west and south-east corners. The main access is established along the gentle curve of the site from the south. Trees planted along the boundary soften the site.

The principal structure of the church is composed of three concrete and masonry shells constructed on foundations beneath the floor of the church to provide the vertical structure, lateral bracing and roof deck of each of the architectural forms. Internally, the dynamic quality is reinforced by vaulted ceiling forms, undulating from 10 to 14 metres. The atrium of the church faces south as an extension of the paved entrance plaza (sagrata); its position close to the altar enhancing the sense of arrival. The pews are arranged laterally in two wings to establish a stronger link with the altar and to create a more intimate space for worship. The baptistery and ambo are located either side of the altar with the choir and organ placed opposite. Services are placed beneath each structure.

Rather than traditional orientation to the east, south to north orientation of the nave and altar maximises natural light for the morning and mid-day services (admitted through glazed openings along the walls and ceilings between the architectural forms). Indirect light is diffused by two sculpted skylights at the south end of each wing.

Peter Eisenman

The iconography of this church is based on two parallel ideas: one, the proximity and distance inherent in the idea of the pilgrimage and the idea of media; and two, the new relationship between man, God and nature.

Eisenman's scheme (not illustrated) presented a 'church in the information age'. It centred on the original concept of the church: the ecclesia, or community of Christ, relinquishing the need for a prescribed space to proclaim one's faith. The intention was to extend one's sense of space rather than to shape it within the confines of a building.

The nave is split down the middle and substituted by two side aisles which are enclosed and provide 'passage' for the community through and into the church. The new nave (the central void) becomes a community space and a connecting artery for a small chapel, community centre, classrooms and auditorium. Each side aisle contains a media wall, conceived as a contemporary expression of the stained glass window of gothic churches.

The media wall enables light and media to penetrate the body of the church and be visible from the central outdoor space, thereby revealing the sacraments to a large assembly. The chapel would be used for daily mass and one of the side aisles for mass on Sundays. All three areas could be used via media for feast days.

Eisenman used the analogy of a liquid crystal and its inherent properties to clarify the condition of 'between proximity and distance' that the scheme is attempting to convey; he explains in his proposal:

The form of the church evolves out of the ground, out of palpable reality toward heaven and the infinite. The church as such becomes the mediator between nature and God, between the physical and the infinite. This then is the iconographic derivation of the new pilgrimage church. The church as a model for the new relationships between man, God and nature at the end of the millennium.

Richard Meier

The jury selected Richard Meier's entry by majority vote. In response to the isolation of the site, his proposal seeks to anchor the community with an enclosure that is part sacred, part secular. The church and community centre are approached by way of a paved entrance plaza at the eastern side of the site near the housing estate. The area to the north is gently landscaped, while the western edge is laid out as two separate courts: a reflecting pool and meditation area correspond with the church. A green area with a paved café terrace is set adjacent to the L-plan community centre which is connected to the church by a conservatory which runs east–west; access between the buildings is provided by first and second level bridges.

The sense of enclosure is expressed by the inward curvature of the church's walls. These fractured shells evolve from a configuration of three circles of equal radius, symbolising the Holy Trinity. The outer shells enclose the side chapel and baptistery while the inner shell contains the main worship space. This is laid out in a traditional manner with two rows of wooden pews and a central aisle oriented vertically towards the altar. The organ and choir loft are located at the east end of the nave and the sacristy at the west end. A block of three reconciliation rooms (entered from the chapel) separates the chapel from the adjacent baptistery. An aperture in the sanctuary wall ensures that the altar remains visible. These ancillary areas are also accessible from the entrance plaza.

The complex is to be constructed of reinforced concrete, cast *in situ*; steel frames and arches provide support for the vertical glass walls and the roof skylights. The inner surface of the shells will enable light to be graduated into interior spaces in an atmospheric way (light diffusing louvres and carefully modulated translucent glass control the effect of natural light entering the interior). Artificial illumination of the church volume is divided into three zones: the main congregational space, the chapel and the altar. Emanating from below, this will create an intimate atmosphere. At night the plasticity of the church will be emphasised by uplighting the three overlapping shells. Underwater lighting of the reflecting pool will also create dramatic surface effects.

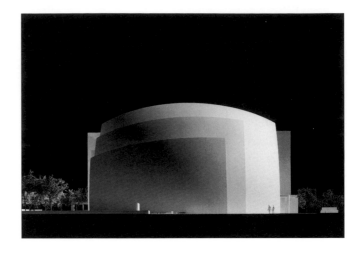

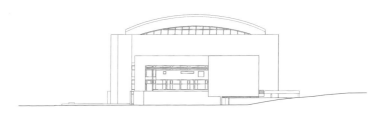

FROM ABOVE, L TO R: Exterior and interior views of model; north elevation; east elevation; west elevation; sections; site plan; ground floor plan; second floor plan

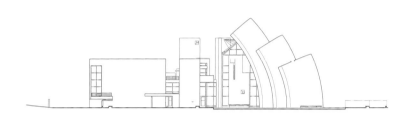

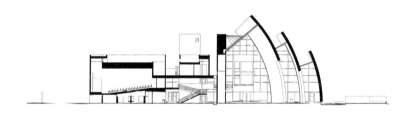

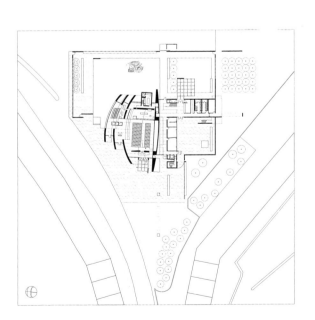

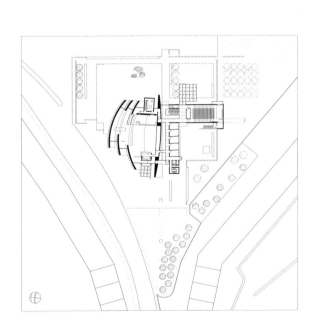

NOTES

Preface

1. Mircea Eliade, *The Sacred and the Profane*, originally published in 1957, Rowohlt Taschenbuch Verlag GmbH; translation 1959, Harcourt Brace and Co, USA, p22.

THE TWENTIETH-CENTURY CHURCH: THE ENIGMA OF SACRED OBJECTIVITY

I. A Matter of Morality

1. Nikolaus Pevsner, *An Outline of European Architecture*, Pelican Books (London), 1943, p381.
2. Robert Furneaux-Jordan, *Victorian Architecture*, Pelican Books (London), 1966, p174.
3. Augustus W N Pugin, *Contrasts; or a Parallel between the Noble Edifices of the Fourteenth and Fifteenth Centuries and Similar Buildings of the Present Day; Shewing the Present Decay of Taste*, Salisbury, 1836.
4. Johann Wolfgang von Goethe, *Baukunst*, essay, 1795.
5. Arthur Schopenhauer, *Erganzungen zum dritten Büch*, 1844.
6. Jean Gimpel, *The Cathedral Builders*, Michael Russell (London), 1983, English translation; *The Medieval Machine*, Victor Gollancz (London), 1976, English translation.

II. Arts and Crafts

1. William R Lethaby, *Architecture*, Thornton Butterworth Ltd (London), 1911, p248.
2. Edward S Prior, 'The New Cathedral for Liverpool', *The Architectural Review*, Vol 10 (London), p143.
3. William R Lethaby, *Architecture*, op cit, p145.
4. *W R Lethaby: Architecture, Design and Education*, exhibition catalogue, Lund Humphries (London), 1984, p40.
5. William R Lethaby, *Architecture, Mysticism and Myth*, London, 1891, p16.

III. Secession: Rationalism and Nationalism

1. Diary of Otto Wagner, quoted in *Otto Wagner 1814-1918*, H Geretsegger and M Peintner, Academy Editions (London), 1979; original version 1964: Residenz Verlag (Salzburg).
2. Otto Wagner, *Moderne Architecktur*, Verlag von Anton Schroll and Co (Vienna), 1895.
3. J A Lux, *Otto Wagner*, Vienna, 1914; quoted in *Otto Wagner 1814-1918*, op cit.

V. German Expressionism: The Star and the Sacred Mountain

1. William R Lethaby, *Architecture*, op cit, p245.
2. Bruno Taut, *Alpine Architecture*, Hagen, 1919.
3. Otto Bartning, *Vom Neuen Kirchenbau*, Bruno

Cassirer Verlag (Berlin), 1919.
4. Bruno Taut, *Frühlicht*, Verlag Ullstein GmbH (Berlin), 1963.
5. Johannes van Acken, *Christozentrische Kirchenkunst, Ein Entwurf zum Liturgischen Gesamtkunstwerk* (Christocentric Church Art: Towards the Total Work of Liturgical Art), pamphlet, 1922.

VI. Auguste Perret: Prophet of the Modern Church

1. Nikolaus Pevsner, *The Sources of Modern Architecture and Design*, Thames and Hudson (London), 1968.
2. Walter Gropius, *Scope of Total Architecture*, New York, 1943, p61.
3. G E Kidder Smith, *New Churches of Europe*, The Architectural Press (London), 1964, p9.

VII. Modernism and Liturgical Reform: A Brief Background

1. Anton Henze, *Contemporary Church Art*, Sheed and Ward, USA, 1956.
2. Otto Bartning, *Vom Neuen Kirchenbau*, 1919, op cit.
3. Rudolf Schwarz, *Vom Bau der Kirche*, Verlag Lambert Schneider. (Heidelberg), 1938; translated as *The Church Incarnate*, Henry Regnery and Co, USA, 1958, pp8-9.
4. Ibid.

VIII. The Church Incarnate: Modernism and the Church

1. Otto Bartning, *Vom Neuen Kirchenbau*, 1919, op cit.
2. Extract from Otto Bartning's dedication speech, 1928.
3. Robert Maguire and Keith Murray, *Modern Churches of the World*, Studio Vista Ltd (London), 1965.
4. Quoted in *Twentieth Century Church Architecture in Germany*, Hugo Schnell, Verlag Schnell and Steiner (Munich), 1975, p48.

IX. Switzerland: The Consolidation of Modernism

1. Peter Hammond, *Liturgy and Architecture*, Barrie and Rockliffe (London), 1960, p62.
2. Quoted in *Modern Church Architecture*, Christ-Janer and Foley, McGraw Hill (New York),1962, p222.

XII. Post-war Germany: A Church Meant for our own Time

1. Quoted in *Contemporary Church Architecture*, R Gieselmann, Thames and Hudson (London), 1972, p160.

XIII. The Church Building as Art: Le Corbusier and the Mediterranean

1. Quoted in Willy Boesiger (ed), *Le Corbusier, Œuvre Complète*, vol V (8 vols), Zurich, 1929-70.
2. Charles Jencks, *Le Corbusier and the Tragic View of*

Architecture, Allen Lane (London), 1973.

3. Christian Norberg-Schulz, *Meaning in Western Architecture*, Electa (Milan), 1974, p213; English translation, Praeger Publishers, 1975.

4. F Boit and F Perrot, *Le Corbusier et L'Art Sacré*, Le Manufacture (Lyons), 1985.

5. Quoted in *Modern Church Architecture*, Christ-Janer and Foley, op cit, p88.

6. Ibid, p98.

7. Giuseppe Vaccaro, quoted in *Spazio* no 7.

8. Quoted in *Connections; The Architecture of Richard England*, Charles Knevitt, 1983.

XIV. United States of America: 'For the Worship of God and the Service of Man'

1. Frank Lloyd Wright, *An Autobiography*, 1932, pp153-4.

2. Quoted in *Modern Church Architecture*, Christ-Janer and Foley, op cit, p259.

XVI. Scandinavia – Modernism: The Organic and the Rational

1. Franco Borsi, *The Monumental Era*, English translation, Lund Humphries (London), 1987, p137.

XVII. Elsewhere in Europe

1. Quoted in *Churchbuilding*, no 8 (London), 1963.

MOVEMENTS OF THE SPIRIT

1. Juhani Pallasmaa, 'The Geometry of Feeling: a Look at the Phenomenology of Architecture', 1986; published in *Theorising a new Agenda for Architecture*, Kate Nesbitt (ed), Princeton Architecture Press (New York), 1996, p453.

2. Ibid.

3. Richard Padovan, *Dom Hans van der Laan: Modern Primitive*, Architectura & Natura Press (Amsterdam), 1994, p144.

4. Ibid, p21.

5. See *Karl Freuler: Architecture for the Church*, Fabrizio Brentini, Verlag Lars Müller (Baden), 1992.

Maguire and Murray

1. Robert Maguire, 'Continuity and Modernity in the Holy Place', *Architectural History* 39, 1996.

Siren Architects

1. Ritta Nikula, *Architecture and Landscape: The Building of Finland*, Otava Publishing Company Ltd (Helsinki), p126.

Justus Dahinden

1. *Architecture*, Justus Dahinden, Kramer Verlag Stuttgart (Zürich), 1987, p29.

2. Ibid, p46.

Suomalainen Architects

1. Malcolm Quantrill, *Finnish Architecture and the Modernist Tradition*, E & FN Spon (London), 1995, p68.

2. Ibid, p155.

Richard England

1. See Chris Abel's recent study of the church, *Manikata Church*, Academy Editions (London), 1995.

Tadao Ando

1. Gunter Nitschke, *From Shinto to Ando, Studies in Architectural Anthropology in Japan*, Academy Editions (London), 1993, p49.

2. Ibid, pp54-57.

3. Quotation from *The Art of Light + Space* by Jan Butterfield, Abbeville Press (New York), 1993, p73.
   For a deep analysis of the Church on the Water and Church of the Light, see Philip Drew's study of the two buildings for the Architecture in Detail series, Phaidon Press Ltd (London), 1996

Juha Leiviskä

1. J Leiviskä, quoted in *Architecture and Urbanism*, no 295 (Tokyo), 1995, p13.

2. Ibid, p74.

Imre Makovecz

1. Edwin Heathcote, *Imre Makovecz: The Wings of the Soul*, Academy Editions (London), 1997. This new monograph provides a very clear interpretation of the architect's work and offers an insight into Makovecz's character.

2. Ibid, p90.

Steven Holl Architects

1. Steven Holl, *Anchoring*, Princeton Architectural Press (New York), 1991, p11.

2. Ibid.

Church of the Year 2000

1. 'The Customer's Intentions', published in *L'architettura, Cronache e Storia* 484 (Rome), p71.

INDEX

A

Aalto, Alvar *62, 63,* 67, 74, 150, 156
Abadie, Paul 10, 12
All Saints, Brockhampton 14, *14,* 16, 27
All Saints, Crewe 70, *71*
All Saints, Margaret Street, London 9, *12*
Ando, Tadao 56, 80, 121, 128-37, 145,
    173, 175
  Church of the Year 2000, Rome 208-19
anthroposophy 23-4
architecture parlante 9, 23, 27-8, 54
Árkay, Aladár 20, *20,* 39, *39*
Art Deco 28, 39, 40, 54, 55
Art Nouveau 16
Arts and Crafts Movement 11-12, 13-16,
    19-20, 21, 23, 61
Asplund, Erik Gunnar 61, *61,* 63, 80
Astruc, Zacharie 11
Austria 17-18, 65

B

Baltard, Victor 11
baptistry 34, 45, 56
Baranzate Church, Milan 50-1, *50*
Barragán, Luis 58, 60
Bartning, Otto *24,* 25-6, 28, 33-5, *35,* 54
Baudot, Anatole de 11, 28
Bauhaus 22, 23, 34, 56
Baur, Hermann 37, 48
Behnisch, Günter 212-13
Behrens, Peter 23
Belgium 32, 40
Bellot, Dom Paul 40, 46, 66-7
Belluschi, Pietro 57-8, 67
Bentley, J F 12, *12,* 13
Beth Shalom Synagogue, Pennsylvania 54
Blomstedt, P E 74
Böhm, Dominikus 26-8, *26, 27,* 34, 36-7,
    37, 41, 43, 55-6, 65, 67
Böhm, Gottfried 41, 43, *44,* 45, 67
Boileau, Louis-Auguste 11
Borsi, Franco 61
Botta, Mario 138-47
Brasilia 59-60, *60,* 65
Breuer, Marcel 56, *57*
Bryggman, Erik 61, 63, 74, 159
Budapest-Gazdagrét Church and Community
    Centre *160*
Budapest-Rákoskeresztúr Memorial Church
    of the Hungarian Martyrs *161*
Butterfield, William 9-10, *12*
Byrne, Barry 54-5
Byzantine 12, 19, 20, 54

C

Cachemaille-Day, N F 39, *39*
Calatrava, Santiago 209, 214-16

Callister, Charles Warren 54
Candela, Felix 59, *59*
Cathedral of Hope, Dallas, Texas 114-17,
    118
Cathedral of the Resurrection, Evry, France
    138, 139-41, 143
Cathedral of St John the Divine, New York
    53, 216
Cathedral of Socialism (Feininger) 22, 23,
    24
Catholic Church 9, 12, 25, 37, 40
Celsing, Peter 63
Chapel on Mount Rokko, Kobe, Japan 128-
    31, 133, 145
Chapel of the Rosary, Vence 48
Chapel of Thanksgiving, Dallas, Texas 117,
    118, *118-19*
Christ Church, Bochum *44,* 45
Christ King, Cork 54-5
Christ the King, Kuppersteig 27
Christ the King, Mainz-Bischofsheim 26-7,
    26
Church of the Light, Ibaraki, Japan 121,
    129, 133, 134-7, 145, 173, 175
Church of the Sacred Heart, Prague 18-19,
    19
Church of the Sagrada Familia, Barcelona *2,*
    21-2, *22*
Church on the Water, Tomamu, Hokkaido,
    Japan 56, 80, 129, *132,* 133, *133,* 135
Church of the Year 2000, Rome 209-19
Circumstantes project (D Böhm) 26, *26*
Cocteau, Jean 48
Colonia Güell Chapel, Barcelona 21, *22*
Colonia Tlalpan chapel, Mexico City 60
Comper, Ninian 11, *12,* 39
conservatism 36, 39
Corpus Christi, Aachen 35-6, *35,* 37
Couturier, Father 46, 48
Coventry Cathedral 63, *64,* 65, 73
Crystal Cathedral, Garden Grove, California
    117, 122-7
Csete, György 65, *65*
Cubism 18, 28

D

Dahinden, Justus 86-97
Daneri, L G 39
Dieste, Eladio 59

E

Ecclesiologists 9, 13
Eiermann, Egon 45
Eisenman, Peter 209, 217
Eliade, Mircea 7
Engelbrecht Church, Stockholm 20-1
England, Richard 46, 52, 108-13

Esleben, Paul Schneider 45
Espoonlahti Church, Espoo, Finland *102,*
    103, *103*
expressionism 21-2, 38, 40, 46, 54-5, 59
    Germany 22-8, 41, 45
    Italy 39, 50, 51
    Scandinavia 21, 63

F

Feininger, Lyonel 22, 23, *24*
First Church of Christ Scientist, Belvedere,
    California 54
First Church of Christ Scientist, Berkeley,
    California 53, *53*
First Church of Christ Scientist, Manchester
    15, 16
First Presbyterian Church, Stamford,
    Connecticut 57, *57*
France 10-11, 28-31, 38, 40, 46-50
Freuler, Karl 67
Freyssinet, Eugène 49, *49*
Friedrich, Caspar David 23, 61
functionalism 9, 33, 35, 38-9, 46, 52, 56-7
Furneaux-Jordan, Robert 9

G

Gaudí, Antoni *2,* 21-2, *22,* 58, 67
Gehry, Frank 209, 217
Germany 10, 22-8, 33-6, 40, 41-6
Gesamtkunstwerk 17, 21, 48
Gibberd, Frederick 65, *65*
Gilbert Scott, Giles *8,* 12, 66
Gill, Eric 39
Gillespie, Kidd and Coia (GKC) *64,* 65
Gillet, Guillaume 48-9, *49*
Gimpel, Jean 11
glass architecture 25
Gočár, Josef 38-9, *38*
Goethe, Johann Wolfgang von 10, 24, 66
Goetheanum, Dornach 24, *24,* 45, 50, 51,
    163
Goff, Bruce 54
Goodhart-Rendel, H S 40
gothic 9-12, 15, 21, 39, 40, 53, 66
    Bauhaus 22, 23
    liturgical movement 25, 31, 32
Great Britain 9-10, 11-16, 39-40, 63-5
Gropius, Walter 28, 35
Grundtvig Church, Copenhagen 21, *21*
Guardini, Romano 35
Guildford Cathedral 73

H

Hagia Sophia 12, 54
Hammond, Peter 37, 39, 46, 67
Harrison, Wallace K 57, *57*
Heilige Familie, Oberhausen 43

222 CHURCH BUILDERS